# Start Your Own Business 2012

Edited by Steph Welstead
& Ian Whiteling

# Start Your Own Business 2012

crimson

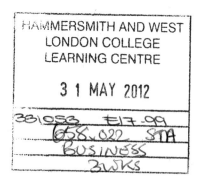
*Start Your Own Business*

This edition first published in Great Britain in 2011 by
Crimson Publishing, a division of Crimson Business Ltd
Westminster House
Kew Road
Richmond
Surrey
TW9 2ND

First edition published by Crimson Publishing in 2008
Second edition published by Crimson Publishing in 2009
Third edition published by Crimson Publishing in 2010
Fourth edition published by Crimson Publishing in 2011

A catalogue record for this book is available from the British Library.

ISBN 978 1 78059 045 5

Typeset by RefineCatch Ltd, Bungay, Suffolk
Printed and bound in the UK by Ashford Colour Press, Gosport, Hants

# Contents

# Contents

# *Introduction*

## 📖 What's in this chapter?

⟶ It's still a great time to start a business
⟶ Becoming an entrepreneur
⟶ Do you have what it takes?

If you're reading this guide then it's safe to assume you're thinking of starting your own business. At Startups.co.uk, we believe there's no substitute for learning from those who have already founded their own ventures. For more than 10 years now we've been interviewing both new and established business owners to share their entrepreneurial insights with you. After all, what better way to learn than from those who have already overcome the myriad challenges involved with setting up a business – and gone on to succeed?

So to kick things off, and before we take you through the journey of starting your own business step by step, we will take a brief look at the current environment for starting up (and explain why it's still a great time to go it alone), before profiling the entrepreneurs behind four great companies – Betfair, Climatecars, Huddle and Moonpig – to look at how the founders turned their ideas into highly successful businesses.

*"A recession and its aftermath can actually be a great time to start a business"*

# It's still a great time to start a business ...

So you're thinking of starting your own business? Well you've come to the right place. In the wake of the economic downturn it may not be the most hospitable environment for start-ups at present, but over the next few pages we will endeavour to argue why it's still a great time to start a business. After that, we will give you a taster of what's to come in the rest of this guide, and the support and guidance we will offer you as you strike out on your own.

First things first, let's not pull any punches – or peddle any false hope – it's not the easiest time to go it alone. The credit crunch, banking crisis and economic downturn have made the last few years a nail-biting time for even the most seasoned of entrepreneurs. And while the UK is no longer technically in a recession, it's still a tough climate for trading. The hangover of economic uncertainty and weakened consumer spending has yet to subside, and access to capital remains scarce.

But it's not all doom and gloom. Starting a business is never an easy option – no matter how robust the economy. In fact, with the right business model, cost management and a healthy dose of hard work, a recession and its aftermath can actually be a great time to start a business. There will be challenges, of course, but economic downturns also present many opportunities for aspiring and established entrepreneurs.

For a start, when budgets are squeezed and spending is weak, there's more scope to negotiate better deals. Whether you're looking for premises, stock or advertising space, if companies are faced with unsold inventory they're more likely to budge on price, while firms are also generally more open to partnerships and more creative deals. Equally, when unemployment is high it is often easier – and cheaper – to find great people.

*"Economic downturns also present many opportunities for aspiring entrepreneurs"*

Starting up during or just after a recession also instils a sense of financial discipline that will stand you in very good stead for the future. While a booming economy can sometimes prop up weaker firms, if you can start – and survive – in a downturn, the chances are you're onto a winner. And even though funding is undoubtedly harder to source than it once was – with banks and equity investors (who take a slice of your company in return for funding) more risk averse – if you keep a tight rein on costs and present a rock solid business plan, it's not impossible to find.

So don't let the economic uncertainty put you off. There will always be risks involved in going it alone, but with the right idea, planning and support you can still make your venture a success. And of course, there are also many benefits to becoming your own boss – which is no doubt part of what drove you to pick up this guide in the first place. In fact, here are 10 reasons why starting your own business beats being an employee.

## 10 reasons to start a business

1. **Being your own boss**

   If you have your own business, the only person you have to answer to is yourself. Being your own boss gives you the freedom to do things your way and implement your own plans. Of course, you live or die by your decisions, but that's what's good about it, isn't it?

2. **Doing what you love – or at least have a keen interest in**

   The good thing about being an entrepreneur is that you can choose what kind of firm you start up, and where. So, provided that you've done your research properly and there is a gap in the market, you can turn a hobby or interest into a profitable enterprise.

3. **Playing by your own rules**

   Start your own firm and you get to set and meet your own deadlines. Of course, you won't be able to just lie in bed until 2pm – you will need self-discipline. But meeting your own targets can be a huge motivation to work hard and drive the business forward.

4. **The freedom to express yourself**

   If you have considered going it alone, you will have thought about how you would do things your way. You will have the freedom to express yourself and develop your concept in any way you choose. Of course, there may be financial constraints, but you will have the opportunity to be as creative as you like.

5. **Plenty of support available**

   The news is full of stories about the amount of red tape and taxes that small firms have to face on a daily basis. However, over the past few years, several measures have been introduced that should make it easier to go it alone and to help small businesses through the downturn. From the government-backed loan guarantee scheme, the Enterprise Finance Guarantee (see Chapter 6), to various inner-city projects, neither the previous nor the current government can be accused of doing absolutely nothing for budding entrepreneurs. With the Prince's Trust, Shell LiveWIRE and other support organisations also up and running, you should be able to secure the help needed to get you started.

### 6. Making a fortune or at least enough to live

There are countless stories of entrepreneurs hitting on a great idea, exploiting it successfully and being well on their way to their first million by the end of the year. Although the start-up process can be tough, with long hours and little money not uncommon, if you run your business well, the rewards can be huge. And, from a purely selfish point of view, you will get most of the profits yourself.

### 7. Doing a variety of things

Dealing with spreadsheets one minute, suppliers the next and then having a look around your new office – an entrepreneur's work is not just busy, it is also extremely varied. If you want a career where every day is different, going it alone could be for you.

### 8. Having a second career

Of course, if you don't want to give up a regular income, you can always get the best of both worlds and remain as an employee while running your own firm. Although juggling the two can be tricky, having a successful sideline should be a profitable option. Do something that you are interested in and go for it.

### 9. Cutting commuting by setting up close to home

Although most small firms operate from offices, many entrepreneurs find that operating from home helps keep costs down in the early stages. As well as having familiar, comfortable surroundings to work in, you don't have to endure the daily tangle with public transport or clogged-up roads.

### 10. Realising your big dream

You may feel that starting up a small firm won't lead to anything more than having your own desk and taking on a few extra staff. However, it's possible to make it really big – just think of the late Anita Roddick, who became a Dame thanks to her entrepreneurial achievements. She started a small shop in Brighton on a shoestring in the 1970s. Before long, she had a chain of The Body Shop stores across the UK and was launching her concept in the USA. Don't dismiss your dreams as a mere fantasy – it really could happen. So what are you waiting for?

So as you can see, if you're willing to put the time, energy and hard work into nurturing your business, becoming an entrepreneur can be highly rewarding – both personally and financially – as well as giving you the freedom to choose when and how you work, and to do something you love.

Indeed, before the downturn, entrepreneurship in the UK was on an upward climb, and while official figures show the number of new businesses fell slightly in 2008 (the year the economy officially went into recession) and more significantly in 2009, early indications suggest start-up activity is on the rise once again, with many people who are out of work choosing to start up their own businesses.

*"Early indications suggest start-up activity is on the rise once again"*

Meanwhile, research shows that start-up activity among the under 35s is now growing at a faster rate than any other age group (see Chapter 2 for more details). Not only is entrepreneurship being promoted as a viable career path for young people more than ever before, through initiatives such as The National Enterprise Academy (the brainchild of *Dragons' Den* entrepreneur Peter Jones) but many school leavers and graduates are responding to the lack of employment prospects by creating jobs for themselves – and others.

At the same time, there has never been more help and information available for people thinking about striking out on their own, and the government has never been so geared up to encourage enterprise. The coalition government has openly pinned its hopes for future economic growth and job creation on the private sector, and both the current administration and its Labour predecessors have launched a number of initiatives in recent years to help small businesses grow.

And of course, Startups.co.uk has been offering advice to budding entrepreneurs for over 10 years now – coupling practical information and how-to guides with a forum where entrepreneurs can share knowledge with each other, as well as interviews with some of the UK's best-known entrepreneurs. From Innocent Drinks' co-founder Richard Reed to John Bird, founder of *The Big Issue*, over the years the entrepreneurial greats have told Startups how they started, and overcame key challenges along the way.

*Start Your Own Business 2012* brings all of this information together in a definitive guide to striking out on your own – in the same jargon-free, no-nonsense style that characterises Startups.co.uk. You'll also find easy to digest tips, action points and case studies interspersed throughout the guide. We will take you through each step of the start-up process, from the preparation you need to carry out: finding the right business idea for you, making sure you're cut out for life as an entrepreneur, evaluating your idea, researching the market, putting your business plan together and selecting the best name and legal structure for your business; to getting everything in place for a successful launch, from people, premises, suppliers

*"The success of your idea hinges on your commitment to seeing it through, during the bad times and the good"*

and marketing to making your first sale. Whether you're looking to start a business to change your lifestyle or to run a multinational operation, we'll help you on your journey as you transform your business idea into a reality.

It won't be easy, and running a business isn't for everyone – indeed, we've devoted Chapter 2 to exploring the reality of life in a start-up, and the personal attributes needed to be a successful entrepreneur. Starting a business is not a decision to be taken lightly. You will face many challenges, and the success of your idea hinges on your commitment to seeing it through – during the bad times and the good. But the hard work you put in will make it all the more rewarding when your venture takes off. So fasten your seatbelt and get ready for the ride of your life.

## *Becoming an entrepreneur*

For some people, the word 'entrepreneur' automatically brings to mind Peter Jones and his ilk – those high flyers who set up and run more successful businesses than most of us could manage in several lifetimes. But in reality, an entrepreneur is anyone who chooses to go it alone and make the most of a business opportunity for themselves, no matter how big or small.

*"Gone are the days when you had to have years of business experience under your belt before you might even consider taking the plunge with a start-up of your own"*

These days, being an entrepreneur is becoming a legitimate career choice for more and more people. Gone are the days when you had to have years of business experience under your belt before you might even consider taking the plunge with a start-up of your own. Technology has advanced to such a stage, it's now possible to start a global business from a laptop, forcing the entrepreneurial doors wide open to everyone from teenagers to the retired and those who quite sensibly want to dip their toes in the water (or at least on eBay) before taking the plunge.

Meanwhile, prime-time television shows such as *Dragons' Den* and *The Apprentice* have raised the profile of entrepreneurship and pushed the idea of running your own business to the forefront of the national psyche – no longer is it exclusive to the daring or the pinstriped, it's for everyone. So before getting down to the nuts and bolts of how to start a business here's a brief insight into why a selection of successful entrepreneurs decided to start their own companies.

People choose to become entrepreneurs for a variety of reasons. For some it's an opportunity to escape their mundane nine-to-five existence and to commit their working life to something that is a lot closer to their heart. For the 'lifestyle' entrepreneurs, the important part of the deal is not how much their business grows, but the effect it has on their life.

**David Creswell**, the founder of comics website ComicDomain.co.uk, falls into this category. 'I don't care if I'm a comic geek, it's my hobby and I've turned that into a small business,' he says. 'I'm proud of the service we provide and our customers are also happy.' For others, the motivation for starting up will come from spotting a gap in a market they know well. Self-confessed 'ski bums' **Tim Slade** and **Jules Leaver** spotted an opportunity for 'been there done that' T-shirts to sell to skiing holidaymakers, and started the highly successful high-street chain Fat Face.

And for **Dee Edwards**, the same kind of insight helped her to launch internet company Habbo. 'I really believed internet business could be made successful by using technology to run a company effectively, and leveraging the different way people were changing their communication,' she says.

Whether it's T-shirts or technology, the world is littered with those who've been able to see a business opportunity others simply can't. In fact, a lack of business experience could well give you the kind of perspective those with a blue-chip curriculum vitae would struggle to attain. Nowhere is this better illustrated than by **Lena Bjorck**. Arriving in the UK from Sweden with no qualifications she landed a job as a kitchen porter, but quickly realised the country's service industry was just not up to scratch. So without a pound in her pocket or even the most basic equipment, she quit. She now runs one of the country's most successful catering companies, Inn or Out.

To help inspire you, here are profiles of four companies, started by entrepreneurs with very different backgrounds and ideas, who took the decision to launch a business for the first time and succeeded.

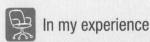 **In my experience**

Company: **Betfair**
Founders: **Andrew Black and Ed Wray**

When **Andrew Black** (pictured), co-founder of Betfair.com says: 'I've had a very varied career and done a lot of job hopping', he's making somewhat of an understatement.
If ever there's an entrepreneur who's trodden an unlikely path to fortune and success, it's Andrew. He had to overcome being expelled from university, being sacked and a personal tragedy to rise to the head of a business that's

7

giving the likes of established bookies William Hill and Ladbrokes a real run for their money. But every experience, Andrew insists, whether it be stocking shelves at B&Q, caddying on the European golf tour, dealing on the stock exchange, gambling for a living, or caring for his dying brother, contributed to the day he thought up Betfair while working on a secret project for GCHQ.

*Building up experience*

Andrew's working life was delayed when his brother developed a serious brain infection. Having only had a handful of dead-end jobs, Andrew stopped working to care for his brother for the final two years of his life. Following his brother's death, Andrew had a brief, and unsuccessful, sojourn onto the European golf tour, before landing his first serious job at 26, working in software. In the following four years, Andrew's natural flair for figures saw him flourish, as he wrote heavy computer code and saw how big business, particularly the stock market, worked. The high-risk stakes of stocks and shares captured Andrew's imagination, and prompted him to start gambling.

'When you're at the sharp end of trading you're trading very much in the short term and it is very, very similar to gambling,' he says. 'When I left, I didn't have enough money to go trading.' Instead, Andrew turned to more conventional forms of gambling for his kicks – and his income. 'I won £25,000 on a £20 bet on a horse and then had a £30,000 win from a £1,000 bet on a race,' he recalls. 'I'd won about £50,000 in three months. Compared to what I was earning at the time it was a lot of money.'

Andrew programmed his own models for betting on football and golf, and also played bridge for substantial figures. But despite doing 'pretty well', it wasn't enough to keep him occupied. So he moved back to buying and selling shares. 'I was seeing the whole mechanics of the New York stock exchange first-hand and getting fantastic experience in this incredibly exciting environment,' he says. But Andrew's excitement was cut short – he was fired after a disagreement over business ethics – and he returned to programming, 'earning ridiculous amounts of money for very little work' in a period where IT skills were in demand. However, his obsession with the stock market and intellectual thirst for a challenge or bet never went away. While working on a secret GCHQ project, he had the time to contemplate how this passion could be twinned with his IT skills.

'We started work at nine and finished at five, and if you weren't out of the office on the dot they got rid of you,' he explains. 'So I had a lot of spare time. I was living in a small remote farmhouse and was lonely.' But the solitude gave Andrew precious time to turn things over in his head and come up with 'the idea'. It was conceived from the way the stock exchange works. 'It's simple,' he explains, 'Betfair is a cross-section of taking stock exchange technology to the gambling market using the internet. In my career I've worked directly with the stock exchange, I've been a professional gambler and I've built websites. I've been there on all three of them.'

### The big gamble
As Andrew's IT contractor job was going well, he was undecided whether it was worth giving up for the risk of starting his own business. Did he really want to leave his excellent lifestyle behind by going out on a betting venture? 'In my heart I knew I had to do it because I couldn't face the thought of going to my grave having had one great idea and not actually putting it into action,' he says. However, before doing anything Andrew wanted a partner. 'I wanted someone who understood business,' he says. But finding one proved difficult, until he met **Ed Wray**, the brother of a friend. 'Ed was talking about a horse he'd bet on but was complaining he hadn't won much,' says Andrew. 'I said: "Well it shouldn't have been like that, soon bookmaking will all change." Ed said: "Tell me more," so I explained the idea.'

A short time later, Ed got in touch to find out if Andrew had done anything about the idea and Andrew asked if he'd like to be his partner. Ed agreed in principle, but not without certain changes. He said Andrew had the right product and the idea was great, but he thought the business plan was totally wrong. He thought if it was going to be done, it needed to be done properly and that they needed to raise some serious finance. The pair spent the next five months working on the idea and carefully planning the business. In the end, Betfair was born. Andrew and Ed wanted conventional venture capital investment, but it turned out they had missed the boat. 'A company called Flutter had got there before us,' says Andrew. 'They were selling the eBay of betting and had got a lot of funding. They didn't have the knowledge or substance we had, but it was still terrible news.'

### Breaking ahead of the game
The rival in the marketplace ruled out interest from venture capitalists, and the pair were about to quit. Then they came up with an idea to present their concept to wealthy individuals they knew in the City who had money to invest. 'We'd pick a bank, do a presentation and two or three would leave the room having invested £25,000,' says Andrew. 'It soon added up and we cobbled together the £1m fairly

quickly.' They added £30,000 each and didn't pay themselves for the first eight months. The site was created and launched in June 2000, the day before Derby Day – one of the biggest days in the horseracing calendar. As funds were tight, Betfair deployed guerrilla tactics to promote the launch.

'We led a procession with coffins saying "Death of the bookmaker" through the City and held fake demonstrations with "Betfair – unfair" protestors to try and get some publicity,' explains Andrew. The antics made the front page of *The Times* business section. In its first week Betfair traded £30,000, but really hit the big time after merging with rival Flutter. 'There was a big fuss when they launched and they had all this money, but it wasn't until six months down the line that it became obvious people were using us,' says Andrew. 'They had a huge advertising budget, but they also had a message board where people were discussing Betfair. Punters were coming into them and leaving to us. About eight months later, they realised we had 97% of the market, despite the fact they'd spent 10 or 20 times what we had. At that point they realised the only way forward was our way.'

A merger was negotiated with Betfair reportedly securing favourable terms, along with access to a 'top-class' chief technology officer, the hardware and most importantly, 'the big punters' that were essential to driving the business forward. So, rather than the establishment of their rival Flutter being the end of their dream, it has proved to be the catalyst to their huge business success.

Since then Andrew and Ed haven't looked back, establishing Betfair as the leading online betting website. In October 2010, the company listed on the London Stock Exchange, in a flotation that valued the firm at £1.4bn. These days, the company is run by chief executive officer David Yu, but Ed still sits on the board as non-executive chairman. Andrew stood down as non-executive director following the flotation.

Betfair's core revenue grew by 8% to £330m in 2011, while its adjusted earnings before interest, tax, depreciation and amortisation (EBITDA) grew 29% to £80.2m. The business now holds licences in the UK, Italy, Malta, Gibralta, the USA and Australia, and remains one of only a handful of companies to have been awarded a prestigious Queen's Award for Enterprise on more than one occasion.

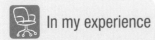 In my experience

Company: **Huddle**
Founders: **Alastair Mitchell and Andy McLoughlin**

Go big or go home – that was the lingering business maxim **Alastair Mitchell** (left in picture) and **Andy McLoughlin** took away from a tech conference they attended four years ago. They'd just launched their online collaboration and hosted workspace start-up Huddle, but from that moment on their ambitions went global. Just a few years down the line and the company topped Startups.co.uk's 2010 'Startups 100' list – the definitive countdown of the UK's most innovative, inspiring and ground-breaking new companies. Clients range from sole traders to multinational blue-chips and public sector giants – Disney, Panasonic, the NHS and the Liberal Democrats are all Huddle converts. And while 2010 may have seen Huddle open up its San Francisco base, Alastair and Andy are quick to emphasise just how much their tech start-up achieved from its Bermondsey HQ, five thousand miles from Silicon Valley.

*A leap of faith*

It took roughly a year of discussion and planning between friends Andy and Alastair before they left their jobs to start work on Huddle full-time. Andy had worked in the online collaboration sector for some time so knew the market well. Alastair's experience working for various web and tech companies also meant he had first-hand knowledge of the collaboration market's shortfalls and it wasn't long before the pair began exchanging ideas on a creating a superior offering.

'The first thing we did was go out for a load of beers and a curry to discuss it, and it became very apparent we had similar ideas about the kind of business we wanted to build,' says Andy. 'We started meeting every day after work. I was wireframing the product while Ali read up on company formation and researched how we could take it to market.'

One of Alastair's 'homework' tasks during this period was to come up with a name for the product. 'He gave me a spreadsheet of 50 different names and all but one of them were absolutely awful,' recalls Andy. 'I saw Huddle and knew instantly that's what we'd use. It was at that point it went from a project we were working on to having a life of its own.'

Six months into working on the venture alongside their day jobs, Alastair and Andy felt confident enough to dedicate themselves to it full-time. A former employer of Andy's came on board as an angel investor which provided the start-up capital to get going, secure office space and the company's first members of staff. Andy admits it was a big leap of faith to give up their salaried roles but says starting up with a friend provided the 'emotional safety net' needed to get through it.

### Honing the product

Huddle's first customers were friends or former colleagues of the pair, who were offered free trials of the software in exchange for feedback. 'We were realistic,' says Andy. 'We knew people weren't going to pay for something they knew nothing about straight off the bat. It also helped us refine the product. You can be a great product designer but, with the best will in the world, you can never accurately predict how everyone will use it, so getting feedback was crucial.'

The Huddle product was formally launched in March 2007 after being honed enough to start attracting paying customers. While the nature of the service allowed viral growth, Andy and Alastair knew they'd need a substantial cash injection to attain that global goal. 'Raising finance is always stressful,' says Andy. 'When you've got a large team you offset that effort but when there's just a few of you it takes time and attention away from running the company. However, after a certain point all VCs start to come up with the same questions so as long you've prepared the answers it becomes less time-consuming.'

### Building relationships

Huddle secured a $4m series A round of funding in November 2007 which saw them through tremendous expansion over three years, and facilitated some great partnerships for the service including deals with professional social network LinkedIn, Hewlett Packard and Intercall. Alongside the securing of clients such as Panasonic and Procter & Gamble, these partnerships meant a US base was necessary. After securing a further $10m in funding from Matrix Partners in 2010, Andy moved out to San Francisco to set up Huddle's stateside office. 'We wanted to develop our partnerships and work with these companies more closely,' explains Alastair. 'Some of our big clients wanted to roll the use of Huddle out within their businesses and those kind of relationships need lots of support.

'The great thing is we were able to grow our user base in the US from a little base in London which even a few years ago wouldn't have been possible. And it's testament to modern technology that being so far away from Andy has felt fairly natural. We work together on Huddle every day so aside from the time difference, it's pretty much business as usual.'

Securing the series B funding from Matrix and opening up the US base also coincided with a major milestone for the company – cashflow profitability. The founders now anticipate significant growth over the next few years, as Huddle fosters its global relationships. But while the company is well on its way to dominating the online collaboration space, these co-founders remain patient. 'With any start-up, when you're small the temptation is to chase the money and go for the short-term benefits,' says Andy. 'But you can't think like that. It's not about today's revenue, it's about what makes you a massive success in five or 10 years' time.'

 ## In my experience

Company: **Climatecars**
Founder: Nicko Williamson

While most of his 13-year-old peers had their heads stuck in the Harry Potter series, **Nicko Williamson** was working from an alternative reading list. His author of choice was Richard Branson and as a result, his business education started early. 'I looked at the Virgins of the world who go into an existing market and provide something else,' he explains. A few years later, still at the tender age of 22, he began his own efforts to disrupt an existing market, launching carbon neutral cab company Climatecars in 2007.

Making cabs greener sounds relatively straightforward. However, with a taxi giant like Addison Lee on your doorstep, a London-based cab hire start-up needs something extra. Climatecars appears to have found that competitive edge, as the company celebrated its third birthday in 2010, replaced its 60-car Toyota Prius fleet with an updated hybrid model, and was featured in Startups.co.uk's 'Startups 100' list.

According to Nicko, Climatecars is more than just a carbon neutral chauffeured car hire service. 'We are the greenest possible car company you can use, but alongside that offer one of the highest levels of service.' Complimentary mineral water, newspapers and smartly suited drivers are all part of the standard package.

### University inspiration

The inspiration for the business came when Nicko was still a student. 'I was studying at Bristol University and kept driving past a gas convergence station that was advertising itself as a green fuel business. The idea was that you could convert a normal car to run on LPG (liquefied petroleum gas), which was much greener and the emissions much lower. 'It was at that point I suddenly thought of taxis, as I had been in and out of London where everybody was using this company called Addison Lee, the biggest in the market, and I just thought "why can't I make this greener?".'

Realising he needed experience in the industry, Nicko got a job at a rival car company which allowed him 'to get a finger on how the business really worked'. However, he was soon itching to get his own business up and running. 'I spent a few months working for the company until I felt I understood the model enough, which was probably naive as I could have done it for longer, but I was eager to start.'

Nicko raised initial funds of £150,000 from friends and family, before contributing £50,000 of his own savings, giving an initial seed round of £200,000. Luckily, Climatecars managed to secure further investment of £300,000 before the recession hit. 'We went into the recession very well capitalised and in a cash rich position. At that point we expanded our operation and grew by aggressively selling. We had to be a bit more competitive on our rates, which I don't think has changed, as all companies have been looking to save.'

### Understated branding

Climatecars stands out in the market predominately as a discreet cab firm, which offers the type of high-end service corporate clients expect, albeit in a more environmentally friendly way. However, while having green credentials is a bonus, Nicko understood that businesses weren't necessarily willing to pay extra to be green. Climatecars' closest competitor in the green space is Green Tomato, a brightly branded car service that uses noticeable eco logos on their vehicles, which, Nicko explains, corporate customers are put off by.

This, according to Nicko, is one of the draw-cards of Climatecars for large corporate firms, along with a competitive fixed rate fee. 'When I started I was determined that we weren't going to price ourselves out of the market. We need to be cost-competitive. While the green angle is great I am very much of the view that people are not going to be pay more for a green service or product. I didn't want environmentally friendly cars where people say "oh great idea but we can't afford it".'

The majority of business (90%) comes from corporate clients, ranging from investment banks and private equity firms to radio stations. 'We have great core customers who spend a decent amount of money every month, and we have built good relationships with them as we try to deliver a decent level of customer service.'

While the average journey in a Climatecar is only around five miles, with clients travelling from one side of the city to the other, many large companies require cars for up to 100 trips a day, which has helped drive up profits.

*Competitive edge*
Nicko anticipates turnover to fly past the £2m mark in 2011, as the company continues its trend of year-on-year growth, and expects to be fully profitable by 2012. 'Our growth has been very driven by the green agenda companies now have', he notes. However, competition for Climatecars has become tougher. 'There isn't a multinational company that doesn't have a green policy out,' says Nicko. 'When I started, the green thing was coming into prominence and it was a relatively easy sell. But we are not alone in the market anymore as other companies have cottoned on and included the Prius cars in their fleet.'

While Nicko remains confident Climatecars still has considerable miles left in the tank he is not opposed to a change in direction – and the rise in competition is one of the reasons he's determined to grow the business by considering courier delivery services for corporate clients. He says: 'Our clients often use those kinds of services so it's a natural fit for us. However, it is a very technical and competitive market – the electric vans are very expensive so we have got to do a lot of work on that one.'

Nicko says an exit isn't on the cards anytime soon – he's still far too concerned with all the market disruption left to do. Green cabs are just the start according to the young entrepreneur. 'We certainly have bigger ambitions, put it that way!'

In my experience

**Company:** Moonpig
**Founder:** Nick Jenkins

When **Nick Jenkins** launched his online personalised greetings card offering back in 1999, he didn't want to compete with the high street on price. He wanted to harness the capability of the web to sell something that simply wasn't available in the shops. Moonpig, which offers a range of over 10,000 completely customisable cards that users can add photographs, names and even their own in-jokes to, is now turning over £40m a year. It's also responsible for one of the most infuriatingly catchy jingles on daytime TV.

Before launching the company Nick had spent eight years in Moscow as a commodity trader for a sugar operation. His decision to return to the UK was in no small part influenced by a death threat nailed to his door after a troublesome deal. 'As homicidal criminals go, the Russians are quite sensible,' says Nick. 'If they give you a death threat and you take notice of it, you're not going to get killed.' The issue with the client was eventually resolved but the incident, coupled with a declining enthusiasm for his line of work and a healthy lump sum gained from a buy-out of the trading firm, led Nick back to the UK where he started an MBA, and simultaneously worked on the business plan for Moonpig.

*Obvious success*

Within a week of graduating Nick had started to piece the business together. One of the most important hurdles he had to overcome at a very early stage was convincing investors and card publishers of the commercial viability of the idea.

'In hindsight, if you look at the business now it seems like a really obvious and outrageous success, but back when we started it wasn't that obvious at all. I really struggled to raise money for the first five years.' Although Nick had an unwavering belief the company would grow organically through word of mouth, it took a while to get everyone else on board.

Securing the rights to the designs in exchange for a percentage of revenue seems like an attractive proposition for publishers considering the sheer volume of sales Moonpig now enjoys, but back when it was X% of nothing, it was a much harder sell. But, as with the investors, Nick was gradually able to win them over, and it's the unrivalled content variety and relationships with so many publishers that makes the business so resilient against competitors today, according to Nick.

Operating with virtually no marketing budget for the first seven years, and having launched before the advent of pay per click or affiliate marketing, Moonpig initially survived on a promotional diet of PR and word of mouth. It's a vastly altered landscape now however, as anyone who's spent more than a couple of hours in front of daytime television will testify.

With its infuriatingly catchy jingle, the ad is viewed as a cheesy classic by some and a broadcasting irritant by others – it's been aired more than 23,000 times since its first outing in November 2006. The real growth of the business however, has been viral. As Nick illustrates: 'If it was as simple as spending lots of money on TV then everybody would be doing it. What's really made it work is customers spread the word about the product themselves. If you buy a card and take it to a party it gets passed around.'

*Patient growth*

The temptation to grow too quickly was the downfall of many of the businesses that imploded when the dot com bubble burst, according to Nick. 'For a few years after the crash I would look around me and think, "when's it my turn?" But I could see why a lot of them went under. Many of them tried to develop too quickly when the online appetite just wasn't there. You can offer a fantastic new solution but it takes time for people to come round – they want to see others using it first.'

As an ecommerce pioneer that outlived so many of the web giants that dwarfed it before the bubble burst, the Moonpig story is the very definition of a slow-burning web success. An offering launched in Australia in 2004, where 'it's proven to be as popular as it is in the UK', says Nick.

More recently, in May 2010, Moonpig launched in America, although Nick says 'it's still early days to see how the market reacts to that'. Following the company's success in Australia, Nick says he deliberately took his time before jumping into subsequent markets. 'Culturally and in terms of sense of humour, Australia is most similar to us, much more so than the US,' Nick explains. 'We wanted to learn how to operate in another country first and Australia has worked very well for us.'

In July 2011, Moonpig was acquired by digital photo printer PhotoBox in a deal worth £120m. Nick owned 35% of the business at the time of the sale, having gone through six funding rounds in Moonpig's 12-year history, with a collection of private investors holding the remaining shares. Nick will continue as an adviser and investor at PhotoBox, and says the deal will build on Moonpig's success through further international expansion and development of the product range.

## *Do you have what it takes?*

The profiles in the previous section highlight the qualities required by an entrepreneur – of which passion is one of the most important. No matter how much potential your business might have for making money, unless you believe in it, how can you expect anyone else to? A bit of self-belief goes a long way.

Hand in hand with passion comes commitment to the cause. From day one you will need to work hard, often forgoing friends and family to get your venture off the ground. Ask yourself whether you are prepared to make that kind of sacrifice and whether you can keep yourself motivated to put in those long, long hours. If you are the sort of person whose New Year resolution lasts until 2 January you might want to think again as to whether you've got what it takes, particularly when things might not be going your way.

Also, as you've probably realised, the chances are you will be going through all of this on your own. While escaping the office might seem like paradise now, you could soon be missing that office gossip and banter. You'll need to dig deep to find the kind of emotional resilience to keep you from losing the plot when there's no one around to lend a helping hand. So, while you don't need qualifications on paper, not just anyone can become an entrepreneur. But if you think you've got what it takes then it could be one of the best decisions you ever make.

# ↰⤴ CHAPTER 1

*What to start*

##  What's in this chapter?

-→ *Choosing the right business*
-→ *Shoestring start-ups*
-→ *Other popular options*
-→ *Franchising*
-→ *Buying an existing business*

Not everyone starts a business following a 'eureka!' moment. Some are simply driven by a desire to work for themselves and then embark on a search for business ideas. To do this, of course, you need to ensure you find the right kind of business for you.

This chapter looks at 20 start-up ideas to give you a taste of what each involves – and hopefully, some inspiration. From starting an eBay business at home to entering the blossoming mobile apps market, we look at what skills, qualifications and attitude are needed to make each venture a success. Then we look at two other routes to becoming an entrepreneur – franchising and buying an existing business – and weigh up these options against starting a business from scratch.

# Choosing the right business

Although thousands of people dream of escaping the nine-to-five grind and becoming their own boss, many are unsure of what sort of business they want to start up and how they can ensure their new venture is a success. Ultimately, this is your choice, but it can help if you initially think about what you want from your business. Before **Kirsty McGregor** launched her web-based company Entertainthekids.com, which provides inspiration for parents looking for ways to keep their children entertained, she laid down her vision of 'business utopia', as she puts it.

'I had quite a strict list of what I wanted any business to be for me, in my circumstances,' says Kirsty. 'These were my requirements:

- The business shouldn't be reliant upon my input to grow. This is a personal thing, as I wanted to start and grow the business and then be able to get 'time freedom' as quickly as possible. It's the whole point of being able to run my own business – flexibility for the family while being financially comfortable and secure.

- It either had to provide a product or service that was niche and high value, or have mass-market appeal with a low price.

- The business needed to be scalable, without any major scarce resource, such as fixed employee or machinery hours, etc.

- Overheads/fixed costs had to be as low as possible, so that I could break even on a fairly low turnover.

- The product should preferably not be a fashionable item or have laws or regulations that will change quickly.

- The business should not have to deal with any stock issues, such as storage, delivery and suppliers – it had to be a service!

- It had to have low start-up costs (unfortunately that also means low barriers to entry for competitors).'

*"Many industries are well suited to budget beginnings"*

Of course, your vision could be completely different from hers, but getting it down on paper can give you key pointers about the kind of business you would like to launch. To give you some food for thought, this chapter gives you 20 business ideas. Some have popped up recently due to certain trends, while others have been around for some time, but all are either very popular now or growing rapidly in popularity. If none of them appeals to you, then at least you know what you don't want to do – and they might inspire you to find the business that is right for you.

A big problem for many people who want to start a business is being able to afford to do it, especially in the current financial climate. But don't let a lack of financial resources put you off. Starting a business on a shoestring may seem like an impossible task, conjuring up visions of compromises and cutting corners that will ultimately undermine your best efforts. But it doesn't have to be that way, as many industries are well suited to budget beginnings. This is not a case of restricting yourself to mean margins. There are several steps you can take to keep overheads down.

-> The most obvious costs in the early days are premises and staffing. If you start by working from home, your office space or workshop budget can go elsewhere. Obviously, this is easier if you are in a desk-bound profession. If it doesn't matter where you are based, rents on out-of-town premises or those in unfashionable areas will also keep costs down. And if you don't have the money for staff immediately, don't forget friends and family. Provided that you don't abuse their goodwill, most will be prepared to help you out on the odd occasion.

-> It's inevitable that you will have to put 120% into the business at first, so try to become competent in as many tasks as possible. It will save you money if you can do things such as basic desktop publishing and accounting yourself. You will also gain a better understanding of the day-to-day running of the business.

-> Where possible, lease rather than buy and purchase second-hand. Tools, machinery and ovens, for example, are widely available to lease if you can provide assurance that payments will be made. You can also make great savings if you opt for used desks, chairs and filing cabinets.

Half of the business ideas that follow are relatively inexpensive to launch, while the other 10 require more capital input. But no matter how much money you have, the points above are worth bearing in mind, because during the start-up phase of a business, every penny counts.

---

### Startups Tips

**The right start-up for you**

- Base it on a key skill or interest.
- Draw up a list of what you are looking for from your ideal business.
- Search out the most successful businesses nationally and locally.
- Find a gap in your local market.
- Canvass opinion of friends and family about your idea.
- Consult business contacts about your idea, such as your accountant.
- Check out local competition and decide if you can do it better.
- Look into the level of finance you will need and whether you will be able to secure it.
- Find out if anyone likes your idea enough to go into business with you.
- Search on the internet or in the *Yellow Pages* for outlets and warehouses. Most large offices refurbish reasonably regularly, so the second-hand market is generally well stocked.

## Shoestring start-ups

### eBay business

Setting up a company on eBay is an increasingly popular choice among would-be entrepreneurs. With millions of potential customers just a couple of clicks away from your products, setting up an eBay store is a cheap and easy way to do business online.

Once you've created a business account, you can set up an online shop by paying a monthly subscription fee. This ranges from £14.99 a month for a basic shop package, to £349.99 a month for the most advanced offering. It costs between 10p and £1.30 to list an item for auction on eBay, depending on the opening value or reserve price of the item. For fixed price listings, the insertion fee is usually 40p (if the seller does not have an eBay shop), or 20p for media items such as books, music and DVDs. With a shop, the listing fee ranges from free to 10p, depending on the shop package purchased.

eBay then takes a slice of the selling price once an item is sold. In a bid to simplify its pricing model, eBay recently changed its business sellers' fee structure. As of May 2011, the tiered model (where the fee charged depended on how much the item sold for) was shelved, in favour of a flat percentage fee depending on what category the item falls into.

For most items, eBay now takes 10% of the final selling price, regardless of how much the item sold for. Fees vary across certain categories though: for instance, on tech items such as computers and consumer electronics eBay takes just 3% of the selling price; for media items the fee is 9%; and for clothing, shoes and accessories the fee is 12%. eBay says the new pricing model will make it easier for sellers to predict and calculate their fees and that fees will decrease overall for many sellers, but concedes that they may increase for some.

Making and receiving payments through PayPal, eBay's online payment system of choice, also incurs a small transaction charge.

For **Wilmamae Ward**, who set up a vintage clothing company on eBay, The Gathering Goddess, an eBay business was the perfect fit. 'I had been buying beautiful vintage clothes on eBay for several years and had amassed a huge collection for which I no longer had room,' she says. 'I decided to sell some of my collection back on eBay. I was amazed at the prices achieved so I began to sell more and more and it just snowballed. eBay allowed me to reach many customers.'

Running her business on eBay allowed her to indulge her fashion obsession and make a great living at the same time, while also enabling her to work from home and set her own hours. 'In addition, unlike a bricks and mortar shop which has to rely on passing trade and extensive marketing, eBay provides all of this on a global basis without the overheads,' she says.

To be successful, the most important thing is to find a niche that few other people are competing in, adds Wilmamae: 'Start with selling something that you know about and/or love doing. Then research the eBay market in your particular sector, as well as on the internet in general, to see what the competition is doing and what is being offered. This will mean you can find a point of difference that will set you apart from your competitors.'

It's also crucial to build up positive feedback on the site, as this will give customers the confidence to buy from you. 'This is the bedrock of eBay and is what sets you apart as a good seller,' says Wilmamae. 'Excellent customer service equals great positive feedback, so never slack on processing orders.'

*"Excellent customer service equals great positive feedback, so never slack on processing orders"*

## Action points

### Launch an eBay business

☑ **Start with selling something that you know about and/or love doing**: This will help to drive your motivation and will be vital in maintaining your work levels, which will be heavy to start with.

☑ **Research the eBay market**: In particular, do this in your sector, as well as on the internet, to see what the competition is doing and what is being offered. Find a point of difference that will set you apart from your competitors.

☑ **Be committed to it**: It isn't easy, but it can be extremely rewarding.

☑ **Build up your positive feedback**: This is vital for successful selling on eBay because it lets potential customers know exactly where you stand among the competition. And remember that excellent customer service will automatically get you this all-important positive feedback. Always aim to provide the best possible customer service.

☑ **Always keep track of your competition**: Don't just research them once or occasionally. Remember they are looking at you and as your business steams ahead, they are plotting and planning to take over. Half of Wilmamae's eBay time is spent researching competitors and new marketing techniques.

☑ **Be as transparent as you can with your potential customers**: Don't hide costs, and describe your items clearly and honestly. Building trust builds business on eBay.

☑ **Don't spend huge amounts of money on stock and setting up**: Start small and grow it slowly. The world of eBay is quite complex and the best way of discovering this world is by experiencing it. If you plough in with a huge store full of stock without knowing the ins and outs of how eBay works, you could be setting yourself up for a fall.

## Personal training

Despite the turbulence of the economic downturn, the health industry has remained relatively stable; in fact, market research firm TGI claims the number of gym members in Britain has increased by one million since 2000. Yet the gym culture is being transformed, as more and more people turn to tailored, one-on-one support from a personal trainer. And, while personal training is now the norm in most health clubs and gyms, there is also an ever-increasing number of people looking to make it on their own by creating their own personal training business. Many are specialising in outdoor training, following the lead of British Military Fitness, the park-based exercise club which now boasts more than 15,000 members.

Personal training is all about specialism – you need to identify an area suited to your skill and expertise (whether it's helping people lose weight, working with pre-natal women or even training elite athletes). Then you need to find a suitable course which will give you the training you need. While there's no singular qualification for fitness instructors, some are more respected than others.

Other than the cost of training, which can be anything from £300 to £6,000 depending on your specialty, other overheads are limited. Insurance is a must, and will usually cost at least £100 per year, but other costs depend on you. Investment in the necessary equipment, such as free weights or a blood pressure machine, is usually an early outgoing. In addition, as of April 2011 Hammersmith and Fulham council in London began charging personal trainers £350 a year to use its parks and open spaces for business purposes (or £1,250 for training large groups of people). While it's as yet unclear how many local authorities will follow suit, this is certainly worth double checking.

*"You have to be willing to work as early as 5am and as late as 8pm because that's when people want to do their training"*

Being a good listener and able to relate to a lot of different people is almost as important as your technical ability as a personal trainer. **Linda Grave**, a fitness fanatic who ran a successful personal training business before recently changing careers, was surprised at the role counselling plays in the health and fitness industry: 'I was shocked at the number of clients who look upon you as a confidante. You have to be very confidential, particularly as many clients know each other.' Meanwhile, **Nick Page**, a self-employed fitness trainer based near Windsor, stresses the need to be flexible: 'On the whole you have to be willing to work as early as 5am and as late as 8pm because that's when people want to do their training.'

Steven Jones, sales manager at Savage Strength, says the average hourly rate charged by fitness trainers is between £20 and £50: 'It depends on several factors such as how well known you are, your location, your specialist skills etc. I know one guy in London who charges £100 per hour.'

"The industry suits someone with a genuine passion for delivering high quality treatments"

## Mobile beautician

The beauty industry is big business. There are currently around 70-80,000 beauticians in the UK, according to the British Association of Beauty Therapy and Cosmetology (BABTAC), and each year, approximately 20,000 new therapists qualify. In today's beauty-conscious world, both men and women are increasingly on the lookout for high quality treatments and beauticians they can rely on, but that can also conveniently fit into their busy schedules. This has led the mobile beauty industry to surge in popularity.

Offering treatments in the comfort of clients' own homes has the added benefit of reduced overheads for therapists, who don't have to pay excessive rates to rent a salon. Beauticians can therefore offer their services at competitive prices, and a mobile beauty business can be extremely profitable.

To be successful, a sound knowledge of everything from the treatments you'll offer to the products you'll be using is paramount, while excellent interpersonal skills are also a must. There's a vast array of marketing tools at your disposal, but according to Natasha Dwyer, founder of London mobile beauty and massage service Return to Glory, word of mouth has been by far the most valuable. 'The industry suits someone with a genuine passion for delivering high quality treatments – if they don't have that they're going to fall at the first hurdle.'

To become a beauty therapist of any sort, you must first obtain the correct qualifications. An NVQ level 3 is the bare minimum certificate you should acquire for each specialty. To be able to perform treatments in somebody else's home you must have public liability insurance, as well as professional indemnity insurance, which covers you in case a client makes a claim against you. You must also attain a licence from each local authority you will be operating in.

As a mobile beauty therapist, you'll spend a lot of time travelling. The most obvious mode of transport is a car or van, bearing in mind you'll probably need to bring products and equipment such as massage couches with you. Time is a crucial factor when making home visits, so it's wise not to set your target area too widely initially. It's also important to assess the local competition – what is it that you are providing that's different to everybody else?

## Market stall

Becoming a market trader is a great way to start your own business, as it's a fairly low-cost and straightforward industry. What's more, according to a 2009 report by the Retail Markets Alliance, markets in major cities largely outperformed high street shops during the recession, as people increasingly sought original and inexpensive bargains.

Before setting up your own stall, it's important to be aware of what the job entails. In particular, be prepared for long hours and early starts. **Matthew Crawford**, who set up his own Caribbean takeaway stall, Easy 'Nuh, in 2009, explains: 'Running a business on a market is rewarding, but also extremely challenging – before you invest too much time and finance into your potential project/career change, you need to know it's suited to you.'

Some markets are outdoors and some are covered, while some run every day, others just at weekends. It's not uncommon for traders to work at a number of different markets during a given week. Your success as a trader will be determined by the product line you choose – most market managers look for a diverse range of stalls selling individual products, so originality is key. There are many wholesale markets around the UK, which often open early in the morning, that are great places to explore and source products. Another worthwhile portal for buying goods is *The Trader* magazine.

*"Before you invest too much time and finance into your potential career change, you need to know it's suited to you"*

You may have to start off as a casual trader, which could mean standing in queues early in the morning waiting for a stall to become available. Permanent stalls can be hugely in demand, but being a casual trader allows the market manager to assess your ability to draw in customers. 'Before committing to a specific market I would strongly advise asking a trader if you can spend a day or two with them so you can see what it's like first hand,' advises Matthew.

You must obtain a licence from your local council to set up your stall. Public liability insurance is a legal requirement, while traders must also adhere to the Trade Descriptions Act, the Sale of Goods Act, and if applicable, food hygiene legislation. Stalls can be set up with relatively low funds, as was the case for **Sebastian Vince**, who started a bread stall on the Portobello Road market in London 13 years ago and now runs a larger more permanent stall on the Northcote Road in Clapham. He recalls: 'I started my stall initially with £200, which I spent on buying ciabatta. Once I sold them, I bought more with the revenue the following week.'

Typical growth routes for successful traders include setting up similar stalls in other markets under the same name, or even moving towards a more permanent retail space, such as opening your own shop.

*"By travelling to your clients' homes you can increase your appeal and income"*

## Tutoring

If you are a good communicator and enjoy passing on your skills, then you may find tutoring attractive. Essentially, you will be offering extra tuition that provides children and young people (from primary to A-level) with the one-to-one or few-to-few attention they can't get in school or college. This is a profession that is ideal for people who need to be at home for certain times of the day, for example those with children. It can be operated from home, although by travelling to your clients' homes you can increase your appeal and income. You must have a comprehensive knowledge across the complete range of your subject, and be at least one level in advance of the level you are tutoring. It isn't essential to be a qualified teacher, but having some teaching experience can reassure parents.

Cost-wise, you will need access to the correct year's syllabus (around £2), sample exam papers (50p to £1) and a range of up-to-date relevant textbooks (£10 upwards). Lessons are generally charged by the hour and fees vary across the country and for different levels, but you might charge between £15 and £20 at home, plus a few extra pounds for travel. This isn't a big money business, but it can easily be built up into much more than a part-time one if you can work at weekends and do longer evenings. To make tutoring a success, it's vital to keep up to date with the curriculum, and as word of mouth is so important for generating more business in this field, make sure you get on well with your pupils and that they get better grades than predicted.

## Public relations

A public relations (PR) and communications agency promotes and represents businesses in the general marketplace, in their specialist fields and within the media. That is, it is concerned with creating a name for its client and helping it succeed. As a PR agent you will work closely with a variety of companies, identifying their needs, while focusing on an area of personal interest and increasing relevance to each client's core business. You will need to understand the objectives of your client's business and identify a strategy for achieving them through increasingly diverse communication channels. Then you have to sell that story effectively to a chosen audience.

The bare essentials are: office premises, computers, printer, desks and other furniture, telephones, print costs and legal expenses, but initially you could run this business from home. A sample hourly rate for executive time is £70 and you should focus on securing retained clients on a regular monthly income. In theory, therefore, two executives should be able to generate an annual income of around £150,000.

It is essential that you identify a market area to focus on that is not only new, but also experiencing growth, as this indicates that there is a proven market and also competition, so that companies will need help to stand out. For example, when **Tim Lewis** and **Greg Moore** set up Synapse Communication in the late nineties (which was acquired by Four Communications in 2001), it was one of the first agencies to specialise in corporate social responsibility (CSR), working with companies that promote responsible practices to benefit business and society. Remember that this is a 'people' business, so you and your staff will need good communication skills, and the ability to be both friendly and persuasive.

*"Identify a market area to focus on that is not only new, but also experiencing growth"*

## *Dog walking*

It's often said that Britain is a nation of animal lovers. However, with credit well and truly crunched, animal care has taken a backseat as many people put in longer hours at work in an attempt to pay off their debts.

There's no doubt, then, that Britain's dogs are crying out for attention, and if you are an animal lover with an entrepreneurial streak, who empathises with these often overlooked victims of the economic downturn, then starting a dog-walking business could be the right move for you.

With around 6.5 million dogs in the UK, walking the canine companions of time-strapped workers seems to be an increasingly viable – and popular – route to self-employment. **William Taylor**, from industry body the National Association of Registered Petsitters (NARP), agrees. 'Although people might not have so much disposable income to spend on a pet sitter, they will have to work longer hours so they will need one in that instance,' he says.

There's good money to be made in the business too, according to William. A survey by NARP revealed that demand rose by almost 60% in 2008; in the same year, one dog-walking business in Philadelphia, USA, grossed US$650,000 (£377,800). Meanwhile, an April 2011 article in *The Daily Mail* named dog walking 'one of the UK's fastest growing jobs'. According to the article, there are now around 10,000 registered dog walkers in the UK, charging between £10 and £30 to walk a dog for an hour, including pick-up and drop-off.

Start-up costs are also relatively low. Your major expenditures at the beginning will be public liability insurance (£80–£150 a year); a police CRB (Criminal Records Bureau) check — which is recommended as it will reassure your clients you are reliable — costing just over £30; and flyers and business cards to spread the word in your local area (you can get 5,000 flyers printed for around £100).

It's also a good idea to join NARP, from which you will get insurance and all the forms and paperwork you need to get the business going for around £450 a year. NARP members are advised to charge around £10 an hour per dog. 'That does vary somewhat, though,' advises William, so do some research into how much competitors in your area are charging before you decide on your fees.

## Debt collection

Debt collectors chase so-called 'delinquent debts', through snail mail, telephone and email, for businesses. The older the debt, the higher the commission you can collect. And with rates running as high as 60%, the earning potential of this business is clear. Although this may not be the first business opportunity that springs to mind, nowadays it is an essential service to businesses and you should ignore any stigma that people may attach to it. You also need to market it in the same way as you would any other business.

Debt collection today requires good interpersonal skills and careful organisation. The 'old school' heavy-handed approach is no longer relevant, as businesses want subtlety, so that they can maintain their business relationships with the companies that owe them money.

It could be argued that debt collection is certainly a business for these times. First, it is a prime example of a sustainable business, requiring nothing more than a telephone in the first instance. Second, these are tough times, and as customer debt grows, the demand for non-court action debt collection is increasing. Also, companies are realising the value of this service more and more, as sufficient cashflow becomes increasingly vital. Many debt agencies operate from a home base, and if you network well, and establish good word-of-mouth recommendations, you can quickly build up a client base.

So, if you are self-motivated, enjoy dealing with people and can think quickly on your feet, debt collection could be the right business for you.

## *Cake making*

Although cake making has been hit by everything from high flour costs to aggressive supermarket pricing in recent years, a 2010 report by Mintel showed the cake market was worth £1.6bn in 2009, after five years of strong growth. So if you are interested in cake making as a business, and can ride out the current economic conditions, the demand seems to be there for you to reap the rewards when the good times return.

Keeping your head above water in this industry will require organisation, a good head for figures and a certain amount of artistic flair. 'We work long hours and it's tiring, because you've got to hit delivery times spot on,' explains **Lynn Oxley**, who has been running Oxley's of Morpeth and its accompanying website, Cake Perfect, since 2003.

Your cakes will need to look as professional as possible, so training in all aspects of the industry, from sugarcraft to marzipan techniques, is essential if you want to compete in a busy market. However, there are several courses available for all levels of cake making, so you should find one which will suit your commitments. Courses start at around £190 for 10 weekly sessions, rising to around £500 for a 30-week NVQ course. Alternatively, The Bakery School has an online course that you can complete at your own pace. A one-year licence for the downloadable software costs between £50 and £250 plus VAT, depending on the modules you require.

*"Your cakes will need to look as professional as possible"*

**Shaz Yousaf's** preparation for starting up his own organic cake-making business, The Healthy Dessert Kitchen, included testing his creations out on friends and work colleagues, and noting down comments and reactions. He also looked for key opportunities to publicise his enterprise, such as appearing on Asian TV channel Sunrise.

Your start-up costs will depend on how big an operation you wish to run. The fewer overheads you have, the lower your expenditure, so working from home initially is a good idea. But you will soon need to trade up to professional catering equipment, and follow the required hygiene and health and safety guidelines.

Pricing is tricky, but you can charge from around £30 for a simple 10-inch diameter sponge, up to £900 for an intricate, five-tiered wedding cake.

## Web design

The good thing about web design is it doesn't take very much to start up an agency – especially if you aim to grow, like many others, organically from your living room. Perhaps the most important qualifications for starting in web design are a certain amount of know-how, an open mind and a thirst for knowledge.

However, low barriers to entry mean stiff competition. 'It's a different industry now to 10 years ago,' **Andy Budd** of Clearleft (which was named Web Design Agency of the Year in 2009) explains. 'Then, the industry itself was quite immature, so you could get a foothold really quickly. Now, the quality of design work is so high that you have to be really, really good to actually get work.'

The current trend for innovation means web developers and designers have to keep up-to-date with the latest technologies in order to gain an edge over the competition. Fine-tuning your expertise and building on your knowledge by reading books, articles and blogs is a key part of developing your business.

For Andy and his two co-founders, establishing themselves as experts in their field by setting up their own blogs before launching Clearleft proved highly successful. 'If your company is perceived as the expert in the particular field, whether it's the UeX field, which is what we're offering, or Java Script, or HTML5, or expert design, then you get the benefit of word-of-mouth marketing. If you don't have that, I think it's much more difficult to get a foothold,' he says.

Not everyone specialises, though: there are a lot of generic agencies out there. Their offer includes the design, the front end programming and the back end programming. Sometimes they do the marketing and the search engine optimisation (SEO) as well. But establishing yourself as a one-stop-shop is not necessarily the best idea. 'I see a lot of generic agencies trying to do it all, and what tends to happen is that if you try to do everything, you don't do anything particularly well,' says Andy.

*"To run a web design business, you need to distinguish yourself"*

When starting out, research what the average daily rates are and be firm with how much you charge, he advises: 'You have a lot of creativity and you should be charging a decent amount of money for it.' It's not uncommon for new designers to charge £500 for a whole website. But if it takes two weeks, and you're charging £50 a day, that is really not enough to cover your costs, let alone make a profit on skilled labour. 'If you're constantly competing on price in a commodity market, you're never going to get out of that,' says Andy. 'So don't focus on price! To run a web design business, you need to distinguish yourself.'

 **In my experience**

Company: **CURB Media**
Owner-manager: **Anthony Ganjou**

*Achieving sustainable growth*
**Anthony Ganjou** founded CURB Media, a groundbreaking venture that harnesses natural resources to create eye-catching marketing campaigns, in 2008. The company has ploughed a unique furrow in its industry by taking under-used or overlooked land, and transforming it into a giant, living ad campaign. CURB has grown logos out of seeded paper, made sculptures for clients in sand, and even created its own branded crop circles.

Anthony's initial epiphany took place in a pub beer garden, where he spotted an advert for a natural product whoosh past on a bus. The contradiction jarred in his mind – a product which claimed to be organic and good for the planet, publicised on a vehicle which powers the grimy, polluted congestion of urban life.

Inspired, Anthony conducted market research, which confirmed there was a gap in the market. 'When we did our research, we found that 99% of the innovation, resource and creativity in the market was focused on the end message; there was almost nothing about how you could actually communicate a message using a green or sustainable channel,' he recalls.

With this as his vision, in early 2008 Anthony began using the internet to build a team of artists, creative visionaries, production experts and sub-contractors. Unlike many new entrepreneurs, Anthony was able to get by without huge loans; his business was funded by loans from friends and family, and personal investment.

Running the new venture from his parents' basement, Anthony was able to avoid expensive office overheads and instead channel money into branding and external assets, such as business cards and media packs, as well as SEO and Google ad campaigns.

By starting small, Anthony sowed the seeds for organic and sustainable growth. Now based in Oxford Circus, London, CURB has six full-time staff and a global team of around 150. Annual turnover exceeds £500,000, and the company commands a truly international profile, having received press coverage everywhere from Japan to Argentina. CURB can count Sony, Microsoft and Smirnoff among its clients, and has even installed natural media in the White House.

## *Other popular options*

### *Online business*

Starting an online business can be as simple as setting up a basic shop on eBay (see 'Shoestring start-ups', above) to sell a few wholesale items, to coming up with a completely new online concept with a novel way of monetising it.

The beauty of the online business is that it's suited to just about anyone. You don't need to be an MBA graduate based in London to succeed. You can start your operation from anywhere, as long as you've got access to an internet connection and a bit of business acumen. You can start off small, work on it part-time or even view it as a hobby before you decide whether to commit to it.

**Claire Lewis** and **Pat Wood** started their online retro T-shirt shop Truffleshuffle.com as a part-time venture. 'It all started after Pat bought a retro T-shirt in the States and friends kept asking where he'd got it,' explains Claire. 'Truffleshuffle was only ever intended to be a hobby – something to bring in a bit of spare cash. It was only when the site went live and started growing that we thought: "There's mileage in this."'

---

## Online business models

After you have decided how much time, money and resources you want to put into your online venture, there are four basic online business models you can follow.

- Ecommerce – which means that customers buy directly from your website
- Advertising – which means you get as many visitors as possible, increasing the amount of customers your advertisers reach
- Subscription – which means users pay to access all or part of your content
- Freemium – which means you offer a basic service for free, but customers can pay for premium features

You can of course base your website around a combination of these models.

---

At the other end of the scale, **Sophie Cornish** and **Holly Tucker** did a five-year profit-and-loss feasibility plan before they started work on their website, Notonthehighstreet.com, an online marketplace where customers can buy from a whole range of independent, quirky and specialised small businesses in a single transaction.

*"Truffleshuffle was only ever intended to be a hobby – something to bring in a bit of spare cash"*

Key factors to consider for an online business are: making sure your domain name reflects your business; choosing the right hosting service; adhering to online trading rules; working carefully on the design and functionality of the site and optimising it for search engines to maximise exposure.

Start-up costs for online businesses vary widely from very little for an eBay set-up to thousands of pounds for a hosted, ecommerce site.

## Crafts business

Austerity chic: thanks to the current economic dip, crafting really is 'in'. Think crochet, soap, cross-stitch, jewellery-making, and wooden toys. Or pottery, glassblowing and tapestry. Home-baked is fast becoming the only way to go: so why not go for a piece of the cake?

If you are one of the recession's newly converted crafters, or even if your grandmother taught you to crochet, knit or sew, the skills you take for granted could well become a promising venture. Don't worry if you have no professional training in your craft, either. Many successful businesses are powered by the enthusiasm of talented amateurs. 'All you have to know is your craft,' says **Amanda Ryan** of craft gifts shop Maisielu.com. 'Everything else can be researched, and gained through experience and the helpful knowledge of others.' In particular, online forums such as Crafteroo and UK Handmade are a great way to source very specific advice from fellow crafters.

*"All you have to know is your craft; everything else can be researched, and gained through experience and the helpful knowledge of others"*

Crafting is a competitive area, so it's important to find a unique selling point. It's imperative to research your product too, to ensure it's original and that there's a market for it. 'eBay is very good for checking up on products that sell well, and to get a general guidance on price,' says **Fiona Morris** of Samigail's Handmade Personalised Gifts.

There are a number of routes to market, and the site of sale will depend on your product. It may need a street presence, or sell better in an established local shop, or at craft fairs at seasonal times. A pottery or wicker workshop could benefit from a studio shop or artisan workspace. Meanwhile, online marketplaces showcasing the wares of small craft businesses, such as Misi, Folksy, Etsy and Notonthehighstreet.com, are also becoming extremely popular. 'With minimal set-up costs, you can set up a store within their site, list your products and off you go. You get support from their forums, an online presence, get to test your products on a target audience and all for a very cheap fee and commission rate,' says Amanda. However, she adds: 'I felt the major breakthrough for my craft working as a business was when I launched my own website. Selling through my own space rather than sales sites, I don't have to pay fees to others.'

Depending on how you choose to sell, there can be sellers' fees, commission taken, insurance, and fete table costs. There can be studio rents, utilities, and so on. Similarly, there is much to consider in terms of pricing your product. 'Don't pitch yourself too low,' warns **Joanne Dewberry** of Charliemoos.co.uk. 'When the work starts flying in and you're up making at all hours and the cash tin is empty you'll struggle to raise them up higher.'

## Photography

For many amateur photographers, running a professional photography business would be a dream come true – and now it can be. The photography industry offers many opportunities for keen amateurs who want to make a living from it.

Wedding photography is the most high-profile money-maker. It is generally recognised by most photographers as being a highly skilled job – not only in terms of taking photographs, but handling all kinds of people at a potentially emotional time. It tends to be seasonal, too. May to September is the busiest time – accounting for 80%–90% of the work – with the rest of the year being relatively quiet, when many wedding photographers will turn to other sources of income, such as passport and portrait work, or commercial and industrial photography. This means it pays to be flexible.

Photography is a business you can run from home, but you will need to set aside some space for administration and storing equipment. Many home-based photographers convert a garage into an all-in-one studio, admin, storage and reception facility. A double garage attached to your home is ideal for doing this; budget around £7,000 for your conversion costs. Alternatively, you can rent a small shop with a display area and a small studio; prices will vary depending on your location. Although more expensive to run, a shop will give you a higher public profile and you may not need to spend as much on marketing your business.

*"The photography industry offers many opportunities for keen amateurs who want to make a living from it"*

You will also need photographic equipment – a reasonable camera and lens, studio lights and back-drops will cost around £5,000. Then there's general administration and marketing costs, which could rise to between £4,000 and £8,000 over the year, especially if you use tools such as promotional stands at locations with high footfall (while expensive, this can be very productive for portrait photographers if done well, according to **Paul Spiers** of photographymarketing.co.uk). However, there are also several low-cost avenues you can explore, such as promoting your business via your own website and using social media sites such as Twitter.

You can learn your trade through a college course or, if you are a gifted amateur, you can pick up professional tips by offering your services to a local business. Your potential earnings will depend on many factors, not least your range of services and your ability to market yourself as a top-notch photographer. However, a reasonably established photographer should expect to earn at least £20,000 a year.

As a guide, **Steven Brooks**, who runs his own photography business based in Kent and Norfolk, provided the following figures for a wedding.

Wedding fee: £1,200–£1,400 (plus a booking fee of between £300 and £350 – due 30 days in advance)

Material costs (processing, album etc): £200–£500

Average profit: £1,000

However, it's far from easy money; as part of his service, Steven meets the couple before the wedding, views the church and other locations, holds a pre-wedding meeting and also a post-wedding meeting of between two and four hours. On the day itself, he spends at least 12 hours on the job.

*"It won't be until you have a large operation that you start bringing in good money, so it could be worthwhile to start up part time"*

## Catering

Whether it's a major sporting event or a low-key wedding, food and drink at gatherings will always be in fashion. In fact, with a growing population of foodies and people becoming more nutritionally aware, it is increasingly a key part of an event. The key to success in catering lies in a passion for excellent quality food and service, along with exploiting any gap in the catering market that may exist in your area.

As an independent, there are two main sectors you can target – private and corporate events. The former category consists of, for example, family occasions such as weddings, birthday parties, dinner parties and funerals. In serving the corporate world, you are more likely to provide food for business breakfasts, business lunches, board meetings and evening receptions. Some caterers specialise in one or the other, while others try to cover both.

Taking into account the professional equipment you will need, you are looking at between £20,000 and £50,000 to start up, depending on the size of business and whether you are starting up at home or moving into premises. It won't be until you have a large operation that you start bringing in good money, so it could be worthwhile to start up part-time. **Sue Roberts** did this and has grown Bristol-based Topline Catering gradually over 25 years, moving from sandwich delivery to business lunches, and finally to corporate and private events for up to 1,000 guests. From first-day takings of £13, the business now turns over £300,000 a year. It obviously takes several years to build up to this size, but a small yet successful business could nevertheless turn over £100,000 and earn a net profit of £40,000.

## *Floristry*

Opening a florist business may be the result of a gardening hobby, but even if you are new to the sector you can start up and make a success of this business. Of all retail businesses, this is one that could probably be almost recession-proof, as people always want to send, and appreciate getting, flowers, whether the occasion is happy or sad. But an online presence is practically a must these days.

*"Florists should emphasise the additional design input and technical skill that goes into their work"*

The flower market has been on the increase since the early 1990s, with UK fresh flowers and indoor plants representing £2.2bn at retail level. Before setting up, carry out thorough market research of the area you want to cover, the people who live and work there and the existing competition. 'Any kind of specialisation is beneficial. Florists should also emphasise the additional design input and technical skill that goes into their work,' says **Andrea Caldecourt** of the Flowers and Plants Association. 'This often has a personal touch – just as artists and clothes designers are recognisable by their work.'

Many florist businesses are members of relay organisations such as InterFlora or Teleflora, which allow people in one part of the country to 'send' flowers to someone in another part of the country or abroad through a network of florists. The benefit of this membership is that you will receive support in marketing and sales, as well as product and design, and as a result of the organisations' international links you may compete with multinational firms and respond to a changing market. Floristry has the classic retail cost base of premises and stock, so the initial outlay can be significant. As with clothing retail, risks are high, but if you get it right, the rewards can be substantial.

## *Hotel*

Whether it's just a simple bed and shared bathroom or full en-suite luxury, a place for the weary traveller to stay the night is always in demand. Obviously, location is the key to success, but the rise of boutique establishments means that many people are increasingly going for style and ambience over five-star blandness.

*"The types of client you attract depend, to a large extent, on the hotel's location"*

The first thing to consider is what type of hotel you want to run. Is it going to be a small, cosy affair catering for couples seeking a romantic weekend break, or a larger, metropolitan establishment servicing the corporate market? Some hotels pitch for both business and private clients. The types of client you attract depend, to a large extent, on the hotel's location. The size of the hotel, its location and the clientele you are aiming to attract will all determine costs. It is possible to rent your premises, but buying means you keep more of the profits.

There are basically two schools of thought when it comes to turnover. The first is to keep earnings below the VAT threshold, which is £73,000; at a usual 40% profit margin you are looking at clearing £29,200. The alternative is to go all out to earn as much as possible. To make it worthwhile you need to earn considerably more than the VAT threshold, which means taking £100,000+.

Having an online presence is also a must for hoteliers these days. As well as having your own website (ideally one that works well on mobile devices; if it has an online booking system, all the better), it is well worth looking into advertising your rooms on third-party sites such as Lastminute.com, Hotels. com and TripAdvisor. These sites typically work on a commission basis, whereby they take a slice of the room fee for every booking they send your way, making it a relatively risk-free form of advertising which can promote your business to a potential audience of millions. Social media sites such as Facebook and Twitter can also be extremely effective low-cost marketing tools, while deal sites such as Groupon and LivingSocial present another opportunity to attract more customers through the doors. As with any promotional activity, make sure you can cope with a potential surge in demand (consider setting a cap on the deal) and ensure that the costing is financially viable.

## *Hairdressing*

*"If you find the right location you are almost certain to make money"*

If there was a service that was always in demand, this could be it. Having said that, competition is fierce, and you do need to train hard to gain the necessary qualifications. It also involves long hours. But if you find the right location you are almost certain to make money. With the variety of customers, from children to adults, it pays to be a people person in this business. However, unless you open your own chain of shops, it's unlikely to make you a millionaire. But as **Linda Heald** from Keeping Up Appearances in Chichester, West Sussex, says: 'Getting paid for something you love doing and working with friends in a nice atmosphere can't be beaten.'

If you are starting from scratch, there'll be the usual outlay for either renting or buying premises, plus fixtures, fittings and equipment. Keeping it basic, Heald spent £1,000 on basic salon fittings and a further £3,000 on chairs and dryers. Having sat down and costed all the equipment she had to buy to fully kit out her salon, she found out that it set her back £1,800. But this could be a lot more expensive depending on the level of ostentation. 'You could stagger these costs though and just get essentials and then buy extras as you begin to make a profit,' she says. 'Also, you must remember to set aside money for the taxman right from day one.' On a good week, Heald can earn around £1,300. But when you take away costs, the figure she will be left with is more likely to be between £300 and £400.

## Day nursery

Day nurseries are a vital service for the many families that can't afford to give up a regular income to stay at home. Clearly, you need the ability to spend long hours with children as well as patience and other child-minding skills, but this is a growing area and one that appears to be increasingly in demand. It is a business that tends to attract working parents – usually either because they have found a gap in what nurseries in their area offer or because there is nothing available in the area at all.

*"Decide from the beginning if you want to run the business as a lifestyle choice or as a profit-making thing; that will determine the size of the operation"*

Running a nursery will not make you quick money. But, if you want a job – and a business – that offers hourly challenges and a lot of rewards then this could be right for you. Finding suitable premises is a must. The regulations set out how much space you will need per child, so once you have worked out how many children you want to have you will know the minimum space required. You can either rent or buy, or build from scratch, but this can be expensive. Some local authorities allow modular nurseries, which are much cheaper to build and can be up and running quickly – for 25–30 children they cost around £80,000.

**Freya Derrick** set up Hopscotch Day Nursery for £600,000 in 2005. The company now operates four day nurseries on the south coast and is turning over £1.5m a year. 'You've got to decide right from the beginning if you want to run the business as a lifestyle choice, or as a profit-making thing, and that will determine the size of the operation,' she says. 'I wanted to have the freedom to spend time with my children, but I also wanted to run a successful business.'

## Restaurant

Despite the downturn, eating out remains big business with a huge variety of restaurants now inhabiting British high streets. However, whatever the climate, many new restaurants won't survive for long due to the sheer amount of competition. But if you can think strategically and find the right niche for your location, the rewards can be great in terms of both job satisfaction and money. For his restaurant, which seats 40 people, **Stephane Luiggi**, owner of the French Living restaurant in Nottingham, spent £5,000 on kitchen equipment, some of which was second-hand, and £5,000 on tables and chairs. Then there are the premises. 'You need to have quite a lot of money, particularly in central London, where an 80-seater restaurant would cost you about £1m,' explains restaurant consultant **Torquil Macleod**. However, if you are going for something slightly more modest, a restaurant on a suburban high street for example, then you should have between £70,000 and £150,000 in your pocket, explains **Mike Rogers**, managing director of start-ups and small businesses at Barclays.

Aside from the equipment, staff will be one of your biggest fixed costs. If you are open seven days a week, you will need more than one chef. Head chefs can command salaries of between £30,000 and £40,000 per year – and getting a good chef will be critical to your business. To avoid being just another restaurant casualty, be prepared to run a business rather than merely indulge a hobby. Market research is essential. 'You need to check out the location and the competition,' says Mike. 'What's your catchment area? What's more, you can't charge a premium when you first open. You need to know what will make people want to come and spend their money with you. With local research you can see what is popular, whether it be Mexican, Thai, Japanese, whatever.' There are also all the hygiene and health and safety regulations to negotiate, and initially long hours to contend with, but if you plan carefully, you will find that there is money to be made.

## Mobile apps

Thinking of starting up a business in mobile applications? Funnily enough, there's an app for that. Search the App Store, Android Market et al, and you'll find plenty of examples: there are applications that offer app development code tutorials; apps that enable you to test your idea through market research; and even more that allow you to submit your app idea to developers.

With thousands of apps to choose from on Apple's App Store and Google's Android Market, and other platforms such as Blackberry, Nokia and Windows Mobile doing their darnedest to catch up, mobile apps is a growing area if ever there was one. It's a crowded and competitive marketplace too, however, and not an easy one to break. While many apps get brought to market, very few mobile app businesses actually make any money.

To top the charts you need a good idea, for sure, but you don't have to be an expert developer yourself. Be warned, though: developing a mobile app is not cheap. A developer's charge may vary according to platform. For a really simple app on Android, £500 is probably the minimum. For a simple app on iPhone, it can cost from around £800. For a more complex app, you could be looking at £4,000. And things can get a great deal more expensive than that.

If you are developing the app yourself, you need technology appropriate to the platform on which you'll be launching. If you want to launch on iPhone, for instance, you need to register as a member of the iPhone Developer Program, which costs, and get your hands on the iPhone Software Development Kit (SDK), which is free. You also need to invest a great deal of time in the development stage. If you are serious about things, two months is really the minimum. Many apps take six months and more to work up to a finished product.

In terms of revenue, the platform generally takes a percentage: Apple and Android take 30% of sales revenue and publishers take the rest. **Tristan Celder** of Zolmo (the developers behind the award-winning 'Jamie's 20 Minute Meals' iPhone app) says: 'In many cases the publisher and developer of an app are one and the same, such is the case with 20 Minute Meals and Zolmo. The reward can be good for publishers, but it comes with its risks – so make sure you do your market research.'

*"While many apps get brought to market, very few mobile app businesses actually make any money"*

Deciding how much to charge for your app can be tough. Many companies struggle to make the numbers tally, although often you can adjust the price and make the decision through learning what sells and what doesn't. Some of the apps The App Factory (a self-funded app development agency and publisher, founded by **David Carter**) produces are free downloads, and money is made back on adverts. The Tweetdeck app is entirely free, without advertising; founder **Iain Dodsworth** suggests developers decide whether they want to make money directly from the product they're building or if they want a lot of downloads. However, if you want to trial this approach, it is best to have funding behind you. Again, there are not many people who make money out of it.

Depending on whether you decide to develop one app and stick with that, like Tweetdeck; or turn your app talents into an agency, like The App Factory, you'll want to grow your business into a bigger venture.

The best start is publishing a great app. 'The key to getting word of mouth marketing is by building a great product – followed up with great PR,' says Tristan.

And think long term from the development stage. So if you've got a game that you think is going to be popular for only three or six months, for instance, then you should plan to evolve it. On the other hand, if you have something you think will be around for the next three or four years, then you need to keep on improving it and iterating so that you can keep your customers engaged. The trick is to drum up numbers when you first launch the app – and then keep interest by iteration and new developments.

 ## In my experience

Company: **Masala**
Owner-manager: **Priya Lakhani**

*Finding a fresh idea*
The common insomniac may spend the early hours channel hopping between the 24-hour news networks, but **Priya Lakhani** found a better use for her sleepless nights – coming up with business ideas. Several concepts were fleshed out with market research and product planning between 1–3am, but it wasn't until the idea for Masala Masala took hold that she mustered enough courage to give up her career as a barrister. Three years later, Priya's range of chilled, authentic Indian cooking sauces is sold by Waitrose, WaitroseDeliver and Ocado.com.

'Being a barrister was risk free,' says Priya. 'I had a very secure income and compared to a lot of my peers, a very comfortable life for a 27 year old. But after I came up with the idea for Masala Masala I just couldn't stop it. It was like an infection.'

Having often used the fresh pasta sauces found in the supermarket chillers, Priya just couldn't understand why an Indian equivalent didn't exist. Keen to be the first mover in the market she started working on the idea straight away, spending weekends researching the industry, developing a brand and forming her business plan.

Priya and her husband worked out they needed £25,000 to take the product through development and secure a supermarket deal. The plan was they'd either sign up a big customer within the first few months or shelve the project until the industry was ready for it. 'I was laughed out of the door by manufacturers, suppliers and people who'd been in the industry for 20 years, but I just knew we'd be in the supermarket within a few months. My product was basically designed – how it looked and tasted – with my suppliers in mind.'

Priya's belief in her idea was well placed. Just as she had predicted, Waitrose was on board within three months of Masala Masala launching. While Priya accepts that launching a premium product in the middle of one of the biggest economic crises in modern history doesn't fit in with everyone's plan, she's adamant there's still a market for quality food. Masala Masala's growth plans are a testament to this: Priya is currently working on new product development, which will soon see ready to cook meals, accompaniments and sauces with a longer shelf life added to the range.

## *Franchising*

Buying a franchise can be a great way to fast-track your way to running your own business. One of the greatest benefits of becoming a franchisee is the opportunity to buy into an established, profitable model that has already been proven elsewhere. The industry has even proved robust throughout the economic downturn. The latest annual survey by NatWest and the British Franchise Association (BFA) suggests that 90% of franchisees traded profitably over the past 12 months.

*"Figures suggest that 90% of franchisees traded profitably over the past 12 months"*

However, there are no golden tickets; as with any business venture, success requires hard work and determination. 'Franchising isn't a get-rich-quick-scheme,' says **Vincent McKevitt**, who founded salad bar chain Tossed in 2005. The company now has seven sites across London, two of which are run on a franchise basis. 'Franchisees are buying into a brand, a set of systems and a successful business model that you know works, because it's been proven in other places and replicated. But if they implement the model incorrectly, or don't work hard enough, it can still fail.'

There are two routes into franchising. Either you buy a franchise directly from the franchisor or you look at an existing franchise for sale. If you opt for the latter, it is important to find out why the franchisee wants to sell that particular franchise. For sale signs are put up for perfectly good reasons, such as retirement, personal circumstances or a desire to move into a different area of business. However, some franchisees might want to sell because the business has not been financially viable. Are you certain that you will be able to make the business profitable if they cannot?

You need to find out the reasons for the business' lack of success. If, for instance, it is in a poor location or the market that it is catering for is not large enough, then you probably should not enter into the deal. Similarly, you must make sure that you are getting good value for money. Compare the costs of the franchise to other businesses of a similar nature. Also, find out how much an original franchise from the same company would be sold for now.

Naturally, there are upsides and downsides to buying a franchise rather than starting your own company. It's worth remembering that a franchise is a hybrid between entrepreneurship and working for an established corporation. Therefore, aspects of both will be evident in the running of your franchise. Here's a look at some of the key differences between buying a franchise and starting a business from scratch.

*"You are paying for a part of an established company's brand: the more established the brand, the higher the fee"*

## Raising finance

Although a franchisor will take much of the financial burden away from you compared with a conventional start-up, there are still significant initial costs to running a franchise. Most franchises incur an initial fee to cover set-up costs and initial working capital. You are paying for a part of an established company's brand: the more established the brand, the higher the fee. However, in return, you will have access to the know-how, systems, experience, value and name – effectively ensuring a head-start on someone starting from scratch. All equipment is likely to be supplied to you, along with premises and help with accounting and insurance. There will be fewer commitments to soak up your money, enabling you to concentrate on growing the business.

**WANT TO KNOW MORE ...**

The British Franchise Association (BFA)
www.thebfa.org

As for investment sources, you will rarely need to look further than your bank. With franchising being a lower-risk option, banks are generally happy to lend money to franchisees. Therefore, finding finance should be easier for a franchisee than a standard entrepreneur.

## Support

Being a conventional entrepreneur means you have to live very much on your wits. If you haven't done it before, you will be taking a trip into the unknown. What's more, the 'safety net' beneath entrepreneurs can vary greatly or not exist at all. Compared to a standard company, a franchise is a different story altogether. Almost all franchisors provide comprehensive training for their franchisees. Before taking on a territory, you should be given a full run-down of the market you'll be working in, advice on any equipment you'll be using and some help on business basics such as accounting, stock-taking and turnover projections.

Having been trained to run a fully equipped business, the support doesn't end there. Most franchise companies offer their franchisees ongoing help in the early days of the business and often put newcomers in touch with more experienced franchise owners for advice. When you consider the support franchisees enjoy compared with their start-up counterparts, it's easy to see why the sector has such a low failure rate.

*"Almost all franchisors provide comprehensive training for their franchisees"*

## Marketing and PR

As a start-up company, it's imperative that you get your message out there to the right audience. Through carefully targeted advertising, you should be able to reach enough people to get some customers through your door. Next comes the ongoing process of building and maintaining a reputation. Get this right and you will begin to thrive from positive recommendations from satisfied punters. It can be a long, time-consuming process and a costly one too – advertising isn't cheap and entrepreneurs often have to think up innovative, quirky ways in which to publicise themselves.

As a franchisee, you'll have the clout of a large, often well-known, brand behind you. You'll generally be given a lot of advice, support and materials to help you spread the word about your business, as well as benefiting from corporate level PR and advertising, sometimes on a national scale.

## Freedom

Franchising provides you with plenty of support, but it isn't exactly the business equivalent of a blank canvas, unlike the experience of conventional entrepreneurs. Franchisors have their own criteria for how each of their outlets should look and operate. However much it feels like you're the ultimate boss on a day-to-day basis, you will always be working to someone else's vision, not your own. The amount of freedom afforded to franchisees varies, but you will almost certainly be briefed on how the company wants to be represented, from the uniforms of staff to what suppliers to use. Generally, the franchise agreement you sign will be

*"However much it feels like you're the ultimate boss on a day-to-day basis, you will always be working to someone else's vision, not your own"*

a comprehensive document, outlining what you will be required to seek the franchisor's approval on, and how you must adhere to the company's standards and systems.

Also, should a franchisor change ownership or fail, the future of your franchise will be thrown into doubt. Likewise, the actions of your fellow franchisees will have an impact upon your image – and therefore sales. It's important that you are comfortable with these circumstances before you purchase the franchise, or you could become extremely frustrated.

## Making a profit

Franchising holds the upper hand here – with one significant drawback. A franchisor will typically demand a percentage of the revenue you achieve as an ongoing royalty fee. But then again, your franchise will provide you with an ideal platform to make profits in the first place. You will be operating a proven business concept that has a solid reputation and a history of making money.

You will also be trained to run a business that is fully equipped, with much of the work done for you in terms of marketing and PR, meaning that many of the time and money-consuming aspects of starting up a business will not be a factor when running a franchise. Moreover, it's likely the franchisor will have projections of how your business should grow, with practical advice on how to achieve profitability.

*"Franchisees should be wary of anyone who requires a flat fee, because then there's no incentive for the franchisor to increase the franchisee's sales"*

For the set-up to work, franchisors should be making money when you do. 'Franchisees should be wary of anyone who requires a flat fee, because then there's no incentive for the franchisor to increase the franchisee's sales,' says **Vincent McKevitt** of Tossed. **Darren Leppard**, who owns two successful Select Appointments franchises in Coventry and Leicester, agrees: 'Look for a company that wants to make money from you making money, rather than the initial fee, otherwise why would it bother supporting you? It would have made its money already. If you're paying a percentage of your revenue, it's in the company's interest to help you.'

The BFA also advocates this approach; marketing manager **Tom Endean** says the average management services fee is 10% – although this varies between franchises.

## Buying an existing business

You want to run your own business. Now the question is: to start up, or to buy? For many, it's obvious. People often start up when they're following a passion – whether it be making cakes or a new piece of technical gadgetry they've invented. Others work for someone else before deciding they could do the same thing better. But another alternative is to buy your own business – could this be the right way for you to become your own boss?

Buying a business is in many ways a much more straightforward proposition. If you buy a business that's doing relatively well, it will be much easier to secure finance for it than if you were starting one from scratch. The proven customer base is a huge bonus both to investors and banks – and to you if you're risking your own finances. Furthermore, it can often take months – if not years – before new businesses start turning a profit and giving you enough to live on. In contrast, buying a profitable business often means you can draw a decent salary much sooner.

You can also acquire many other assets with the business – suppliers, employees, systems and credibility being among them. In other words, all the unknown quantities that would deem a start-up a risky venture have been worked out by the business' previous owners. However, it's important to note that while funding may be easier to access, the initial purchasing cost of an established business is usually much greater than the cost of starting up. You have to know what you can afford, and this has to take into account other costs such as accountants, lawyers, valuation specialists and so on.

*"You have to know what you can afford, and this has to take into account other costs such as accountants, lawyers, valuation specialists and so on"*

## Why not to buy a business

Buying a business isn't always the easy option. It takes as much hard work to take over a business as it does to start one up, and you have to be extremely dedicated. Furthermore, it can be much more expensive than starting a business, especially if you buy a profitable firm that's performing well, and which comes with advantages such as trained staff and a good customer base. And, if the business has been neglected or run badly, costs are likely to mount up. You may have to carry out repairs, buy new equipment or redecorate to give it a chance of succeeding.

Furthermore, there could be many other hidden problems with an established business – and they could be difficult to find and solve. Although the business may come with staff, easing recruitment worries, they may not be happy with a new boss. The way the business was run previously may have depleted morale. This leaves you with a big job: you'll have to find ways of unlocking their potential and getting them used to new ways of working. The previous owner will also have contracts in place that you will either have to honour or renegotiate.

Buying a business can also be a long process. It can take months to identify a business that is on the market and suitable to your aims and desires. It's important to resist the temptation to buy one that isn't what you had in mind just because it's available and at the right price. Negotiating the purchase can also take a long time, and lots of hard work is involved, mainly around researching the business and the market.

*"It takes as much hard work to take over a business as it does to start one up"*

However, if you think you can deal with these potential problems (and let's face it, nothing worth having comes without difficulties) then buying a business might just be the option for you. The main thing to avoid is picking up a business which seems too good to be true. It is. If a business is going for a song, it's likely that it's failing, and all the advantages that should come with buying your own business will disappear.

## What can you afford?

It's crucial when looking at the type of business you want to buy to make sure you're only paying what you can afford. No matter how attractive the business appears to be, if you overstretch yourself financially you're likely to run into problems. Use a professional adviser to help you work out what you can afford, and what kind of financing you should consider. The loan you're able to get will help you decide what business you can acquire, but you have to take into consideration the terms that the financing will come with.

It is likely you may experience a drop in income as well. How long can you afford to be earning little or nothing? If you're looking at a particular business to see whether you can afford it, look at its cashflow to get an idea of the money you will need to see you through. Does the cashflow have peaks and troughs – eg is it seasonal? Can you afford to cope with this, or will you need an overdraft for some periods?

And, as always, hope for the best but expect the worst. Unforeseen problems and expenses will inevitably crop up, and not having the cashflow to be able to deal with these could destroy your plans, and cause serious difficulties. For example, is the landlord able to raise the rent for the premises? Could you afford it? Cashflow problems are the biggest cause of failures for start-ups, but newly-bought businesses are not immune either. Try and plan for the unexpected, therefore, and budget accordingly.

Having the upfront cost for the business then isn't enough. There are also fees for solicitors, accountants, and other professionals and any repairs, equipment, wages or suppliers you might have to pay for before you see any profit, and all the unexpected expenses that crop up. Taking all this into

consideration then, how much does the business you want to buy
really cost? Make sure it is as good as it first appears.

 **Startups Tips**

**Buying a business: what to look out for**

- → Is the buyer in a hurry to sell? If so find out why. There may be hidden problems such as debt or a large fall in profits.
- → Do the numbers add up? Look closely at turnover, profits, and accounts.
- → Look at the customer base. How big is it? What's repeat business like? Is the location or sales strategy bringing in a sufficient number of customers?
- → Is there a strong team? Experienced employees who can help you learn about the market are a huge benefit. Look at their salaries, and enquire whether they're likely to stay on once you've bought the business.
- → Assess the competition. How is the company performing against its rivals, and what threats do they pose?
- → Is there growth potential? Can you expand the business by adding new products or services, entering new locations or improving the existing proposition?

## Valuing a business

The valuation is one of the most important things to get right in the process of buying a business. Unfortunately, it's also one of the most difficult. You need to know that you're paying the right price for the business you've set your heart on. The only way of doing this is to carry out in-depth research.

One of the best ways to start your research is by talking to people. Speak with customers and suppliers as well as the vendor. They may give you information about the business, or even the market in general, that you wouldn't have considered checking. You need to know how healthy the business is. Things to find out include the business' history; its current performance including turnover and profit; and its finances: debts, expenses, assets, and cashflow. You should also find out why it's being sold. If the previous owner has to sell it because of a fall in profits, for example, it will bring the price of the business down.

Apart from the aspects listed above, there are also intangible assets to value. These could include the business' relationships with suppliers and customers, its reputation or intellectual property. Don't necessarily rely on the seller's profit projection figures when working out the business' value – make your own forecasts.

Other factors to consider when evaluating the business include stock, employees, products, premises and competition. Once you've looked at all these factors, you should be able to work out a return on investment. A business is really only worth anything if it can pay for itself over a reasonable period of time. You want to make a profit as soon as you can.

Unfortunately, the general rule is that the higher the risk, the higher the potential return should be. When you have a good idea of how much the business is worth, you'll be in a position to know what you're prepared to offer for it. For your own peace of mind, it's a wise move to get a valuation from an accountant or a professional business broker too. An expert opinion could well be worth its weight in gold.

And remember, as with starting your own business, drafting a business plan is a crucial part of your groundwork. Not only will this enable you and the bank to decide on the best course of action in proceeding with your purchase, having your research findings and strategy down on paper will help you to assess the viability of the business, as well as providing a template to work from in the future. For advice on how to put together your business plan, see Chapter 3: 'Business plans and market research'.

 ### What to do next

- Assess your business options carefully. Be sure that your chosen business sector or industry is one you're willing to dedicate your life to.

- Decide whether you want to start a lifestyle business, one that provides you with a steady income and a career, or a growth business that you expand over time.

- Consider your budget and how much money you're willing to put into your business idea. Do you want to start something you can grow organically or will your ambitions require outside investment?

- Make sure you've considered online opportunities. Your business may not primarily be an internet venture but the online world influences every modern day business in one way or another.

#  CHAPTER 2

*Are you an entrepreneur?*

## 📖 What's in this chapter?

→ What it takes to be an entrepreneur
→ The average UK entrepreneur
→ The entrepreneurial personality
→ Female entrepreneurship
→ How and when to quit your job
→ So you've made your decision ...

A great idea is not the only component of a successful business. Your fledgling company will require a massive investment of your time, energy and probably your money if it is to flourish, so before you take the plunge you have to be certain you have what it takes to be an entrepreneur. In this chapter, we look at the reality of starting up, the commitment and sacrifices a new business demands and the personality traits you need to set up and grow a profitable business. If that doesn't put you off, you're already displaying the characteristics of an entrepreneur. Read on for advice on how to quit your job without burning your bridges.

# What it takes to be an entrepreneur

Although it's critical to carefully consider what kind of business you would like to launch, having a good idea doesn't automatically lead to success. An original concept or a company that you are confident has a strong market is a great start, but the key to making it a going concern is, quite simply, you. No matter how good your idea, it will only be a success if you have the necessary drive to turn it into a profitable business. Having what it takes to be a successful entrepreneur ultimately comes down to three factors:

⇢ **Are you sure you want to start your own business?**

You shouldn't view becoming your own boss as simply an escape route from your current job – and it certainly shouldn't be viewed as an easy option. In all probability, you will be working harder than you are at the moment. You need to be prepared to work long hours and be totally committed to your business idea.

⇢ **Is it too great a risk to give up a secure income?**

Initially, starting up is likely to put pressure on your financial stability, as it will be a big risk no matter how good an idea you've come up with. Be sure that you have the resources to survive, otherwise the fear, stress and an inability to support yourself could mean that your business never gets off the ground.

⇢ **Are you cut out for it?**

Launching your own business will probably be the most exciting and rewarding thing you have ever done – it's also likely to be the biggest challenge you have ever faced. So be honest about whether or not you think you will be able to cope. This is such an important factor, in fact, that this chapter is dedicated to defining what qualities an entrepreneur needs and helping you recognise whether you have them.

## The reality of starting up

Setting up a business will change your life: the way you think, the way you work, the way you spend money and the way you socialise. You will most likely need to work every hour possible to get your business off the ground, and even longer to keep it afloat during the early days. You probably won't have another holiday for a couple of years and virtually your entire life will become focused on making your business venture succeed. If you are in a relationship, it will likely feel the strain, and if you've got a family, prepare to be repeatedly torn between them and 'the business'.

This is the reality of starting your own business. However, if what you have just read hasn't curbed your enthusiasm, keep reading — you are now showing the attributes an entrepreneur needs when starting up in business. Sure, you will still have plenty of anxieties and unanswered questions, but like every successful entrepreneur starting a small business, the thought of a challenge excites and inspires you.

If you are going to succeed, you will most likely need to concentrate all your energy into the new business, because it will be 'your baby' and you and your family will be the ones reaping the rewards. You will also need the enthusiasm and ideas to find solutions to the obstacles in your path. But remember, you won't be the first person to have to cope with anxieties or to face the challenges involved in starting your own business. Every successful entrepreneur has overcome many barriers and continues to do so every week with whatever new business he or she is bringing to market.

Many successful entrepreneurs have no business qualifications or experience prior to starting up. And many spent months, even years, formulating their idea into a viable business proposition. Every single one will have made mistakes, accepted help and learnt lessons as they've gone along.

## *The average UK entrepreneur*

Over the past decade, statistics on business start-ups in the UK have tended to reveal that the majority of entrepreneurs are white males in their forties, who live in the south-east. They are likely to have been educated to degree or A-level standard and to have previous work experience in the same sector as their business — although they are not necessarily experienced in owning or managing a business. If you don't fit this profile, take heart: the greater proportion of entrepreneurs may be white, middle-aged and male, but figures suggest that the UK's entrepreneurial landscape is changing, and there is considerable scope for increasing the extent of entrepreneurship among women, those from ethnic minorities and younger people. Here's a look at the current make-up of the UK's early-stage entrepreneurs:

*"Many successful entrepreneurs have no business qualifications or experience prior to starting up"*

## Age

Historically, most small business owners in the UK have fallen into three age ranges: 35–44; 45–54 and 55–64. However, starting a business is now being promoted as a viable career option for young people more than ever before. While in the past young people have been more likely to consider starting up as a sideline venture, or as something to do later in life, figures suggest that start-up activity among the under 35s is growing at a faster rate than any other age group.

The 2010 UK Global Entrepreneurship Monitor (GEM) found that individuals aged between 25–34 years display the highest rate of early-stage entrepreneurial activity in the UK. Meanwhile, a study of 160,000 UK small businesses by insurance broker Simply Business found that the number of young people choosing to start their own business grew significantly between 2007 and 2010. The proportion of UK small businesses owned by 18–25 year olds rose by 4.2% over this period, while those owned by 25–34 year olds rose by 6.5%. Meanwhile, the proportion of small businesses run by owners aged 35–44 fell by 3%, along with a 3.6% fall in the proportion of companies owned by 45–54 year olds.

*"I soon realised that I would have to make a job for myself, rather than just waiting for one to land in my lap"*

While initiatives such as Peter Jones' National Enterprise Academy, which launched in 2009, have no doubt helped to boost entrepreneurship among young people, **Jason Stockwood,** CEO of Simply Business, largely attributes this rise to the recession – or rather, the current dearth of employment prospects for school leavers and graduates. 'This data shows that young people are adapting to a challenging employment landscape by taking their destiny into their own hands and starting a business. It's a really inspiring picture,' he says.

**Rebecca Holder,** the 24-year-old founder of online handmade craft company The Emporium Oundle, is a case in point. 'Having graduated from university in 2010 with a good degree, I spent months trying to find employment but with no success. I soon realised that in order to find employment I would have to make a job for myself, rather than just waiting for one to land in my lap,' she says.

'Initially it was a very daunting process as I had no idea about how to run a business. However, with the support of family, friends and third parties such as The Prince's Trust, I have significantly improved my understanding of how to manage a company. It's been a steep learning curve but I'm having a great time and enjoying the challenge.'

## *Gender*

Only 14% of small and medium-sized businesses are led by a woman or by a management team mostly comprising women. But the gender gap is slowly closing, with the figures up since 2005, when just 12% of start-ups were led by women. With the government keen to encourage women in business, there's every indication the upward trend will continue. On a wider level, the UK has some work to do, as figures released in 2010 revealed the UK to be 15th in the gender gap index, out of 134 countries surveyed. Although this may seem a respectable position, this is down from 11th in 2007, and 9th in 2005. For more on female entrepreneurship, see later in this chapter.

*"Only 14% of small and medium-sized businesses are led by a woman"*

## *Education*

Educational background clearly has a large impact on entrepreneurship, and rising levels of education can be associated with higher relative rates of enterprise activity. Figures show the highest proportion of owner-managers tend to be educated to A-level or equivalent (29.4%) followed by a degree or equivalent (21.8%). However, a significant minority of owner-managers (11%) have no educational qualifications whatsoever. Almost two-thirds of entrepreneurs say that before working in their business they had no prior experience of owning or managing a company, although half of active entrepreneurs have previously worked in the sector they start a business in.

## *Ethnic background*

Although the majority of entrepreneurs may indeed be white, aspirations to start up in business run higher among ethnic minority groups than among their white counterparts, according to the Ethnic Minority Business Task Force's 2009 report. However, conversion to start-ups remains low and ethnic minority groups are still under-represented in business. Despite high levels of entrepreneurialism, the reality is that many ethnic minority groups report problems relating to access to finance and to public sector business support – issues which the government task force was set up to address.

*"Many ethnic minority groups report problems relating to access to finance and to public sector business support"*

In 2010 a new independent body – the Ethnic Minority Business Advocacy Network (EMBAN) – was set up to influence, inform and represent ethnic minority businesses across the UK (following the recommendation of the 2009 task force report). A key part of EMBAN's remit is to ensure that mainstream services are appropriately targeted and accessible, as well as working to influence future government policy by building up the evidence base on the economic contribution of ethnic minority businesses. The organisation also hopes to raise the profile of ethnic minority businesses, to inspire a new generation of successful entrepreneurs and unlock the latent entrepreneurial energy within this group. In particular, EMBAN is currently urging the coalition's Local Enterprise Partnerships to develop new ways of engaging with and supporting business run by entrepreneurs from ethnic minority communities.

**WANT TO KNOW MORE ...**

Global Entrepreneurship Monitor
www.gemconsortium.org

According to the most recent Department for Business, Innovation and Skills (BIS) figures, around 310,000 UK small and medium-sized businesses are led by a member of a minority ethnic group (MEG), or have a management team with at least half of its members from MEGs. These companies contribute around £20bn a year to the economy, but they make up just 7% of all UK small and medium-sized businesses. This figure has grown since 2004, however, when it was closer to 5%. London is the focus of MEG entrepreneurial activity, with 22% of small businesses run by MEGs, compared with 8% across the UK as a whole.

## Location

*"London and the south-east is the focus of nearly a third of all entrepreneurial activity in the UK"*

London and the south-east is also the focus of nearly a third of all the entrepreneurial activity in the UK, boasting more than 1,400,000 businesses. In the GEM UK 2010 report, respondents in the 'South' – the area comprising London, south-east England, south-west England and the east of England – were much more likely to think they had the skills to start a new business than those living in Scotland and Northern Ireland. Similarly, a relatively high proportion of Londoners expect to start a business over the coming three years. So it seems as if the north–south divide still exists. However, government initiatives to decentralise enterprise funding, along with schemes such as the coalition's National Insurance (NI) holiday for start-ups outside of London, the south-east and the east of England (a three-year scheme exempting new businesses from NI contributions for their first 10 employees during their first year of business) mean there should be greater support for entrepreneurs outside the south-east in coming years.

## The entrepreneurial personality

The differing attitudes of entrepreneurs aren't recorded – but perhaps they should be. Regardless of your age, background, gender or ethnicity, your success as an entrepreneur is most likely to be down to your attitude to business. If you're determined, prepared to make personal sacrifices, have the ability to plan ahead and take on board advice while remaining focused on your goal and also, of course, have a decent business idea, you will have every chance of success wherever you're from and whatever age you are.

To be a successful entrepreneur you need more than a viable business plan. Crucially, you also need the essential skills and personality traits required to make that plan work. To help you determine whether you have what it takes, we have described the core skills you need to possess, or develop, to make your business a success in the sections below, from commitment to self-motivation. But remember, while starting up does demand an array of talents, the trade-off is the freedom and flexibility of running your own show.

## Commitment

Can you work incredibly hard, all day, every day? It isn't about putting in a couple of late nights, or making an extra effort for a one-off project. By launching your first business, you could find yourself on the wrong end of a potentially gruelling timetable that could go on for weeks and weeks, if not months. Or, in the case of **Dylan Wilk** a whole year. When Dylan was setting up Gameplay.com during the 1990s, he claims he was permanently 'doing 24/7 . . . I was working every single second of every single minute,' he says. 'Sure I had to give up a few things, like sleeping and eating, but I was willing to do that.' Are you prepared to make the same commitment?

*"Sure I had to give up a few things, like sleeping and eating, but I was willing to do that"*

## Motivation

Linked to your level of commitment is your ability to be motivated, and crucially, self-motivated. Being self-motivated is not the same as being pushed by someone else to do something. This motivation has to come from within. It has to come from your energy, your discipline, your focus. This is difficult enough when things are going well, but what about when things are going badly?

'It's really tough,' admits Dylan, who recalls just a few things that went wrong in the early days. 'We were burgled around eight times; we had tens of thousands of pounds in stock stolen; we had someone register our name and then try to slap a writ on us – that was pretty hairy; we had moments where it looked like the business was going to go under. And, at times, I didn't really know what to do.' So even the most determined of entrepreneurs have moments when they are not sure which direction to take. Even if they do know, some have simply had enough and can no longer be bothered to take it.

'This can affect all of us,' admits **Alan Denbigh**, former executive director of the Telework Association, who is now business liaison partnership manager for the School of Psychology at the University of Exeter. 'To succeed in self-employment you have really got to be a self-starter.' Dylan adds: 'You have to really believe in yourself and decide that, no matter what, you will not be beaten.'

**WANT TO KNOW MORE …**

The Breakthrough Network
www.breakthrough-network.net

## *Emotional resilience*

Belief in yourself is not enough, however. You must also have a capacity to work for yourself, often by yourself. At first this might sound like bliss, with no more workplace politics and gossip. But what about the banter, the social life, and more seriously, the brainstorming of solutions and the bouncing around of ideas? If you are like most solo entrepreneurs, you will miss this. 'The simple fact is that it can be very lonely,' says **Andrew Ferguson**, founder of the Breakthrough Network which counsels people on new ways to work. 'You can feel, professionally at least, very isolated at times.'

*"You can feel, professionally at least, very isolated at times"*

## In my experience

Company: **2B Interface**
Owner-manager: **Beatrice Bartlay**

*Bulldozing through barriers*
Setting up a business in the UK on your own is no easy feat, especially if you're from Poland and don't speak the language. Add the biggest financial downturn in post-war history to the scenario, and your chances of success look slim, or so you'd think. Luckily, **Beatrice Bartlay** has the aforementioned motivation, drive and and resilience required to be a successful entrepreneur in spades. Beatrice bulldozed through the tough trading conditions and the language barrier to build a booming recruitment business, 2B Interface, which now has a turnover of £4.2m.

On a visit to the UK in 2005, Beatrice began casually helping a friend to find joiners to work in his carpentry shop. 'I realised there was a shortage of skilled workers over here, so I found joiners from Poland and sorted out their contracts and accommodation,' she recalls. Beatrice soon saw the business potential of a recruitment firm for skilled and professional workers, and so 2B Interface was born.

The first big breakthrough came in 2007, when 2B Interface was named Best New Business by the London Chambers of Commerce. However, just three weeks later her main client went bust, leaving Beatrice with a £90,000 unpaid invoice.

Ignoring advice to close the business, she refused to admit defeat, and set about recovering the money owed to her. 'I realised that if our client still had customers waiting and orders to fill, I could help them find the staff for their production line. I managed to save jobs for the workers and negotiated the best way of payment for the client, who paid in small instalments – it took me three months to be in the black again.' 2B Interface survived, but not without months of long hours, hard work and minimal income: 'I almost lost a stone and was working 16-hour days.'

Launching a business in a foreign country has been one of the hardest battles, according to Beatrice. But the founder puts her company's survival down to the 'best team of workers'. Months before the credit crunch struck, her employees were designing packages for their clients that would weather the financial storm and offer a service they needed. The workers on her books retained temporary contracts with a number of companies, providing them with steady income, and the companies with less financially draining contracts.

Thanks to Beatrice's (and her team's) determination and adaptability, 2B Interface has not only surmounted huge obstacles, it has bucked the downward trend in the recruitment industry.

**Gwen Rhys**, founder and director of networking organisation Networking Culture, agrees. 'But there is a solution,' she says. 'You need to build up a virtual team. You need to develop a circle of colleagues that you communicate with in much the same way you did in the office, except now it may be over the phone, via email, or face-to-face, but once a month rather than every day. You also need to make sure that you do get out there and mix with people. It is worth joining a professional group you connect with, even if it is only to learn that there are others who have been through what you are going through and identify with how you are feeling. This in itself can be a great source of support.'

## Optimism and opportunism

All this talk about what can go wrong may sound daunting, and the last thing you will probably expect to be feeling is optimistic. However, Dylan says that this is exactly what you have to be. 'There is no point doing something if you think it will not work,' he says. 'But sometimes you just have to think of ways of making it work better.'

Andrew is equally encouraging. 'It's an opportunity to do something you've always wanted to do but never quite found anyone to pay you to do it. It's your big chance to do something that makes you happy.'

# Female entrepreneurship

As a woman interested in starting your own business, you may be faced with some stiffer challenges than men, mainly due to your gender. In recent years, the annual Global Entrepreneurship Monitor (GEM) has revealed some interesting facts about women's route to self-employment.

Female entrepreneurs worldwide, for example, are much more likely than men to start their businesses while still employed. This may not only have benefits in terms of resources and social capital, but also act as a safety net, as women often express less self-confidence in their entrepreneurial ventures than men (although perhaps men are simply far less willing to admit their fears).

*"Women are still a lot less likely to believe they have the skills, knowledge and experience to start a business than men"*

Early-stage entrepreneurship among women continues to grow globally, although start-up rates among men are still higher. According to the 2010 GEM, Australia has the highest level of female entrepreneurship among the high income (or 'innovation-driven') economies, with equal numbers of men and women going it alone. The USA also has a relatively high number of female entrepreneurs, with a ratio of about 85 to 100.

However, in most high-income countries, men are almost twice as likely to be early-stage or established business owners than women. In the UK, for example, the level of female early-stage entrepreneurship is just 44% of that of men: independent start-up activity among women is 4% of the adult female population, but 9% among men. The 2010 GEM report also found that women are still a lot less likely to believe they have the skills, knowledge and experience to start a business than men – and have a greater fear of failure.

Female entrepreneurship is an increasingly important part of the economic profile of any country. But the male/female gap is still significant, especially in high-income countries and technology-intense sectors. A white paper entitled *The Observed Characteristics of Outstanding Women in Business* found that while businesses run by women contribute £70bn to the UK economy and employ more than one million people, there would be 750,000 more female-led start-ups if entrepreneurship rates matched those in the USA.

## Access to finance

Access to investment is unfortunately one of the biggest barriers facing female entrepreneurs. Research from the Women's Enterprise Task Force highlighted the scale of the problem. The task force found that when starting up, businesses owned by women access an average of only £10,000 worth of funding, compared with £15,000 for men. According to the research, the under-capitalisation of women-owned businesses results in under-performance and slower growth. Meanwhile, it has also been found that women tend to be charged higher rates of interest when taking out loans.

According to Women Unlimited, a network for female entrepreneurs in the UK, around 60% of women will seek to bridge the gap between what they have and what they need to finance their business through a bank loan. Very few women currently seek outside investment via a business angel or a venture capital (VC) firm, and just 2% of the VC funds available are currently invested in women-owned businesses.

*"Very few women currently seek outside investment via a business angel or a venture capital firm"*

Clearly, improving access to finance for female entrepreneurs remains a key issue. As the 2010 GEM report says: 'Women entrepreneurs also need to rely on the cooperation and willingness of stakeholders like investors and creditors, employees, suppliers and customers. When these factors act as impediments, society misses an opportunity to gain from the entrepreneurial energy of half its population.'

But this isn't to say that women aren't finding funding opportunities. Female entrepreneurs generally make better use of alternative sources of funding, with the British Chambers of Commerce (BCC) finding that although

**WANT TO
KNOW
MORE …**

British Chambers of
Commerce
www.britishchambers.
org.uk
☎ 020 7654 5800

women put in less of their own money than men in the start-up stage
(£10,106 compared with £13,500), 27% of women will obtain further funding
from family, compared with just 17% of men. What's more, 33% of women-
owned businesses, compared with 20% of firms owned by men, had used
government programmes to fund their business start-up.

## Women in business

The world of business is changing. But there's still a lingering attitude which
assumes that a successful business is owned by a man. Women, especially
young women, often report coming away from meetings or pitches feeling
patronised or not taken seriously. As an entrepreneur though, a thick skin
is something of a necessity.

**Claire Nicholson**, co-founder of marketing agency More2, finds her job
surprises people even in a social environment. 'When I meet new people
socially they often assume you are at home bringing up the children and
not running a business,' she says. It's not just Claire's gender, but also her
age that surprises people, with the combination of the two causing looks
of disbelief. 'We set up More2 when I was just 28 and so many people
don't expect you to have your own business at that age,' she adds.

*"As an
entrepreneur,
a thick skin is
something of a
necessity"*

Despite these challenges, many female entrepreneurs never experience
any form of prejudice or negative reaction on account of their gender. 'I
do feel that male/female prejudice is a bit of a red herring – the main
problem with start-ups is access to good advice and supportive subsidised
incubators, as well as government bureaucracy and anti-competitive
practices from large incumbents,' says **Katie Allcott** of FRANK Water. 'I
am aware of a few situations where it has taken longer for me to gain
respect, but I think this is not just because I am a woman, but also because
I am considered to be young and that I run a very ethical, values-driven
company.' It's important to remember that every entrepreneur faces specific
problems, and whatever you battle through will leave you even more
determined to succeed. As Katie articulates: 'Varying problems exist for tall
people, short people, thin people, fat people, men, women, young people,
old people – if you look for them. But the important thing is to not focus
on obstacles but on goals.'

## Becoming self-confident

Findings show that women are more put off by the fear of failure when it
comes to starting a business. Women are less positive about their skills,

according to Prowess (an advocacy network for women's business) and perceive fewer opportunities than men. However, this may just demonstrate that women are more honest or realistic than their male counterparts! Entrepreneurs are by their nature confident people who like taking risks, and anyone with these qualities won't be held back for long by a fear of failure. 'I think that as long as women have plenty of support around them they can be very successful,' says Katie. 'That's support from friends and family as well as colleagues, support agencies, bank managers, suppliers and customers. Whether a man or woman, you do need a reasonable amount of self-confidence, even more so, total confidence and passion for the business or idea itself . . . then with good support networks you have a great start.'

 ## In my experience

Company: **Skimlinks**
Owner-managers: **Alicia Navarro and Joe Stepniewski**

*Innovation from desperation*
Being part of a rare breed of female tech entrepreneurs in the UK has its benefits, according to **Alicia Navarro**. For one thing, you get noticed more. 'People often trust you quicker too,' she says.

Skimlinks was launched by Alicia and co-founder **Joe Stepniewski** in 2008 after the recession forced them to reconsider their business strategy. The concept for affiliate marketing network Skimlinks evolved out of Alicia's first company, Skimbit, a decision marketing tool.

As with most entrepreneurial success stories, the founders' resilience and ability to see opportunities when faced with challenges have played a key role in the company's survival and growth. 'I was about to be made bankrupt and I was unbelievably stressed, and the recession wasn't going to make funding any easier,' recalls Alicia. 'But it was actually the best possible thing that could have happened as out of that desperation grew innovation. Skimlinks fills a massive void as any type of publisher who wants to make revenue from their content can use us.'

Skimlinks converts links into affiliate revenue for online publishers, who add a line of code to their site template which makes it possible for links to products and services to be tracked and monetised.

'Previously companies have made very good use of banner and text ads, but what we do is monetise the actual content,' explains Alicia. 'You could do it yourself, but it requires a massive human resource investment and is prone to errors, whereas Skimlinks aggregates everything.'

Alicia raised initial funds from generous friends and family, before embarking on a second round. To date, Skimlinks has raised around $2m; the company's main investors include Sussex Place Ventures, NESTA and The Accelerator Group. Skimlinks has also scooped an impressive number of business and industry accolades.

# How and when to quit your job

Like many entrepreneurs, you have probably come up with the idea to launch your own business while still in employment. As mentioned above, many people launch start-ups into a market similar to that in which they were previously working as an employee. Of course, starting up by yourself will have serious ramifications on your existing job, and you have probably decided to quit it. But what is the best time to hand in your notice, and what exactly do you say to your boss?

## The right time to quit

A lot of research and planning will need to be put into your business before you can give up that monthly salary. Continuing to earn while you are planning the business will allow you to save up some cash to act as a buffer. That way you will be able to focus your attention on the business rather than worrying about next month's gas bill.

*"Continuing to earn while you are planning the business will allow you to save up some cash to act as a buffer"*

**Tina Jesson** put away half her salary for two years before quitting her job to set up property development company Home Stagers, so she had personal income to cushion her through the first year of the business. She spent two years researching and planning, so her move from employee to business owner was a gradual one. 'I was spending about 30 hours a week on the business. I told my company that I either wanted to go part-time or leave, and I guess they thought that by allowing me to work part-time they could keep my skills for a while,' she explains.

Before you make the leap to self-employment, get as much done as you possibly can. You may have been using your spare room to sell a couple of items a week through your website while you were working, but if you are going to make a living out of it, perhaps you need to think about commercial premises. You might also want to use this period to prove the business model, through an eBay shop or some other form of ecommerce selling and marketing. Potential investors will have far more confidence in an idea that has been tested.

Ask yourself if your revenue predictions are accurate, too. If you've budgeted for selling more than is realistic, you could find yourself in a tight spot when your last pay cheque gets used up. 'You should have some idea of at least two or three potential customers who can provide the beginnings of an income stream,' says **John Lees**, author of *How to Get a Job You'll Love* (McGraw-Hill, 2006). 'Only when you get customers saying "yes" to your offer should you really consider making the leap.'

**Jeremy Martin**, co-founder of men's health drinks brand For Goodness Shakes, says he and his business partner **Stuart Jeffreys** did as much work as possible while still in full-time employment. But eventually you need to make the move. 'It was definitely the right thing to do,' argues Jeremy, adding that cutting the cord 'commits you 100%. When you make the leap, it's surprising how fear gets you working harder and makes you more committed than ever before.'

## How should you do it?

If your business is going to compete with the company you work for, it's probably not a good idea to mention it until you've handed in your notice, if at all. 'It's best to say as little as possible if you are becoming a competitor,' recommends John. In addition, if you are likely to compete with the company you work for, you need to check your employment contract carefully for competition clauses, notice periods or anything else that could cause legal problems if you decide to start your own business. If there's nothing threatening in your contract, though, and your employer's biggest worry is losing your skills, it may help to talk about your idea. 'Thank your boss for his or her support,' says John. 'Make it clear that you are leaving for entirely positive reasons. Your previous employer could be in a position to refer you new business, so if you can, be as clear as possible about what you plan to do.'

When **Liz Jackson** left to set up Great Guns Marketing, her employers provided her with a few days' worth of work a week, which gave her crucial income while she was trying to win new clients. The lesson here is don't burn your bridges. There are just as many risks as rewards when setting up your own business, but if you plan your exit carefully, you may just manage to tip the balance in your favour.

---

###  Startups Tips

**Leaving your job without burning your bridges**

-➢ Don't do it immediately after your 'eureka!' moment.
-➢ Get as much preparation done as possible first.
-➢ Consider going part-time for a period.
-➢ Make sure you have at least some customers before ditching your income stream.
-➢ Keep your venture quiet before you leave if it's in a similar market.
-➢ Check your contract for possible legal issues relating to your start-up.
-➢ Talk to your boss about your idea if he/she could be a possible customer.
-➢ Leave on a positive note – thank your boss for his/her support, etc.

---

*"There's no better time to start planning your next move than the present"*

## *So you've made your decision …*

You started reading this chapter with an idea that you think you can turn into your own business, or because you simply want to be your own boss. If you now think that the trials and tribulations of entrepreneurialism are not for you, then simply close the book and walk away, safe in the knowledge that you've at least carefully considered setting up on your own. However, if the last few pages have made you even more determined to launch your own company, then it sounds like you have decided to join the ranks of entrepreneurialism, and there's no better time to start planning your next move than the present.

So where should you start? The next step is easy – simply keep on reading and you will be guided through the key steps of starting your own business, from evaluating and researching your idea to writing a business plan and raising finance – as well as how to deal with the upheaval. Work–life balance is an over-used term you will hear from every business coach and all the business start-up services you will encounter. But if you've worked 20 hours a day for two months in a row you will be physically and mentally drained and appreciate the need for striking that balance.

The next chapter will take you through the research stage, to help you test drive your idea to see if it's commercially viable and if there's the market demand for it. Then you will learn how to make cost and revenue forecasts and to present your idea in the form of a business plan that you can then take to prospective investors and partners. Further chapters deal with naming your venture and how to register that name, as well as the format your business should take, from a limited company or partnership to a sole trader.

There is also advice on developing the key skills you will need when starting up. For instance, there's a guide on safely negotiating the minefield that is tax and the practices, products and systems that will help you organise your accounts efficiently. If you are raising finance, there are plenty of sources from which to choose. There's a rundown of the advantages and disadvantages of using different financiers, from high-street banks to venture capitalists and business angels – and how best to impress them while still getting a good deal. There's also guidance on whether to work from home or seek premises, along with finding the right space for your business and how to get the best from your chosen location.

You will also find advice on how to get the most from your working day and ways that you can ensure your time is put to good use, such as the best way to take calls when you are in a meeting with clients. Do you need to use a virtual secretary, and would it be cost effective? There are tips on tracking down reliable and affordable suppliers, which can be one of the hardest tasks for new business owners, as well as talking to other entrepreneurs. Networking is a word that often strikes fear into the hearts of new business owners. Walking into a roomful of people who've been in business for decades can be quite daunting. But select the right networking groups and a format that you are comfortable with, and it will help you build a valuable source of contacts that can drive your business forward.

Word of mouth may not be enough to get your business working to its full capacity and it's likely that you will need at least some marketing and public relations (PR). There are clear explanations of all the options available to you, what is most likely to prompt the best response rates and advice on how to handle PR companies. You will also gain an insight into the type of marketing and PR that you can do for yourself for very little money.

If you are launching an online business, website design, marketing and internet connectivity will be important issues from day one. Even if you are not starting an internet business, you might want a website or even to sell online too. You will find guidance on the process of getting a website designed from one of the thousands of companies now specialising in the service. There's also help on deciding how complex your website needs to be, along with advice on how to drive traffic to it.

If you will need to take on one or two people straightaway, do you think you are experienced enough at recruiting? You might know a friend of a friend who can help out, but you need to make sure that you can entrust this person with your business' future. So read on and you will be taken through all the issues involved with recruiting and employing staff, along with health and safety issues, employer liability insurance and general employment legislation. Red tape is the bugbear of every business owner, but the weight of the problem is significantly lessened if you are organised and know what's expected of you.

 **What to do next**

- Assess your attitude towards risk. Decide if the uncertainties involved in starting a business are ones you can live with.

- Be aware that the first few years after launching a business could mean the temporary end of your social life. Make sure you're prepared.

- Talk through your plans with family and friends. It's important to get their support.

- Consider whether you have all the required experience to start a business in your chosen field. If not, get out there and learn from others, even if it means working for someone else for a short period.

- Don't burn your bridges. If you're leaving a job to start a business, leave on good terms. Former employers or colleagues may become your customers one day.

# ⤶ CHAPTER 3

## Business plans and market research

## 📖 What's in this chapter?

→ Evaluating your idea
→ Market research
→ Working out your USPs
→ Why write a business plan?
→ Preparing data for your business plan
→ The key elements of a business plan
→ Forecasting your sales
→ SWOT analysis
→ Making your plan investor-friendly

Once you're confident you've found the right business idea – and you're certain you're cut out for life as an entrepreneur – the next step is to put your idea through its paces to see if it really has legs. Not all great ideas have what it takes to become great businesses – you need to conduct extensive market research to establish whether there is indeed a market for your business, as well as finding solid evidence to support your key assumptions before you launch, such as whether your business model, cost base and pricing structure are viable.

This chapter will take you through the planning and evaluation stage step by step, from the key information you need to acquire to assess your idea, to putting together a killer business plan.

# Evaluating your idea

Sadly, not all great ideas translate into great businesses. Even if you've thought of a fantastic product or service, you still need the right business model, pricing, funding, marketing and people to make it work – and of course, enough customers willing to pay for it. As discussed in the previous chapter, setting up a business is a massive undertaking, and may well require a significant injection of capital from your own savings. Success is never guaranteed, but through careful research and planning you can certainly get a good indication of whether or not you're on to a winner before risking it all and diving straight in – or indeed, whether certain areas of your strategy need to be tweaked and honed.

So how do you know if your idea is viable and worth pursuing? Below is a summary of the main areas you need to consider when assessing the strength of your business idea. These areas will be explored in a lot more detail later in the chapter.

## Is there a market for it?

The first step towards determining whether your business idea has legs is to carry out extensive market research. You need to establish if there is a market for your business, and whether this is big enough to make the venture a success. Many great ideas have been scuppered by a lack of research and this stage should never be overlooked. Not only do you need to work out whether there is sufficient demand for your offering, you must also determine what marketing, pricing and business model will work for your target market.

To do this, you need to find out as much information as possible about your potential customers: how many are there? What type of people are they? Where do they shop? How do they behave and what drives their purchasing decisions? If they are consumers, how much do they typically earn and how much disposable income do they have? How often would they buy your product or service?

Thankfully, you can carry out much research yourself at little or no cost. Market research falls into two main categories: primary (which you conduct yourself) and secondary (analysing data published by secondary sources). The research can be quantitative (based on numbers and statistics) or qualitative (based on attitudes and opinions). Ideally, you want a mixture of all of these sources to gain a reliable picture of the market.

Remember, the goal is to arm yourself with as much information as possible about the state, size and needs of your market. Do enough research to ensure the results aren't one-sided, and take feedback on board. Be prepared to change your idea according to what your customers want, not what you prescribe as the best solution.

## Is there room for you?

Is your idea original or are you building on an existing concept? If it's the latter, is there really room for another player in the market, and is your idea sufficiently distinct and compelling to lure business away from your competitors? You need clear unique selling points (USPs). Similarly, if no-one else is doing it, is there a reason for this?

In addition, is there anything about your technology or approach that couldn't be easily copied by a rival with big buying power? If the answer is no, think carefully before moving forward. Mitigate the threats by protecting your intellectual property where you can. You can't protect the idea itself, but you can safeguard your name, brand, designs and inventions through trade marks and patents. Equally, run a search on the trade mark and patent databases on the Intellectual Property Office's website to ensure you're not treading on anyone else's toes. For more on how to protect your intellectual property, see Chapter 4: 'Business names, brands and intellectual property'.

## What's the business model?

It's what you do with a great idea that counts: you need the right execution. Google wasn't the first search engine and Facebook wasn't the first social network, but by finding the right business model and honing the offering, these companies were able to build on an existing concept to become market leaders.

You have to be able to monetise your idea if you want a sustainable business. You also need the right marketing, pricing and cost base, and a product or service in tune with how your customers want to use it. Often there will be different business models and revenue streams to consider; for instance, a web business could charge end users a monthly subscription fee, or make the website free for the user but earn a commission for every 'lead' or sale that it generates for another company (eg Toptable, price comparison websites), or sell advertising space. The freemium model,

*"Is there really room for another player in the market? Or, if no-one else is doing it, is there a reason for this?"*

*"You have to be able to monetise your idea if you want a sustainable business"*

where a basic service is offered for free but customers can pay for a premium service, could also be an option.

Again, research is vital to test the viability of your model – what are your customers willing to pay for and how much would they pay? Can you charge enough to cover your costs and turn a profit?

## Can you fund it?

*"Can you sell enough at the right price to make it viable?"*

Do you have the funds in place to get your business off the ground? You need enough to support yourself and to provide sufficient working capital until your company hits profitability. Undertake some honest and thorough analysis of how much it will cost to set up and run your business, how much you expect to sell each month and when you expect to break even. What are your margins? Can you sell enough at the right price to make it viable?

Think about how to keep costs down without cutting corners and avoid unnecessary extravagances. Operating online or from home initially; negotiating with suppliers; shopping around for the best deals; being ruthless with spending; trying to exchange your products, expertise or services for those of others and using freelance or part-time staff could all help to keep your start-up costs down.

Unless you have savings, minimal costs or you're starting a business while still employed, you may need to raise external finance. You will need a watertight business plan that includes your detailed cost analysis, cashflow forecast and sales projections backed up by solid research. Crucially, if you are looking for a bank loan, remember to factor debt repayments into your forecasting. For more advice on raising finance, see Chapter 6: 'Raising finance and business banking'.

## Have you got what it takes?

Last but by no means least, have you got the right attitude and skills to make your idea a success? As the previous chapter illustrated, setting up a business is an endurance challenge. The success of your idea hinges on your commitment to seeing it through – during the bad times and the good. Your idea needs to be something you're passionate about, and you then need the skills, drive and belief to make it work.

*Startups Tips*

**10 questions to ask yourself before launching a business**

Think you've got the makings of a great business idea? Here are 10 key questions to help you determine whether you're on to a winner.

1. **How is it different?**

   Your underlying business idea doesn't need to be original, but you need to establish unique selling points (USPs) if you want people to buy from you rather than your competitors. You have to offer something new. Is your proposition solving a problem? Are you filling a gap in the market, or building on an existing offering?

2. **Is there a market, and is it big enough?**

   Thorough market research is needed before moving forward with your business idea. You need to ensure there will be sufficient – and sustainable – demand to support your business and enable it to thrive.

3. **What's the business model?**

   How will you charge your customers, and what for? Can you think of additional revenue streams? Research is vital to determine whether your business model is viable; this should include analysis of how your competitors have structured their businesses.

4. **Is the price right?**

   It's no good having a winning product or service if your customers can't afford it, but you need a decent margin for a sustainable business. Talk to your potential customers to find out whether your pricing is feasible.

5. **What will stop others from copying you?**

   If you've ever watched *Dragons' Den* you'll have heard no doubt heard this question: 'What's to stop a big company coming along and stealing your idea?' Have strong USPs – such as exceptional customer service – and wherever you can protect your intellectual property.

6. **Do you know your customer?**

   Arm yourself with as much information as you possibly can about your target customer, and listen to them at every opportunity. What does a typical customer look like? How do they behave? What do they most value from a product or service like yours? Where can you find them? What marketing methods do they respond to?

7. **Can you turn a profit?**

   How much will it cost to produce your idea? (taking into account manufacturing or supplier costs; salaries; overheads; office equipment, etc). How much can you sell your product or service for, and how much do you need to sell to not only cover your costs, but make a profit? Is this achievable?

8. **Do you have sufficient funding to get the venture off the ground?**
   You need enough cash to support yourself and your business until it becomes sustainable. If you don't have the funding in place, can you raise it?

9. **Do you have the necessary experience, attitude and skills to pull it off?**
   Even if you have the best idea in the world, without the passion, drive and commitment to see it through, it still stands a good chance of failing.

10. **Is there scope for growth?**
    Can you expand on your idea in the future by adding new products or services, entering new locations, or improving your original proposition?

 In my experience

**Company: Moonfruit**
**Owner-manager: Wendy Tan White**

*Learning the hard way*

The dot-com crash of 2000 was the kiss of death for many web businesses which, buoyed by soaring market confidence and plentiful venture capital investment, had focused on attracting users rather than establishing a viable business model. Many were also guilty of reckless cost management.

The crash would have claimed self-build web company Moonfruit too, were it not for a fast and deep programme of cutbacks initiated just in the nick of time.

**Wendy Tan White's** vision for Moonfruit was a user-friendly web development tool which would allow anyone to build a good-looking website (even with no prior web design experience) without having to pay for it. Driven by advertising revenues, the business would also take on the responsibility of hosting its sites.

Her idea soon started turning heads. In 1999 management consultants Bain agreed to incubate the company, which also attracted significant private and venture capital backing from a number of investors.

Moonfruit splashed out on a £2m advertising campaign, which generated huge publicity, and within six months of its launch in January 2000 the business had built up 40,000 users. But collecting eyeballs was one thing; making money from it was another. Because Moonfruit was free, it was hard to commercialise the venture, and overheads were starting to mount – particularly following a move from its original attic into plush Soho offices.

Then the crash came, and Moonfruit's main investor pulled their funding. Losses escalated, and the management team were forced into a two-year period of brutal bootstrapping. The company retreated to its original attic, and the staff roster was cut from 60 people to two. At one stage Wendy even had to fill out insolvency files at Companies House.

However, her faith in Moonfruit survived. She began to develop a new business model, doing away with the old free model in favour of a tiered subscription-based service. The strategy worked; by 2001, Moonfruit was profitable again.

Yet the lessons of the crash left a lasting impression. Recognising that the company 'grew too fast', Wendy kept a tight leash on growth: staff numbers did not return to double figures until 2004. Meanwhile, recent growth has been fuelled by clever, low-cost marketing techniques using social media sites such as Twitter.

Ten years on from the crash, Moonfruit is now turning over more than $4m a year, while over 3.5 million websites have now been created using the company's software.

## *Market research*

Properly targeted market research is the key to a thriving business and can mean the difference between success and failure, say experts. Market research can be a cost-effective way of discovering what your customers want and matching products and services to this demand. Even better, it can help a business grow by keeping you up to date with current trends and with what your competitors are doing. Knowing the state of the market and how to improve your position within it can revolutionise your business, but this can only be achieved through proper market research.

*"Market research will help you to determine the viability of your venture"*

If you are looking to start a company, market research will help you to determine the viability of your venture. First, it will provide key material for your business plan, which is an essential part of attracting the investment you may need to launch your business. Second, it will help you assess the chances of success.

A lot of companies already succeeding in the area you'd like to enter doesn't automatically mean you are on to a winner. It could mean the competition may be too fierce and there may not be a demand for what you are offering in the specific location you plan to launch your business. Equally, you may have had a highly original idea and there may be little or no competition around, but this could be for a very good reason. In either case, market research can help provide the answers. One key area you need to look at is demand:

- Do people want what you plan to offer, and if not, is it simply down to their profile in the particular location where you planned to launch?
- If there is demand, can you put a figure on it?

You also need to examine the competition:

- Which other companies are offering something similar to what you are proposing?
- How successful are they?
- Can you improve on their offer, or strategically differentiate your proposition from theirs, while maintaining demand?

Further research can provide key information on pricing, location, size of premises, etc. Securing this data early not only shows potential sources of investment that you are serious about your proposal, but also reassures them that you are organised and motivated, making them more likely to want to back you. And, of course, it also increases the chances of your launch being a success, if after carrying out the research you decide to go ahead.

For many would-be owner-managers of small businesses, the cost of commissioning a market research agency can be prohibitive, so you will most likely want to conduct basic market research yourself for the purposes of informing your business plan and providing an early indication of the viability of your venture. But remember that it needs to cover all the points discussed above so, depending on the market you are considering entering, you may find the process too complex and time consuming, and that calling in the experts could save you money through producing more accurate results.

## How important are trends?

**WANT TO KNOW MORE ...**
Department for Business, Innovation and Skills
www.bis.gov.uk

Before discussing the key market research techniques, here are some useful official start-up figures, published by the Office for National Statistics (ONS), which offer a key insight into the types of business that are on the increase or decline. The Department for Business, Innovation and Skills (BIS) Enterprise Directorate also publishes a lot of business statistics, which are a useful starting point for you to make a quick assessment of the viability of your idea before embarking on more thorough research, while also informing you of the most popular sectors for business start-ups.

When looking at the sector you intend to enter, consider:

→ How many businesses were started in the current year, and how it compares with the previous year. Is it a growing market?

→ If so, has that now been fully exploited and will it drop in the coming year?

→ If it's less than in the previous year, why is that?

Also consider the changes to the total number of businesses that occurred during the current year. For instance, while around 21,000 new retail businesses were started in 2009, around 26,000 folded. If you are looking to enter a market that's losing businesses, you will need to consider why this is so and find out which particular firms are suffering and why.

Evaluating the statistics doesn't mean that you shouldn't enter into a sector that is shrinking, but it should alert you to whether important changes are afoot. In addition, you should think about the outside influences that are likely to have affected start-up business figures. For instance, how much have the fish, agriculture, hotel and restaurant trades been affected since the start of the economic downturn?

*"Evaluating the statistics doesn't mean that you shouldn't enter into a sector that is shrinking, but it should alert you to whether important changes are afoot"*

## Starting up in the downturn

According to the ONS figures, around 236,000 new businesses were started up in the UK in 2009, compared to 267,000 in 2008 – the year the economy officially went into recession. This marks an 11.7% decrease in the number of new start-ups. In addition, 2009 also saw a record number of business closures. Provisional figures suggest that 279,000 businesses closed in 2009, which is up 26.2% on 2008, when 221,000 UK businesses failed. This represents the highest number of business closures since current records began in 2000. 'Not only is it the highest number of businesses closing in a single year, it is also the first time that business deaths have outnumbered business births since the series began,' says ONS statistician **Andrew Allen**.

*TABLE 1: Business Demography 2009: Enterprise births, deaths and survival*

| | Active (000s) | Births (000s) | | Deaths (000s) | |
|---|---|---|---|---|---|
| | | Count | Rate (%) | Count | Rate (%) |
| Production | 157 | 11 | 7.3 | 16 | 10.1 |
| Construction | 336 | 29 | 8.7 | 44 | 13.2 |
| Motor trades | 76 | 6 | 7.9 | 7 | 9.2 |
| Wholesale | 120 | 10 | 8.1 | 13 | 10.5 |
| Retail | 221 | 21 | 9.6 | 26 | 11.6 |
| Transport & storage (inc. postal) | 82 | 7 | 8.5 | 11 | 13.2 |
| Accommodation & food services | 163 | 20 | 12.0 | 23 | 14.3 |
| Information & communication | 171 | 19 | 11.1 | 23 | 13.3 |
| Finance & insurance | 35 | 3 | 9.5 | 4 | 12.6 |
| Property | 87 | 8 | 9.1 | 11 | 12.7 |
| Professional, scientific & technical | 380 | 48 | 12.5 | 42 | 11.2 |
| Business admin & support services | 206 | 29 | 13.9 | 31 | 14.8 |
| Education | 34 | 3 | 10.1 | 3 | 9.2 |
| Health | 87 | 7 | 7.9 | 6 | 7.2 |
| Arts, entertainment, recreation & other services | 187 | 15 | 8.0 | 19 | 10.2 |
| Total | 2,342 | 236 | 10.1 | 279 | 11.9 |

*Source: Office for National Statistics. Note: the death counts reported in this table are provisional.*

The ONS figures show that the highest number of business deaths in 2009 occurred in the construction industry, with more than 44,000 closures. This was closely followed by the professional, scientific and technical sector, which saw over 42,000 firms going under; however, this sector also saw the highest number of births, with just under 48,000 new businesses launching in 2009. In fact, this was one of the few sectors where births outnumbered deaths.

While ONS figures on the number of business births and closures are not yet available for 2010, figures released by the Insolvency Service for 2010 suggest that closures peaked in 2009. The statistics showed that company insolvencies were down by 15.9% on 2009. However, figures for the first quarter of 2011 suggest that closures crept back up again, with an increase of 2% on the same period in 2010.

With so many companies going out of business, this is clearly a challenging time to launch your own company no matter what sector you'll be entering – although some are clearly feeling the strain more than others. However, it's unwise to launch without preparation in any kind of economic climate, so as long as you have done the groundwork there's no reason why you can't launch in a recession. And if you can turn a profit in tough times, you should be ready to go full steam ahead when the recovery arrives, and hopefully grow significantly. Also, there are some businesses that have been doing well in the downturn. Pharmacists traditionally do well when times are hard, perhaps because people are feeling more down and under stress. There have also been reports that takeaway restaurants and home movie rental companies are performing well, as more people are staying in to save money.

*"If you can turn a profit in tough times, you should be ready to go full steam ahead when the recovery arrives"*

## *Relevance of trends to your circumstances*

Although national start-up statistics are important to consider, they are by no means relevant to every situation. For instance, trends may vary in different parts of the country and at different times. The local economy will also affect your chances of success. Unless you are about to launch on a national scale, probably the most valuable research you can do is to investigate what need exists for your business locally. Look at how many other similar businesses are in the area; can you find an area where there are few companies offering the service or products you are looking to launch, or where there's room for competition, either in terms of better quality service or on price?

There's also the argument that trends should be made and not followed, and there's some truth to this. The telecommunications industry is full of very young, bold, and now wealthy, individuals who proved a lot of sceptics wrong, and it can pay to be at the forefront of the latest movement. However, over-confidence can also be perceived as arrogance or naivety, and it's always worth checking the state of the markets even if you then choose to ignore them.

## *Sizing up the competition*

*"There's no better way to establish the quality of the competition and how successful it is than by sampling it"*

Finding out about your competition is a key part of the market research you need to carry out before starting up. However, before you can assess your rivals, first you need to find out who they are. A good place to start is online. Make a list of keywords that people would use when looking for companies that provide your potential product or service. Remember to keep a note of these words and phrases as they will prove useful in the future to help with optimising your website. Internet searches should throw up the range of companies across the UK that you will be competing with if you launch. If there are none, you have an original idea – but is there a market for it? If there are lots of competitors, is there room for you? To find this out, look at what your competitors are offering and whether you can improve on this. You can get much of this information from company websites, initially.

Depending on the business you are proposing to launch, in the next level of assessment, get out of the office and check out the competition first-hand, either personally or by enlisting the help of others. There's no better way to establish the quality of the competition and how successful it is than by sampling it. If you are well known in the area, ask your friends to help out.

**WANT TO KNOW MORE ...**

Companies House

www.companies
house.gov.uk

☎ 0303 1234 500

If you do your market research fully enough, you can organise your business in a way that gives you a clear advantage. You can even play detective and go on a stake-out to observe how busy your rivals' premises are, and subtly question customers about what they are looking for in this kind of business.

You can also investigate the performance of your rivals by tracking down their annual accounts at Companies House. Although the data is likely to be at least a year old, you can source turnover and profit and loss details, which will give you an idea of how successful each business is. If your rivals are having problems, try to find out why this is. It could be that they are not very good, or that there are simply too many companies offering this service in the area, or that the service isn't in demand.

Remember, collecting information isn't enough; it's vital that you gain an in-depth understanding of your potential competitors. We will look at how to conduct a detailed competitor analysis and work out your own unique selling points (USPs) later in the chapter.

 **Startups Tips**

**Three facts about market research**

- ⇢ It's one thing recognising the importance of market research, and quite another carrying it out properly.
- ⇢ Of those companies that do conduct research, many simply don't approach it in the right way.
- ⇢ This can be just as dangerous as not doing any research at all, as it produces inaccurate results, which can lead to the wrong business decisions being made and false confidence on the part of the entrepreneur.

## Primary research

Primary research is research that you can conduct yourself or commission someone else to do for you, instead of using information that is already published. You can carry out research into your market or competition using the internet as mentioned previously, or through direct contact with your potential customers. The latter falls into two broad types of research: quantitative, which focuses on a broad cross-section and produces a numerical result, such as '36% of the target audience think this', which can be useful figures to show a potential investor; and qualitative, which is more in-depth, often using a smaller, but representative, sample, and covers not only what people do, but why they buy a certain product, how they feel about it and how they would like to see it improved.

An example of qualitative research is a focus group. You gather a small number of people who represent a cross-section of your target market for a discussion with an assigned leader to assess their opinions of the product or service you will be offering. If this can include giving the focus group members first-hand experience of that product or service, their opinions will be better informed. To entice people to attend a focus group, you will need to give them some kind of inducement, such as a small payment or gift.

If structured correctly, it can be an extremely useful exercise. Focus groups enable people to bounce ideas off one another and build upon each other's suggestions. The set-up takes the pressure off individuals to come up with a compelling answer, and can deliver the type of spontaneous reactions that a survey never could.

### ⟨ᴦ Startups Tips

**Using focus groups to evaluate your business idea**

Here are some tips for getting the most out of focus groups.

**Objectives**: What do you want to get out of the exercise? Focus groups tend to work well when you have something tangible to show (eg a prototype of a product, an ad campaign or logo) and specific aspects of your proposition you want feedback on, such as your branding, pricing or sales strategy. Have a structure for the session to keep the discussion on track.

**Questions**: The value in market research comes from asking the right questions. What do you want to know? Use open-ended questions (which can't be answered by a simple 'yes' or 'no'), which aren't loaded (pushing people towards a desired response). A useful question could be: 'What would you pay for this product or service?'

**Consider using a third party**: You can enlist research companies to organise focus groups for you, and this is worth looking into. One major benefit is access to a trained moderator (experts agree that this role is crucial), who will keep the session focused, make sure everyone's voice is heard and will usually be an expert in analysing behaviour, so can help you to interpret the results.

**Environment**: Encouraging people to speak freely requires the right atmosphere. Find a quiet, relaxed location where the discussion won't be interrupted, arrange people in a circle so everyone feels included and try not to make it too formal.

**People**: Invite people who represent your target market. Think about your extended network – reaching out to people via social media could be an option. Generally, you need to offer some kind of fee or incentive to attendees.

**Numbers**: You want enough people to get varied input; but not so many that the discussion becomes difficult to control. As a general rule of thumb, go for at least three and no more than 10.

**Use the results**: If you dismiss views that contradict your own then it becomes a pointless exercise. Instead, try to remain objective, take the comments on board, hone your proposition and seek further opinions and advice.

However, there are limitations to this type of research. For a start, small numbers can sometimes lead to inaccurate conclusions about the viability of an idea. Likewise, there is sometimes a disparity between how people say they behave and how they actually behave. To mitigate these risks, try to ensure the people you invite are relevant and representative of your target market. Also, try to run more than one focus group and use this as just one part of your market research.

A simple direct survey of your target audience (the bigger the sample, the better) is an example of quantitative research, where you either send questions out to a database (either by post or via email), go doorstepping or ask people in the street. There are also a number of online survey tools, such as Survey Monkey, where you can set up a basic survey for free and then post a link to it on Facebook, Twitter, your website or blog, or email it out to contacts.

**Michael Warren**, former director general of the MRS and now a freelance researcher and consultant, says it is misleading to suggest that one kind of research suits certain goods and services better than others. 'Qualitative and quantitative research are complementary to each other, and should be used together,' he advises. 'Qualitative research, in particular, can be used to give a greater understanding of the figures.' The key to success for both types of research, though, is the kind of questions asked and how they are put across. So a properly devised questionnaire can be an invaluable marketing tool, as long as you avoid the common pitfalls. A good market research agency with experience in your sector can help with this. Alternatively, you can consult marketing guides for advice, but bear in mind that this is something of a skill and getting it wrong can mean that you have wasted any effort you put into doing the research.

For example, questions such as 'Would you buy this product?' can give misleading answers. The answer might be 'Yes', but the respondent could mean that they would pay £1 whereas the price might actually be £10. So avoid closed questions with yes/no answers, as you're likely to get more information by eliciting a fuller response. Michael adds that it's important to think carefully about what other brands you're asking people to compare your offering to: 'In sectors such as fast-moving consumer goods, where market researchers are trying to explore the image of one client's products against those of its rivals, it is usual for respondents to be asked about other products, some of which they may never have used,' he says. 'You might ask them about a range of variables, including smoothness, price, levels of satisfaction, but you have to be careful about what you compare the product to. Asking people how a new car, say, compares to a Rolls-Royce really gets up respondents' noses because they have probably never driven a Rolls.'

**WANT TO KNOW MORE ...**

**Market Research Society**

www.mrs.org.uk
☎ 020 7490 4911

## In my experience

**Company: Shortlist Media**
**Chief executive: Mike Soutar**

*Finding a niche*
It wasn't long ago we saw the introduction of media tycoon
Rupert Murdoch's online paywall for News International's
newspaper *The Times*. Elsewhere in publishing, however, a group of
guys eschewing consumer cash for their work are making a pretty penny.

While most publishers struggle to stay in the black and advertising spend continues
to freefall, Shortlist Media is boldly carving out a niche in periodicals. In just under
four years, the company, which produces *Shortlist*, the most widely circulated men's
magazine in the country, has not only clinched over 30% of market share, but also
secured that elusive publishing industry prize: commercial success.

With the men's newsstand market in decline, chief executive **Mike Soutar**, the
former editorial director of publishing giant IPC, and his senior management team
(who between them have worked on some of the biggest titles in the men's market,
including *FHM*, *Men's Health* and *Nuts*) were eager to determine whether this was
linked to growing detachment from the magazine as a format, or just distaste for
the content on offer.

The laddism of the 1990s had faded, but the sector was still saturated with titles
aimed at teens, where bare female flesh occupied the majority of page real estate.
'It was an interesting time,' says editorial director **Phil Hilton.** 'That kind of content
was a massive turn-off for affluent men in their late twenties and early thirties, and
they'd walked away from the newsstand leaving this massive *Shortlist*-shaped hole.'

A whole generation had grown up with the internet, expecting high-quality content
for free. By targeting this audience, who had abandoned the newsstand, and going
directly to them, they took a compelling proposition to advertisers.

However, despite the team's confidence in the idea, *Shortlist* still went through
a lengthy research and development process before launch. Content ideas were

tested on focus groups over a three-month period, and the feedback fed into the initial launch product.

Not only did the research confirm there was indeed a gap in the market, it helped the team create a product that was in tune with what its readers wanted – and as a result, advertisers have flocked. With its strapline, 'For men with more than one thing on their minds', *Shortlist* has proved a commercial triumph. Shortlist Media, which turned over more than £10m in 2010, has also gone on to launch *Stylist*, another free, successful weekly magazine aimed at women.

## *Secondary research*

Secondary research is information others have acquired and already published which you may find relevant, for example the BIS start-up statistics mentioned above. Often you can access valuable secondary data free of charge simply by asking for it via a phone call or email, or for a nominal charge to cover postage or photocopying. Much of it is also available online: trade associations and government departments often publish data such as sales figures, economic trends, and other statistics and reports. When in doubt, call or email the organisations' offices and ask what information is available.

*"Industry–specific business publications can offer a wealth of information on your proposed venture and your market"*

Industry-specific business publications can also offer a wealth of information on your proposed venture and your market. Aside from the major general-interest business publications, such as *Business Week* and *The Economist*, many trade publications look at specific industries.

**Tim Berry** and **Doug Wilson's** book, *On Target: The Book On Marketing Plans*, advises: 'specialism is an important trend in the publishing and internet businesses. Dingbats and Widgets may be boring to the general public, but they are exciting to Dingbat and Widget manufacturers who read about them regularly in their specialised magazines. The titles are an important medium for industry-specific advertising, which is important to readers as well as advertisers. The editorial staff of these magazines have to fill the space between the adverts. They do that by publishing as much industry-specific information as they can find, including statistics, forecasts and industry profiles. Consulting these magazines or websites can sometimes produce a great deal of business and market forecasting, along with key economic information.'

Action points

## Key steps to doing your own research

Whichever type of primary research you decide to undertake, there are a number of factors you should bear in mind before you start.

☑ **KISS (keep it simple, stupid!)**: Long-winded questionnaires are likely to put respondents off, and will distort the response – the only respondents may be those with nothing better to do that day, which may not be your target market. 'Telling them that a survey will take five minutes is likely to get a better response than one lasting 25 minutes,' says **Michael Warren**, former director general of the Market Research Society. 'If it does last longer than that, it is bad for the industry and not good for your product image.'

☑ **Choose a representative sample**: It's no good working hard on producing a good questionnaire if you present it to the wrong people, so you need to make sure that your 'sample' represents a cross-section of your potential customers.

☑ **Circulate the questionnaire appropriately**: Via the internet is usually the best way to do this.

☑ **Offer a prize draw for completed questionnaires**: Remember that a low response rate will distort figures, and often people need an incentive to complete questionnaires, because they take up valuable time.

☑ **Respect confidentiality**: The Market Research Society's code of conduct specifies that respondents should not be misled over what they are being asked about. Do not use their responses for follow-up sales once you are trading.

If you don't know which magazines focus on your business area, the best place to start looking is on the internet. For traditional printed directories, several reference sources list magazines, journals and other publications. They also offer indexes to published articles which you can use to search for the exact references you need. These will be kept in the reference section of most libraries. Once you have identified the right magazines, contact the editorial departments using their website, phone number and published contact information. Use the indexes to identify useful published information. When you find an index listing for an article that forecasts your sector or talks about industry economics or trends, jot down basic information on the publication and ask your local library if it has a copy or contact the title directly. Many business magazines will send back issues for free.

Finally, special industry sector reports are regularly published by independent research companies such as Mintel and Key Note, which have been producing reports for more than 35 years. The reports are very expensive and tend to be written from a certain perspective, which may not be your own. However, you can access Key Note and Mintel reports in your local library and carry out desk research yourself by using the index to search for the relevant sectors.

## Market research agencies

For many start-ups, the costs of using an agency may be prohibitive, and good ones are likely to start at four figures, according to **Michael Warren**. But those costs should be set against the real benefits to your business of getting right the product, retail layout or new restaurant. Good market research should pay for itself and, as with anything, there are also ways to keep costs down.

*"Sharing the cost of a survey with other organisations can help to cut costs"*

First, shop around. The Market Research Society offers much advice on its website to help you select the right market research agency. Contact three or four; outline what you need; then compare prices and service. A good agency should have detailed proposals about ways to carry out the research and should also be happy for you to contact existing or former customers for testimonials. Sharing the cost of a survey with other organisations, who have their questions included in the same questionnaire, can also help to cut costs.

When approaching an agency, be clear from the outset about what you want to discover, whether it is testing a new product during development, or gauging customer needs and people's responses to different products. Going to a market research agency with a definitive set of objectives, and a good sense of how you will use research results to improve your business, can make the agency's task much simpler.

> **Startups Tips**
>
> **Where to find key market information**
>
> –▷ The internet.
> –▷ Trade associations.
> –▷ Government departments.
> –▷ Local libraries for reference directories.
> –▷ Industry magazines.
> –▷ General-interest business titles.
> –▷ Market research firms.

*"It's important to know who you will be competing with for your potential customers' time and money"*

# Working out your unique selling points (USPs)

It's important to know who you will be competing with for your potential customers' time and money, in order to determine how to set your business apart. What are your rivals' strengths and weaknesses? How are they positioned in the market? How can you improve on what they are offering? A good competitive analysis varies according to what industry you are looking at and your specific marketing plan and situation, but there are some common themes.

Begin by thinking about the general nature of the competition in your type of business, and how and why customers seem to choose one provider over another:

–▷ Price or billing rates

–▷ Reputation

–▷ Image and visibility

–▷ Use of technology

–▷ Are brand names important?

–▷ How influential is word of mouth in providing long-term satisfied customers?

For example, competition in the restaurant business might depend on reputation and trends in one part of the market and on location and parking in another. Alternatively, for the internet and internet service providers, speed of connection and response rates to problems might be important. Meanwhile, a purchase decision for a car may be based on style, or speed or reputation for reliability. For many professional service practices, the nature of competition depends on word of mouth because advertising is not completely accepted and, therefore, not as influential. Is there price competition between accountants, doctors and lawyers?

Next, think about the factors that make the most difference for your business and why:

→ How do people choose travel agencies or florists for weddings?

→ Why does someone hire one gardener over another?

→ Why would a customer choose Starbucks over the local coffee house?

→ Why select a Dell computer instead of one from HP or Gateway?

This type of information is invaluable for understanding the nature of competition. Compare your potential product or service in light of those factors of competition. For example:

→ If you are planning to open a travel agency, will your agency offer better airline ticketing than others, or perhaps be located next to a major university and cater to students? Are existing travel agents offering good service, better selection or better computer connections?

→ The computer you plan to sell is faster and better, or perhaps comes in attractive colours. Do existing computer vendors offer better prices or service than you have planned?

Once you have established what factors are most important to your customers when it comes to influencing their purchasing decisions, you can work out your unique selling points (USPs) – that is, reasons why customers would want to buy your product or service instead of your competitors'. In other words, you should know how you plan to position yourself in the market. What benefits will you offer at what price, to whom, and how will your mix compare to others?

*"You should know how you plan to position yourself in the market"*

Think about specific kinds of benefits, features and market groups, comparing where you think you can show the difference. Describe each of your potential major competitors in terms of those same factors. This may include their size, the market share they command, their comparative product quality, their growth, available capital and resources, image, marketing strategy, target markets, or whatever else you consider important. Make sure you specifically describe the strengths and weaknesses of each competitor, and compare them to your own plans in terms of service, pricing, reputation, management, financial position, brand awareness, business development, technology, or other factors that you feel are important. Consider the segments of the market in which competitors operate and their strategy. How much are they likely to affect your business, and what threats and opportunities do they represent?

As indicated earlier, you can find a wealth of market data on the internet. The hard part, of course, is sorting through it and knowing what to keep. Access to competitive information is variable, depending on where you are and the nature of the competition. Competitors that are publicly traded may have a significant amount of information available, as regular financial reporting is a requirement of every serious stock market in the world. Competitive information may be limited in situations where your rivals are privately held. If possible, you may want to play the role of a potential customer and gain information from that perspective. Industry associations, industry publications, media coverage, information from the financial community, and their own marketing materials and websites may be good resources to identify these factors and 'rate' the performance and position of each competitor.

*"It's vital to establish just how much you intend to spend and when"*

## *Why write a business plan?*

Having a well-researched and logical business plan will not only get your venture off the ground, but also keep it on track when it is up and running. In the first instance, unless you have a strong plan, you are unlikely to secure any funds and your idea could fall at the first hurdle. Your plan will serve as a structured form of communication to your investors, whether it's the banks, business angels or even family and friends, and it will provide reassurance as well as a means for everyone, yourself included, to measure your business' performance.

A business plan will help you to prioritise what exactly needs to be achieved and when. Do you need to find premises for your business before you hire staff? Should you be talking to wholesalers before your product has been finished? In the current climate, it's also important to outline what strategy you have in place for getting your venture through the downturn –

perhaps you consider it recession-proof, or you have done your research and have started in a sector where companies are growing, or you have strong measures to control expenditure. The answers will be different for each business, but it certainly helps if they are clear in your mind. 'If objectives are clearly flagged up, they are more likely to be achieved,' says **Tim Berry**, founder and president of business planning software company Palo Alto.

By using your business plan to prioritise key tasks, you can also use it to plan your cashflow. It's vital to establish just how much you intend to spend and when. Whether it's to buy stock, order uniforms, lease equipment etc, unless your finances match your requirements at the right moment, your business could stall.

Clearly, compiling a business plan should be at the top of your 'to do' list. If you are in a partnership or part of a potential management team, then decide early on who will write the plan, and then the same individual should be assigned the task of making the business stick to it. How far ahead to plan will again depend on your own aims and the type of business, but a year, broken down month by month, will be a minimum.

Once you've established responsibility and a timeframe, you need to decide on certain criteria, on which your business' success will be determined, and how these can be achieved. For instance, it could be hitting a given number of sales by a set date through an aggressive marketing campaign, or expanding to three more product lines through extensive market research. Whatever these achievement criteria turn out to be, you need to think hard about them without making too many assumptions. Consider your business failing in two or three years' time and try to imagine the reasons it might do so.

 In my experience

Company: **Ariadne Capital**
Owner-manager: **Julie Meyer**

*What sets a great business plan apart*
**Julie Meyer** cemented her position within the European start-up community when she launched networking club

First Tuesday in the late nineties. After selling it in 2000 she started investment and advisory firm Ariadne Capital, whose portfolio of companies includes Monitise, BeatThatQuote.com and Zopa. Alongside running Ariadne, Julie is now an investor in the online version of *Dragons' Den*.

With extensive experience as both an entrepreneur and investor, Julie has learned a great deal about how to put together and then present a killer business plan – and the pitfalls to avoid. So what's the most common mistake she comes across? 'One very common one is not knowing the plan intimately enough,' she says. 'Sometimes people hand it to their accountant to do, but when it comes to sitting across from a bank manager, they can't answer basic questions about what drives the business. If the business plan has been done by someone else, you never really own it yourself.'

However, Julie also often sees entrepreneurs being too optimistic about sales and costs: 'I don't believe in thinking small, but you do need to present reasonable and achievable figures. A good business plan should allow you to point to fixed costs, variable costs and forecasts for the next 12 months, which you should monitor on a month-by-month basis to see if you're on track with them. If you're wildly off base with your forecasts then you'll know something's wrong with the thought process.'

There are really three different business plans you should prepare, advises Julie: the best-case scenario, the worst-case scenario, and 'the one in the middle which you roll with'.

'If a bank manager asks you what the biggest thing that could go wrong with your business is and you stare back blankly, that's an instant giveaway you haven't stress tested your plan,' she says. 'It doesn't need to be bulletproof. You just need to think about what could go wrong and how you'll mitigate against that risk.'

And finally, Julie is also a big advocate of gaining as much feedback as possible on your business idea during the concept-testing stage: 'Some ideas are so revolutionary they need patents and confidentiality clauses around them, but there are very few businesses like that. One of the best ways to test an idea is to socialise it. Run it by people you respect in the market. You need to risk sharing your idea in order to get feedback on it. Some entrepreneurs work in isolation either through fear, competitiveness or because they don't have a network to discuss it with, but you need input to build a better concept.'

# *Preparing data for your plan*

This section will describe the key data you will need to compile before you start putting together your business plan, some of which you will be able to get from your market research, discussed earlier in this chapter.

## *The legal structure of your start-up*

While understandably the focus of most entrepreneurs is on their 'idea', it is vital that the operational and logistical requirements are not neglected. For example, decisions regarding whether you intend to trade as a sole trader, partnership or limited company are very important. (The options available to you are discussed in Chapter 5: 'Business structures and registering your company'). Similarly, you should understand and cover issues such as your potential VAT (value-added tax) obligations, registering a trade mark and drafting employment contracts.

## *Managing the numbers*

Whether you like figures or not, having a thorough understanding of 'the numbers' that will impact on your business is a crucial component of running a successful company. At the outset, it will be important to understand:

- ⇁ **Your start-up costs.**
- ⇁ **Your funding requirements.**
- ⇁ **Your cashflow forecast for the following months.**

### *Your start-up costs*

How much will it actually cost to get your business up and running? Think about what you will need to pay out before the launch date, such as legal and administrative fees that may be involved in registering your company, and any marketing, ranging from pre-launch advertising to the design of your logo and stationery. There's also the cost of renting premises if you are not working from home and any stock or equipment you may need, such as general office and IT items, to specialist tools that may be required for your particular business. You will also need to consider how much money you will need during the early months, once you are up and running – this is known as your cash reserve and covers you initially when you are likely

*"How much your cash reserve will be depends on how quickly you can start to bring revenue into the company"*

to be making a loss. How much your cash reserve will be depends on how quickly you can start to bring revenue into the company, so you need to consider carefully how long it will take until you reach the break-even point (see below) and move into profit. Here's an example of typical start-up costs and how you can itemise them:

| | |
|---|---|
| Initial expenses (legal costs, stationery, sales literature, logo and branding design) | £2,500 |
| Money in the bank as reserve for early losses | £16,500 |
| Start-up stock or raw materials (if required) | £900 |
| Other short-term assets (leasehold improvements, fixtures, signage, etc) | £700 |
| Long-term or fixed assets (land, machinery, IT equipment, etc) | £10,000 |
| **Total start-up requirements** | **£30,600** |

## Your funding requirements

To get your business off the ground, you will most likely need financial help to cover some of the start-up costs outlined above. Your business plan will be a vital tool for convincing lenders or investors to support your company. So, you will need to have carefully worked out how much money you need to raise, and explain your reasoning behind the figure. It's important to remember that once you have secured finance, it won't be easy going back to ask for more, so it's vital that you get it right first time. Although it's wise not to overestimate how much funding you need, as it's likely investors will react unkindly to such an approach, you do need to make sure you don't ask for too little either, as this will put a lot of pressure on your company. This is when working out the amount of cash you will need in reserve becomes important, and when you are likely to reach your break-even point.

## Your break-even point

Your break-even point is the critical milestone at which your new company stops making a loss and is about to move into profit, once all the additional expenses have been taken into account. Estimating as accurately as you can when you will reach this point is an expected part of your business plan. Before you can work this out you need to formulate your start-up costs and monthly running costs, taking into account any repayments on loans, salaries, etc. You then need to build in your projections of how many products you will sell, or how much demand you will have for your service, per month. By comparing your projected monthly revenues against your total monthly costs, you should be able to come up with a point at which you start to move into profit, that is, your break-even point.

Calculating the break-even point will give you an excellent idea of the costs involved in your business and the level of sales you will need to generate, which in turn will affect your overall business strategy. How much business you have to generate (either number of products or units of service) in a given time to break even can be calculated using the equation below:

Total revenue per month = Total costs per month

Unit sale price × Unit sales = Total monthly fixed costs + (Unit variable cost × Unit sales)

(Unit sale price × Unit sales) − (Unit variable cost × Unit sales) = Total fixed costs

(Unit sale price − Unit variable cost) × Unit sales = Total fixed costs

Unit sales per month = Total fixed costs/Unit sale price − Unit variable cost

Once you know how much you need to sell in one month to break even, you can work out from your sales projections how long it will take for your business to reach this point. You can also see in the table the elements of the equation that you need to change to reach the break-even point sooner if you want to.

## Your cashflow forecast

Estimating the amount and origin of cash coming into your business, together with how much is being paid out and where it's going during any given period, is a vital part of good business management. This is known as a cashflow forecast, and it's also what many lenders or investors will be looking for before they decide to invest in your business, making it a key part of your business plan. Once your business is established, it's usual to produce cashflow forecasts for a quarter or even a year in advance. However, during the early stages of your business, it's probably wiser to do this more frequently – say a month in advance. When formulating a cashflow forecast, it's critical that you don't overestimate your incoming cash. You will find it easier to get an accurate indication of your outgoings as you should be able to itemise them, as described above. The problem is, you are unlikely to be able to accurately identify how much money is going to be coming in, as you can only estimate how much business you will generate each month. This means it's vital to err on the side of caution, keeping your forecast on the conservative side.

## In my experience

**Company: 2B Interface**
**Owner-manager: Beatrice Bartlay**

*Being pedantic about overheads*

Having already set up an events and PR company in Poland, **Beatrice Bartlay** understood the importance of rigorous planning when starting up her recruitment business for skilled and professional workers, 2B Interface, in 2005.

Beatrice spent six months preparing the business plan, dividing her goals up into years, months and even weeks, all the while abiding by her philosophy that smaller goals are easier to achieve. 'In order to reach your targets, you have to work long and hard,' she explains. 'Business runs through your veins and is always in your head, regardless of what time it is or what you're doing, because there is always something you have to do.'

Beatrice stresses the importance of keeping your costs down, and admits she's 'pedantic about overheads'. Keeping a tight rein on cashflow is certainly crucial to any business, especially in the current economic climate, and Beatrice ensures she invests at least 20% of the income back into the company: 'If clients pay late, you always know you've got this money as back-up,' she says.

Indeed, Beatrice's diligent planning and careful cost management enabled her company to stay afloat when her main client went bust back in 2007, leaving her with a £90,000 unpaid invoice (see Chapter 2). The business has since flourished, recording a turnover of £4.2m last year.

*"There are niches you can occupy where price is not the most significant consideration"*

## Pricing

One of the most important decisions to be made when you start a business is how much to charge for your products or services. Customers buying standard products that are available from numerous sources will look for the supplier with the cheapest prices. This makes it difficult, if not impossible, for the small firm to compete with major suppliers who have the advantage of bulk purchasing or mass production. Fortunately, there are niches you can occupy where price is not the most significant consideration, being outweighed in the eyes of the customer by quality, service or uniqueness.

'Small companies often make the mistake of charging very low prices because they feel they must compete on a price-only basis,' warns marketing consultant **Annmarie Hanlon**. 'But there will always be a large company that can afford to drop its prices to squeeze the small company out. Instead, you should compete on product or service quality. A small company can give an attention to detail which is difficult for a big company dealing with 20,000 customers to achieve.'

## Pricing confidence

Having spent five years as a director of the Prince's Youth Business Trust, Annmarie speaks from the experience of being midwife at the birth of numerous businesses. 'There is less confidence in a cheap service than in a more expensive one,' she says. 'Hairdressing is a good example, where there is an idea that if you are paying your hairdresser more you are getting a better hair-do. I know a hairdresser in the Midlands who charges more than anyone else in the area. Customers receive a welcoming neck and shoulder massage on arrival and are given a hot towel to wipe their hands. With these added attentions, a premium price is perceived as appropriate.'

## Location and environment

Annmarie points out that location and environment are also important: 'If an establishment in a back street and with no reception area charged the same prices as a lush Mayfair location, its customers would feel they were being ripped off. It's all about ensuring the price is appropriate for the service.'

This is illustrated by what she calls 'the salmon sandwich issue'. She explains: 'If you buy a salmon sandwich from your local sandwich shop to take away in a paper bag you are happy with a price of £1. If you go to a well-known department store, the sandwich is nicely packaged and you have a perception that the quality is better, so £1.50 might be acceptable. Then there might be a premium product with finest Scottish smoked salmon and delicious trimmings. For that you might well accept a price of £2.10 because you think it is right for what is being offered. But if the same £2.10 sandwich was being sold for 45p you would wonder what was wrong with it.'

## Offer a specialised service

*"Compete on product or service quality. A small company can give an attention to detail which is difficult for a big company"*

In the retail sector, specialisation can sidestep price competition. Offer a wide selection in a narrow field. Observe what is lacking in an area and not encompassed by the big chains. It's a matter of finding a demand in your area that's not catered for, where your customers will feel they are getting value for money as opposed to cut prices. Family convenience stores that buy from middlemen – wholesalers and cash and carries – cannot match the prices of supermarkets, which buy in vast quantities direct from manufacturers. But their strength can be their location. They usually serve a localised market, such as a housing estate, or they may be situated on a route used by people going to and from work. Open for long hours, they are handy for people calling in for newspapers, confectionery or snack foods, or an 'emergency' purchase such as milk or sugar, aspirin or cigarettes – items that do not justify a trip to the supermarket. And people who call in for just one item often make other impulsive purchases. It's a case of convenience outweighing cost.

Ultimately, when you launch your business, to maximise your profits you will need to think creatively and strategically about your pricing structure to make sure, if possible, that you can charge the maximum by offering a premium product or service that is niche to your area. If there are larger companies offering a similar service, this will be a must.

## In my experience

**Company:** MyBuilder.com
**Owner-manager:** Ryan Notz

### *Finding a profitable model*

Let's be honest, the builders' industry doesn't have the best reputation. Picking a tradesman at random out of the phone book can be a gamble. Word of mouth recommendations are invaluable, but can be hard to come by.

**Ryan Notzp**, a self-employed stonemason, realised the solution lay online. Launched in 2008, MyBuilder.com is an online marketplace that brings together builders and homeowners. Customers can post a job on the site for free and registered builders offer them quotes. What's more, tradesmen post profiles on themselves where customers can leave reviews in a similar system to the eBay feedback model, bringing accountability and trust to an industry that often gets a bad press and enabling reliable tradesmen to build their reputation on the web.

The site has proved incredibly successful, scooping numerous business and technology awards. However, Ryan has gone through several different revenue models for the business over its lifespan. Initially, it was free for builders to register and income stemmed from charging customers £30 to post a job. 'Believe it or not, people paid,' says Ryan. 'It was pretty exciting when you got six people posting in a single day, but then there were days when nobody did and you can't grow a business that charges people up front with no guarantee of them finding a suitable builder.'

Ryan eventually adapted the business model so builders were charged a quarterly fee to register on the site, as well as a percentage of every job they secured through the service. Meanwhile, homeowners could post jobs free of charge. It was a tough call to make and cut the number of tradesmen registered from tens of thousands to a select 5,000. However, Ryan says it was the best move they could have made: 'Putting up a pricing barrier cut out most of the tradesmen but all the best ones were staying. Suddenly our payment rate went up.'

Now that the company has a profitable model, Ryan has turned his attention to heavily promoting his offering – with impressive results. There are now more than 47,000 tradesmen registered on the site, and more than 10,000 jobs are posted each month.

## Identifying the right people

Along with financial predictions, the people entrusted with putting your plan into action will be subject to particular scrutiny by potential financiers. Regardless of the entrepreneur's/founder's skill-set, he or she will invariably need help. While many non-core activities can be outsourced, certain functions, such as sales, will need full-time attention. You should outline the various skills required to run the business, price them into the model, and also identify any gaps and prospective candidates to fill them.

## Defining the customer benefits

Many entrepreneurs fail to clearly articulate the benefits of their new venture. As a result, the term 'elevator pitch' was introduced into modern lexicons as a proposed solution to this. An elevator pitch is your idea, supported by your business model, company solution, marketing strategy and competition, all stated in the length of time it takes for a short elevator ride. This simple idea encourages entrepreneurs to think carefully about the language they use when describing their new venture (particularly technological ones). It also reminds you to remain customer-focused and ensure that you concentrate on describing the benefits.

## Getting a mentor

Many start-up entrepreneurs are paranoid that their idea will be stolen and behave secretively prior to launch. Often the idea is closely guarded and only discussed with close confidantes. However, your confidantes (often family or friends) may find it difficult to pose sufficiently rigorous questions to you, either because they don't want to offend you, or because they lack the relevant experience or judgement to critically analyse your new venture. Hence, an idea with serious flaws, which could have been rectified early on in the process, can move ahead only for the wheels to come off at the most important phase. It is highly recommended that you engage an independent mentor or plan reviewer at an early stage. This person can help hone your idea before you present to investors or bankers.

# Key elements of your business plan

Your business plan should give a concise description of what your company will sell or the service it will offer, the buyers you will be selling to and how you will be filling a gap in the market, by touching on pricing and existing competition. It should be prepared to a high standard, be verifiable (meaning that you need to be able to back up your statements with facts), with no jargon or general position statements. It should offer the reader a combination of clear description and analysis, including a realistic SWOT (strengths, weaknesses, opportunities and threats; see later in the chapter) test of each area. This will demonstrate to investors that you are realistic about your company's prospects. So, ensure that you have a full appreciation of the risks, and you know how to grab your market share – all of which, of course, should have been covered in your market research. For your own benefit as well, it should contain details of how exactly you intend to meet your key objectives, as well as sales forecasts, target dates and who, apart from yourself, is to be responsible for this.

Then comes the boring, but just as necessary part – a financial analysis that shows clearly how much finance you need and where you plan to source it from (see Chapter 6: 'Raising finance and business banking'), a summary of start-up costs, your break-even point and cashflow forecast (as described above), plus profit and loss and balance sheet projections.

The key to all of this will be striking a balance between covering your business in enough detail and keeping the plan clear and to the point, so that it becomes useful to refer to time and time again rather than just sitting on a shelf gathering dust once you've started trading.

The key features of your plan are described below in brief, and then explained in more detail later in the chapter.

## The length

The length of a business plan depends on individual circumstances. It should be long enough to cover the subject adequately and short enough to maintain interest. Unless your business requires several million pounds of venture capital and is highly complex, the business plan should be no longer than 15 pages. The British Venture Capital Association (BVCA), the members of which you may well be pitching your plan to, recommends erring on the side of brevity. If investors are interested, they can always call to ask for additional information.

**WANT TO KNOW MORE …**

British Venture Capital Association
www.bvca.co.uk

## The look

The plan should look professional. Ensure there are no grammar or spelling mistakes. Use graphs and charts where appropriate and titles and subtitles to divide different subject matters. Although the aim is to make the plan look good, do avoid expensive stationery, as this could suggest unnecessary waste and extravagance.

## The company

The business plan should detail all the important aspects of your company: the market and customers; the products/services; the strength of the management team – and if there are any gaps in talent, identify how you will fill them. The plan should also explain how products will be made or services provided. Realistic financial projections should be outlined and you should provide different scenarios for sales, costs and cashflow for both the long and short term.

## What ifs and ways out

A number of possible scenarios should be presented, along with how your company would cope in different situations. These 'What if?' questions will show how your business will react to or counter the effects of an unexpected drop in sales or an increase in costs. The business plan should also detail potential exit strategies.

> ### Startups Tips
>
> **Areas to include in your business plan**
>
> → Executive summary (including mission statement)
> → Products and services (detail on your offer)
> → The market (customer and competitor analysis)
> → The proposition (why customers will buy from you)
> → Marketing strategy (how you will get your message across)
> → Sales strategy (how you plan to convert interest into sales)
> → Financial data (sales forecast, cost base, profit estimates)
> → Management and personnel (profiles of key people behind the business)
> → SWOT analysis (strengths, weaknesses, opportunities, threats)
> → Ownership and legal structure (shareholders and whether limited, partnership or sole trader)
> → Summary (brief overview and round-up)

## The executive summary

*"If you are looking for a loan, say so in the executive summary, and specify the amount required"*

The last thing to be written is the first part of the business plan: the executive summary. This is the most important section and summarises in two pages what you have written in detail in the proceeding 10–15 pages. This is where, among other things, you lay down the company's mission statement – a few sentences encapsulating what the business does for what types of client, your aims for the company and what gives it its competitive edge. In other words, the mission statement should combine the business' current situation with your aspirations. As with the main part of the business plan, the executive summary should be clearly written and powerfully persuasive, yet it should balance sales talk with realism in order to be convincing. It should be no more than 1,000 words long and should also state your company's legal status.

The executive summary presents the highlights of your business plan, and even though it opens the document, it's often the final part to be completed – for obvious reasons. The executive summary is the doorway to your business plan, so it's important to get it right or your target readers will go no further. As a general rule, for a standard plan, the first paragraph should include:

- ⇾ **Business name.**

- ⇾ **Business location.**

- ⇾ **What product or service you sell.**

- ⇾ **The purpose of the plan.**

Next, highlight important points, such as projected sales and profits, and keys to success. Essentially, you should include the news you don't want anyone to miss. This is a good place to put a 'highlights' chart – a bar graph that shows prospective sales, gross margin and profits before interest and taxes for the next three years – as well as drawing attention to them in the text. As you are starting up, one of the main purposes of your plan is likely to be to secure investment, so say this in your executive summary, and specify how much investment is required and the amount of equity ownership offered in return. It's also a good idea to add highlights of your management team and your competitive edge.

If you are looking for a loan, say so in the executive summary, and specify the amount required (but leave out other details about the loan).

# *Forecasting your sales*

Developing your sales forecast isn't as hard as most people imagine – assuming you have carried out sufficient and effective market research to inform and support your projections. Think of your sales forecast as an educated guess. It requires good working knowledge of your business but is much more of an art than a science. Remember that even if you don't have business training, you can guess your own business' sales better than any expert device, statistical analysis or mathematical routine. Experience counts more than any other factor.

A business plan should usually project sales by month for the next year, and annual sales for the following three years. This doesn't mean businesses shouldn't plan for the longer term, it simply means that the detail of monthly forecasts doesn't pay off beyond a year, except in special cases. It also means that the detail in the yearly forecasts probably doesn't make sense beyond three years. It does mean, of course, that you still plan your business for five, 10, and even 15-year timeframes, but you just don't do it within the detailed context of business plan financials.

Break your sales down into manageable parts, and then forecast these different elements. Estimate the figures based on line of sales, month by month, then add up the sales lines and add up the months, presenting your estimate graphically in a table or chart – but remember that you still need to explain them. A complete business plan will usually include some discussion of your sales forecast, sales strategy, sales programmes and related information. The text, tables, and charts will provide some visual variety and ease of use, but remember to position the tables and charts near the text covering the related topics.

Ideally, do three different forecasts, covering your best-case and worst-case scenarios, and your likely results.

"Make sure you discuss important assumptions in enough detail, and that you explain the background sufficiently"

## Drawing up a sales strategy

Near the sales forecast you should describe your sales strategy, which should deal with how and when to close sales prospects, how to compensate salespeople, how to optimise order processing and database management, and how to manoeuvre price, delivery and conditions. It should answer questions such as:

- How will you sell? For example: through retail, wholesale, discount, mail order or over the phone?
- Will you maintain a sales force?
- How will you train your salespeople, and how will they be compensated?

Your business plan text should summarise and highlight the numbers you have entered in the sales forecast table. Make sure you discuss important assumptions in enough detail, and that you explain the background sufficiently. Try to anticipate the questions your readers will ask. Include whatever information you think will be relevant and that your readers will need. Details are critical to implementation and your business plan should include specific information related to sales programmes, for instance:

⇢ How is this strategy to be implemented?

⇢ Do you have concrete and specific plans?

⇢ How will implementation be measured?

Business plans are about results, and generating results depends in part on how specific you are in the plan. For anything related to a sale that is supposed to happen, include it here and list the person responsible, dates required and budgets. All this will help to make your business plan more realistic.

---

### Marketing versus sales strategy

Don't confuse sales strategy with your marketing strategy. Sales should close the deals that marketing opens. To understand the difference between marketing and sales strategies, think of marketing as the broader effort of generating sales leads on a large scale, and sales as the efforts to bring those sales leads into the system as individual sales transactions. Marketing aims to build the business' image, customer awareness and propensity to buy, while sales involves getting the order.

---

# *SWOT analysis*

SWOT analysis is a method of describing your future company in terms of those factors that will have the most impact on the business. Strengths and weaknesses are internal factors, such as the quality of your product or the skills of your management, whereas opportunities and threats are external factors, which may include the development of a whole new market (opportunity), the arrival of a clutch of new competitors or the impact of the recession (threats) or the eventual economic recovery (opportunity). SWOT is an easy, understandable way of identifying key issues and communicating them to others. To make things even simpler to grasp, the typical SWOT analysis is done on a four-cell grid.

*"SWOT is an easy, understandable way of identifying key issues and communicating them to others"*

| Strengths | Weaknesses |
|---|---|
| **Opportunities** | **Threats** |

Sometimes it helps to start without the grid and list any issues at all that might affect the business – internal or external, real or perceived. Then, when the flow starts to dry up, organise the chosen items into the SWOT categories. Here's a guide to help you complete the categories.

## Strengths

In the first box list all the strengths of your company:

- ⇢ **Why should you succeed?**
- ⇢ **What will you do well?**
- ⇢ **Why will customers do business with you?**
- ⇢ **What distinct advantages does your company offer?**

*"The important consideration is honesty"*

The important consideration is honesty. Avoid being too modest or too optimistic. Any SWOT analysis is essentially subjective, but try for a third-party viewpoint: what strengths does the outsider see? A jump-start trick, especially for a group SWOT session, is to begin by brainstorming adjectives that characterise your business, writing them down as quickly as people say them, and then using those words to construct a more considered profile of your company's strengths. If you are the sole proprietor or the prime mover in the business, try starting with a list of your own positive personal characteristics.

## Weaknesses

A weakness is something that could seriously impede your company's performance – a limitation or deficiency in resource, skills or capabilities. These could be factors that you will be able to address on launch. For example, a weakness could be a lack of awareness in the marketplace compared with your competition, which means you will need to promote your company heavily to raise its profile, ideally before you launch the business or immediately after. Also, although you may list your personal knowledge of the market as a strength, the fact that the company will initially be heavily reliant on you could be seen as a weakness. If you can spot the key weaknesses of your proposed venture now, you can address them in time for the launch, and it shows investors that all-important element of realism in your approach. So don't try to disguise weaknesses, simply acknowledge them and ensure you have a strategy in place to tackle them.

## Opportunities

Under opportunities, think about where the openings are for your business, or the customer needs not being met by your competitors. You will probably start with marketing issues, presumably because your business fills a niche or can compete effectively, but do include all the possibilities. For instance, think of the interesting trends in your business sector – in terms of not only markets but also technology changes, the legislative and regulatory environment and social patterns.

## Threats

Threats are key impediments that your company will face on launch. What are the more apparent obstacles in your way, both actual and potential? Obvious candidates would include the economic downturn, a sudden rush of bad debts or a slack sales period leading to cashflow problems. But try to think further than that:

*"It's important to include a couple of worst-case scenarios . . . to consider how possible damage may be overcome"*

→ **What is your competition doing that could take business away from you or stunt your company's growth?**

→ **How might your competitors react to any moves you make?**

→ **What trends do you see that could wipe you out or make your service or product obsolete?**

→ **Might technology changes threaten your products or services?**

→ **What happens if a key customer goes under before paying a sizeable invoice?**

It's important to include a couple of worst-case scenarios. Weighing threats against opportunities is not a reason to indulge in pessimism, but rather a question of considering how possible damage may be overcome, bypassed or restricted.

## Using SWOT data

Once you have the results of your own SWOT analysis and at least one (but preferably more) from another source, combine them on the grid. Sort each category first by relative importance, then in terms of reality – this is an interesting exercise, which might well require some soul-searching. For example, ask yourself what evidence you really have for saying that

*"A SWOT analysis helps identify the critical issues in any situation and organises them in a way that enables you to come up with a sound strategic approach"*

customers will choose your product over your competitors'. Finally, trim the categories to around no more than five or six items each per category, homing in on the really critical issues. You can use this as the basis for some strategic planning. This cut-down SWOT summary and a description of your sound strategic approach to address the points listed should appear in your business plan. This will cover how you plan to:

-> Build on the strengths

-> Minimise the weaknesses

-> Seize the opportunities

-> Counter the threats

## Action points

### Four key recommendations for a flawless SWOT analysis

☑ **Be comprehensive**: This means picking up small details. A minor weakness could be too few filing cabinets, while a major threat could be a decline in the value of sterling following an election. Of course, this could also be a key opportunity if there was a rise in currency value instead.

☑ **Be prepared**: Put real effort into background preparation and gathering information. Be self-critical, but don't be too defensive. SWOT analysis is there to stimulate ideas, not stifle them.

☑ **Include others**: SWOT works well in group sessions. To get a real brainstorm going you need more than four people, but to keep it manageable limit numbers to around 10.

☑ **Test your analysis**: Ask an outsider (your accountant, perhaps, or a family member) to conduct the same exercise and compare their views with your findings. The more people who look at your SWOT analysis, the more ideas you are likely to get.

**Using SWOT analysis to clarify your business goals**

After a SWOT analysis you might see things in terms of answers to these four questions:

- How can strengths be used to take advantage of opportunities?
- How can strengths be used to avoid or defuse threats?
- How can weaknesses be overcome to take advantage of opportunities?
- How can weaknesses be overcome to counteract or minimise threats?

Remember to try to be objective at all times when writing your strategic approach.

## *The people*

Anyone who runs a business knows that none of the areas covered by a business plan can be tackled without people. Why then do so many business plans feel that it's sufficient to insert an appendix with the CVs of the managers? This token gesture does not give any feel for how the business will be run, what the potential gaps in expertise may be or what essential skills will be needed in the future. It all comes back to strategic planning versus day-to-day fire-fighting.

*"If you are launching solo, the people section will initially revolve around your skills and experience"*

If you are launching solo, the people section will initially revolve around your skills and experience. But this model can still help you to draw up a list of the kind of people you will need to meet your projections for the business, either at start-up or beyond, which will show that you have a clear understanding of what is required to realise your vision. Here is a model that might help you to analyse the 'people' section of the plan.

1. Draw up a table with four columns: (a) people, (b) experience, (c) skills and (d) functions.

2. Make a list of all the people who are involved in your business in column (a) and summarise their experience and skills in columns (b) and (c), so that you can clearly see who you have on board and what they each bring to the business.

3. Make a list of the areas of sector and functional expertise required for the business and see who is ideally placed to fill each of these roles. Are there any functions that can't be undertaken by the people who are within the team and, if so, how do you propose to fill these gaps?

4. Draw up another table showing the business in three years' time. How will the management team be different? What steps will you need to take to both keep existing staff satisfied and recruit new staff of sufficient calibre to deliver your ambitious future plans as described in other sections?

Businesses change over time, and it is unusual for an early-stage company to have a full management team. Generally an entrepreneur will endeavour to fill many roles, some of which they will be particularly unsuited to. Why not explore in the business plan what roles could be performed better by others, such as a finance director, sales director or even the chief executive? How are you going to afford people of sufficient calibre to deliver what you want? Perhaps you will need to raise some further finance to cover this at a later date. One of the most valid reasons for raising equity capital is to pay for people who are good enough to take a company to a higher level, and yet entrepreneurs generally leave such recruitment too late.

## The mission statement

*"It's vital that the mission statement is original and accurately reflects your business"*

An effective mission statement should be able to tell your company story and ideals in less than 30 seconds, and, as such, it can be one of the more challenging elements of your business plan. The readers should be able to gain a clear understanding of what your company's about from the mission statement, so it's vital to think it through very carefully. Essentially, it should only be around three to four sentences long, defining what your company is, what it does, what it stands for and why, and it is often best developed with input from everyone involved in the launch.

It can help to examine other companies' mission statements, but don't be tempted to copy any, because it's vital that the mission statement is original and accurately reflects your business, not someone else's. You should also make sure that you believe in your mission statement, as it will provide the basis for your business going forward, inspiring both you and your future employees to succeed. If it's a lie, it can be demotivating for your employees and put off customers once this becomes apparent.

## Mission control: example mission statements from famous companies

### IBM

'At IBM, we strive to lead in the invention, development and manufacture of the industry's most advanced information technologies, including computer systems, software, storage systems and microelectronics.

'We translate these advanced technologies into value for our customers through our professional solutions, services and consulting businesses worldwide.'

### Amazon.com

'To be the most customer-centric company in the world, where people can find and discover anything they want to buy online.'

### Apple Computers (1984)

'To produce high-quality, low cost, easy-to-use products that incorporate high technology for the individual. We are proving that high technology does not have to be intimidating for non-computer experts.'

### Sainsbury's

'Our mission is to be the consumer's first choice for food, delivering products of outstanding quality and great service at a competitive cost through working faster, simpler and together.'

 **Startups Tips**

### Writing your plan

- Write from the audience's perspective – tell them what they need to know.
- Research the market thoroughly – it proves the viability of your business.
- Understand the competition – and how you will beat it.
- Pay attention to detail – it shows you really care.
- Focus on the opportunity – talk it up, but be realistic.
- Ensure all key areas are covered – be comprehensive.
- Make sure your figures add up – they won't take it seriously otherwise.
- Write a killer executive summary – it's the bit that gets them interested.
- Get it reviewed – ideally by an experienced independent source.
- Implement the plan – don't leave it on a shelf and forget about it.

# *Making your plan investor-friendly*

Although many people work hard to produce business plans that are technically perfect, because they recognise the importance of the document in securing essential finance and other support vital to getting a business off the ground, many business plans still fail. This is because often they need to show more than technical excellence. Remember that potential investors receive lots of business plans and so are looking to be inspired by those that offer more than the ordinary. So while you should include the necessary sales forecast, SWOT analysis and mission statement, here are some tips that could provide the key to unlocking a target reader's interest and encouraging them to venture beyond the executive summary.

*"Tell them who you are, how you got into this position of writing the plan, and engagingly unfurl your vision for the business"*

## *Research your target reader*

The more you know about the reader and their requirements, the better equipped you will be to give them what they want – and so get what you want. The bank manager, the equity provider and whoever else you may be pitching your business plan to are likely to all have different needs and concerns, but will probably have one thing in common: they are busy, short of time, impatient and hassled. So spoon-feed them. Make their lives easier and they will appreciate it. Once you have excited the finance provider with your vision, give some background about the business. Don't make assumptions about what they know about your potential company, your ambitions and your plan. Tell them who you are, how you got into this position of writing the plan, and engagingly unfurl your vision for the business. In short, put it all in perspective. Frame the plan, and the reader will have some reference points straight away.

## *Explain your proposition*

Once your readers know two things – where you came from and where you are going – next comes the crucial bit: can you explain what your value proposition is to your customers in no more than 30 seconds or a few lines of text? If you can, you will be among a very small minority of entrepreneurs – even some of the successful ones have never managed it. Succinctly summarise:

→ **Who will buy your product or service and why will they buy?**

→ **How many will they buy?**

↠ Why will they continue to buy over time?

↠ Why will they buy from you rather than someone else?

↠ In short, what value are you really delivering to your customer?

*"Can you explain what your value proposition is to your customers in no more than 30 seconds or a few lines of text?"*

It can often help to test yourself. For example, bore your friends with your proposition, or if you get the chance, try it out on prospective customers, and once you have it off pat, write it down. It will be one of your most valuable assets. If all this sounds quite simple on paper, remember that many have found it impossible to achieve in practice. But after all the time spent researching your market, working through your sales forecasts, constructing your SWOT analysis and other relevant details and then committing them to paper, you may just crack it. Working on producing a killer value proposition will be well worth the effort, as it could prove decisive in gaining the investment you need to launch your company.

## *Presenting your plan*

When the business plan has been prepared and it has received input from a financial adviser, the next step is to put it in front of investors. If you are using a business angel network, which match young businesses with private investors, there should be plenty of advice on offer as they will know exactly what a business angel is looking for. Try also to run through the plan with any business contacts you have, as they may spot something you hadn't noticed. Asking friends and family to help can also be useful.

At this point, you may send just a copy of the executive summary. This has the advantage of saving costs and increasing the chances of receiving attention. Response times to the business plan will vary, but can take as little as a week. If the answer is no, you should find out the reasons why and then consider incorporating those ideas into a revised business plan, changing and strengthening the management team or carrying out further market research before approaching other potential investors.

And remember, the business plan is a living document. Don't think of it as a fixed route and be prepared to adapt it to suit your audience. Even if you are in an established business, you must be prepared to adapt the plan as your market or customer base changes, or if disaster strikes.

Action points

## Common business plan mistakes

While including the necessary items in a business plan, make sure you don't commit any of the following common business plan mistakes.

☑ **Putting it off**: Too many entrepreneurs make business plans only when they have no choice in the matter. Unless the bank or the investors want a plan, there is no plan. Don't wait to write your plan until you think you will have enough time. It should play a key role in the development of your business, creating a strategic framework to build your company around, and not just created in response to a specific need, such as securing funding. This is why it is essential to review your plan regularly — it should be an organic document that develops as the business grows and as the influences on it change, such as marketing conditions.

☑ **Cashflow casualness**: Most people think in terms of profit instead of cash. When you imagine a new business, you think of what it would cost to make the product, what you could sell it for, and what the profit per unit might be. We are trained to think of business as sales minus costs and expenses, which equals profits. Unfortunately, we don't spend the profits in a business. We spend cash. So understanding cashflow is critical. If you have only one table in your business plan, make it the cashflow table.

☑ **Idea inflation**: Don't overestimate the importance of the idea. You don't need a great idea to start a business; you need time, money, perseverance and common sense. Few successful businesses are based entirely on new ideas. A new idea is harder to sell than an existing one, because people don't understand a new idea and they are often unsure if it will work. Plans don't sell new business ideas to investors, people do. Investors invest in people, not ideas. The plan, although necessary, is only a way to present information.

☑ **Fear and dread**: Although preparing a business plan can seem daunting, if you approach it carefully and strategically, and have carried out the necessary research into the viability of your business beforehand, there is no need to fear anything — in fact, fear and dread could mean you put it off until the last minute and then don't dedicate the time and energy to it that it deserves. There are also plenty of resources available to help you get it right.

☑ **Spongy, vague goals**: Leave out the vague and the meaningless babble of business phrases (such as 'being the best'), because they are simply hype. Remember that the objective of a plan is to secure results, and for results, you need tracking and follow-up. You need specific dates, management responsibilities, budgets and milestones. Then you can follow up. No matter how well thought out or brilliantly presented your business plan may be, it means nothing unless it produces results.

☑ **One size doesn't fit all**: Tailor your plan to its real business purpose. Business plans can be different things: sales documents to sell an idea for a new business; detailed action plans; financial plans; marketing plans or even personnel plans. They can be used to start a business, or just run a business better.

☑ **Diluted priorities**: Remember, strategy is focused. A priority list with three to four items is focused. A priority list with 20 items is certainly not strategic, and rarely, if ever, effective. The more items on the list, the less the importance of each.

☑ **Hockey-stick shaped growth projections**: Sales grow slowly at first, but then shoot up boldly with huge growth rates, as soon as 'something' happens. Have projections that are conservative, so you can defend them. When in doubt, be less optimistic.

 **What to do next**

- Don't ignore the importance of market research. Analysing the current market will shape your ideas on how to launch your offering and help you avoid competitors' mistakes.

- Assess the competition. Is the market saturated with other players? Is there a need for your services in certain areas?

- Highlight your USPs (unique selling points). It's important to identify these clearly in your own head before you can effectively communicate them to others.

- Remember business plans aren't just for investors and bank managers, they're also a map of where you intend your business to go.

- Be realistic with your numbers. Be careful not to underestimate how much funding you'll need to get the venture off the ground.

 **CHAPTER 4**

*Business names, brands
and intellectual property*

# What's in this chapter?

→ What's in a name?
→ Naming a limited company or LLP
→ Naming a sole trader business
→ Checking your name is original
→ Choosing your domain name
→ Protecting your intellectual property

Choosing your business name is one of the most important things you will have to decide upon. Unfortunately, it is also one of the first decisions you will have to make. This chapter offers advice on how to select the perfect moniker for your start-up, from making sure your chosen name is original – and what to do if it's not – to the different rules for naming a sole trader business and a limited company. Read on for advice on how to choose and register the right web domain name for your business, as well as key information on how to protect your intellectual property – such as your name, brand, designs and inventions – through trade marks and patents.

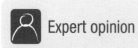 Expert opinion

## Brands and effective brand protection

**Roger Lowe from ip4all offers advice on how to protect your brand**

Regardless of the size of your business, the nature of the goods it supplies or the services it provides, your business will create and as a consequence, it will own some forms of intellectual property (IP). One of the most important forms of IP any start-up business will own is its brand.

A brand describes the personality of a product, service or company, and in its broadest sense, a brand will consist of a collection of intangible values as perceived by a customer which are attributed to a distinctive name, a logo or symbol, and possibly a colour pallet which immediately identifies the brand within its particular market. A brand may incorporate a slogan or strap line, or a certain form of advertising which can include a particular celebrity, or corporate relationship. It may also be defined by a particular house style which includes a well-defined form of packaging, jingle or even scent.

All of these diverse component parts of a brand can be and should be protected by appropriate forms of intellectual property rights and these are described below.

### Copyright
Copyright protects the physical expression of ideas. As soon as an idea is given physical form, eg a piece of writing, a photograph, music, a film, a web page or a logo, it is protected by copyright. There is no need for registration to claim copyright, protection is automatic from the point of creation.

Copyright is normally owned by the creator of the work, eg an author, composer, artist, photographer etc. If the work is created in the course of an employee's employment, then the copyright owner is usually the employer. In each case, it is imperative that copyright in a logo or jingle used by your business is owned by your business, and advice should be taken to ensure that such ownership is captured.

### Design
There are currently four types of design protection in the UK, two of which you are able to register and two which do not require any form of registration. In the case of

the UK Registered Design and the Community Registered and Unregistered Design Rights, a 'design' means the appearance of the whole or part of a product resulting from the features of, in particular, the lines, contours, colours, shape, texture or materials of the product or its ornamentation; and a 'product' means any industrial or handicraft item other than a computer program, and, in particular, includes packaging, get-up, graphic symbols, typographic type-faces and parts intended to be assembled into a complex product.

It is therefore apparent that where a logo or device is to be used on an industrial or handicraft item, thought should be given to the registration of the logo or device as a design. The UK Unregistered Design Right is of less use or interest to brand owners, but it should not be entirely neglected.

### Goodwill and passing off

The law of passing off prevents one person from misrepresenting his or her goods or services as being the goods and services of another, and also prevents one person from holding out his or her goods or services as having some association or connection with another when this is not true. Business goodwill is protected by the common law tort of passing off and while this may be associated with a particular name or mark used in the course of trade, this area of law is wider than trade mark law in terms of the scope of marks, signs, materials and other aspects of a trader's 'get-up' that can be protected. The owner of goodwill has a property right that can be protected by an action in passing off.

What is goodwill? It is a thing very easy to describe, very difficult to define. It is the benefit and advantage of the good name, reputation and connection of a business. It is the attractive force which brings in custom.

Goodwill is created by trade and in certain circumstances, evidenced through the extent of advertising. Therefore once a product or service has formed the basis of trade, sufficient goodwill may have been derived in order to bring a claim for passing off.

### Trade marks

A trade mark is defined as any sign capable of being represented graphically which is capable of distinguishing goods or services of one undertaking from those of other undertakings. A trade mark may, in particular, consist of words (including personal names), designs, letters, numerals or the shape of goods or packaging.

The proprietor of a registered trade mark has exclusive rights in the trade mark which are infringed by the use of the trade mark without his consent. The proprietor of a registered trade mark can sue for infringement if a person uses the same or similar mark on the same or similar goods or services for which the trade mark has been registered.

Once a sign, mark or logo has been identified, then the best advice is to attempt to seek registration of it as a trade mark in all jurisdictions in which trade is going to be undertaken.

*Conclusion*

All of the intellectual property rights identified above overlap when considering the best possible forms of protection for a brand. All of them should be considered at the earliest possible time in order to ensure that the appropriate forms of protection are secured and to make sure that the rights of third parties are not being infringed by their use.

In addition, the recent reconstitution of the Patents County Court allows more affordable access to the enforcement of all intellectual property rights concerned with a brand or otherwise.

Dr Roger Lowe at ip4all
3-5 Wormalds Yard
off King Street
Huddersfield
West Yorkshire
HD1 2QR
Mobile: 07800545089
Huddersfield: 0148 481 7770
Leeds: 0113 278 9974
Manchester: 0161 939 0141
Email: roger.lowe@ip4all.co.uk
Website: www.ip4all.co.uk

# *What's in a name?*

In a rational world, a company with a strong product, service, or niche idea could expect to make a healthy profit. However, it takes more than that to get across to customers the benefit of using your business instead of your competitors'. The name is the first thing that any potential buyer is going to encounter and, in this respect, is more important than your sales pitch or even your end product. You might have the best idea in the world, but if people are going elsewhere because your competition 'looks' more attractive, then no one will ever know.

As the name is the entry point to your business and, superficially, the only differentiator between you and your competitors, customers will make instant judgements on where they want to buy from. Therefore, it's essential that you strike the right tone with your business' name.

However, in today's world, you also need to take it one step further – successful companies do not just have good names, they develop a brand. And, in time, brands can literally sell themselves. Company branding specialist, **Jim Fowle**, of Red Mullet Design, explains: 'When starting a company, your brand is of vital importance. Branding is not just a memorable logo, but also an effective, memorable name that can really help people remember you. This can be portrayed strongly visually as well. In the initial stages, we find it's good to envisage your name and branding, making sure it's recognisable, simple and reflects your business.'

It's easier said than done. You don't just want to stand out from your competition; you also need to be taken seriously. When you are choosing a business name it's essential to remember that this is a name that you will have to say dozens of times each day and it is something you will be known by. Make sure that you like how it sounds and how it looks before committing. 'Initially, in the early stages, the best option is to be experimental,' suggests Jim. 'Sometimes it's easy to get too clever and lose sight of what you are trying to achieve. It is about getting the balance of a good name and having good branding at the same time. This encapsulates the perfect package.'

It's tempting to incorporate your own name into your business' moniker, but remember it won't add any information about the company. A safe and trustworthy method is to link your business' name to the area in which you operate – customers associate such firms with strong local roots and a friendly approach to the public. Therefore, the Acton Sandwich Shop or Govan Records would be perceived as well-established, reputable businesses.

*"Names should be snappy, original and instantly informative as to what your business does"*

> ## There are essentially three types of business name:
>
> **Descriptive:** these describe what the business does, or may be named after the owner; for example Design and Print Centre
> *Pros:* Provides information about your business or who runs it
> *Cons:* Can lack creativity and be less memorable
>
> **Associative:** these aim to create positive associations in customers' minds; for example Ocean Fish Bar
> *Pros:* Can help to generate a positive image of your company
> *Cons:* If not original or creative, they can come across as clichéd
>
> **Abstract:** these may have no meaning at all, and could be just words joined together; for example Shoon (shoe shop)
> *Pros:* Easier to be original and can attract attention
> *Cons:* Provides no information about the company

Meanwhile, humour or a nice play on words is an effective way to stand out from the crowd. While a fish and chip shop called Your Plaice or Mine or a hairdressers named Hair Today, Gone Tomorrow would elicit predictable groans from passers-by, puns can be used to good effect, so long as they are not overly cheesy and don't digress from whatever image you are trying to convey for your firm. Ideally, names should be snappy, original and instantly informative as to what your business does.

*"Rebranding can be expensive, so try to avoid a name that is too specific if this will inhibit your future growth plans"*

## Choosing the right name

Firstly, think about your brand values and the image you want to portray. Do you want a name that says traditional or modern? Should it suggest well-established reliability or an innovative approach? Ideally you want a name that is memorable and unique, yet relevant and clear. A descriptive name avoids confusion about what you do and can be beneficial to search engine rankings. On the other hand, a more creative, abstract title can inspire curiosity and set you apart, but there needs to be some reasoning behind it if you want a credible brand. How does your name encapsulate your brand values? Could it be qualified by a clever tagline?

Think about how your name will work in your logo, signage, advertising and when answering the phone, too. Try to remain objective, put yourself in your customers' shoes, and get as much feedback as you can from trusted sources. And don't forget to factor in the development of the company. Rebranding can be expensive, so try to avoid a name that is too specific if this will inhibit your future growth plans.

 ## In my experience

Company: **easyJet**
Owner: **Sir Stelios Haji-Ioannou**

*easyJet and the simple approach*
In classic abstract style, **Sir Stelios Haji-Ioannou**, who founded low-cost airline easyJet in 1995, called his first business (a shipping company) Stelmar, which was an amalgamation of Stelios Maritime. The reason he wanted to incorporate his name was to stamp his own personal credentials on the company. 'I wanted to achieve something specific and for it to be known as Stelios' company and not my father's,' he says.

In the same vein, Stelair was the working title for the airline he planned to set up, once again trying to involve his name in the business. But then he changed his mind. 'I decided that I shouldn't be so self-centred,' he says. 'And it was also difficult to pronounce . . . I also decided that the brand had to be extendable over several industries.'

There were also considerations of longevity behind his decision to call this business easyJet, as well as consideration for his shareholders. Stelios, who departed from the easyJet board in 2010 (although his private investment vehicle, easyGroup, remains a major shareholder) wanted to create a name – and a company – that would continue to work whether he was in charge or not.

Stelios has gone on to set up 16 other 'easy' branded companies; easyGroup owns the 'easy' brand and licences it to the various ventures, including easyJet.

## *A great name is good marketing*

The small business insurance company More Th›n Business conducted a survey into the impact of business names on potential customers. First, the company asked for nominations for the most creative company name, with entries coming not only from the companies themselves, but also their customers, giving a clear indication of just how much attention a great company name can attract.

Once a list of the best names had been compiled, they were then tested on the general public. Three-quarters of those surveyed admitted to being influenced by a catchy name, while 58% said it would make them remember the business. In fact, names were found to be most important to the younger people, with three-quarters of 18–24 year olds stating they would notice and remember a shop with a humorous name. 'Our research confirms what the UK's most creative business owners already knew – that the right business name can offer a real advantage in the battle for customers,' says **Mike Bowman**, head of insurance at More Th›n Business. 'With [thousands of] new start-ups each year, it is becoming increasingly difficult for business owners to settle on a catchy yet original name, but the research shows that it's definitely worth putting in the time and effort to get the right name.'

Citing the great marketing potential of a good, creative business name, Bowman adds: 'A creative name plays a huge role in setting a small business apart and getting it noticed. Small businesses and independent high street retailers may not have massive marketing budgets, but this doesn't mean there is a lack of creative flair.'

More Th›n Business awarded the title of most creative British business name to Aisle Alter Hymn, a wedding shop for gay and lesbian couples in South Shields, Tyne & Wear. While you don't have to use a pun to achieve a memorable name, if you are in an industry where it's hard to market your unique selling point, it may just help you stand out from the crowd – as William the Concreter would probably agree.

## The top 20 creative business names

Here's a rundown of the best business names in the UK, as found in the survey by small business insurer More Th›n Business:

1. Aisle Alter Hymn (UK's first wedding shop for gay, lesbian and heterosexual couples in South Shields, Tyne & Wear)

2. Battersea Cods Home (fish and chip shop in Sheffield, South Yorkshire)

3. Mad Hakkers (hairdressers in Leven, Fife)

4. Mr Bit (window cleaners in Derby and Coventry, West Midlands)

5. Only Foods and Sauces (takeaway in Walsall, West Midlands)

6. Spruce Springclean (window cleaners in West Byfleet, Surrey)

7. Tree Wise Men (tree surgeons in Wallington, Surrey)

8. Vinyl Resting Place (second-hand records shop in Croydon, Surrey)

9. Walter Wall (carpet sales in Exeter, Devon)

10. Plaice Station (fish and chip shop in Manchester)

11. William the Concreter (concrete suppliers in Hastings)

12. Carter, Whey and Tippet (refuse collection service in London)

13. Dustin Often (cleaning service in Leicester)

14. C Thru Cleaning (cleaning service in Middlesex)

15. Give us a Break (window fitters in Leicester)

16. R Soles (Bootmaker in London)

17. Floral and Hardy (gardeners in Hayes, Kent)

18. Sarnie Schwarzenegger's (sandwich shop in Liverpool)

19. Abra-Kebab-Ra (kebab shop in Dublin)

20. Wok This Way (Chinese takeaway in Glasgow)

There are also some other serious contenders. These include north-east entertainers Amps and Decks and arborists Tree Amigos, as well as: Pimp my Pet, Fishcoteque, Pain in the Glass, Junk and Disorderly, Curl up and Dye, Spice Boys, Bubble n Chic and The Head Gardener. Can you guess what these businesses do?

Once you've selected the perfect title for your business, you then need to ensure that it complies with certain rules and regulations before you register your company or begin trading, and crucially, that it hasn't already been snapped up by somebody else. Below, we will look at the different rules and considerations you need to be aware of when naming a limited company or limited liability partnership (LLP), and when selecting a name for a sole trader business or partnership. Which structure you choose for your company is another key decision you will need to make. We will explore the differences between the business structures themselves in Chapter 5: 'Business structures and registering your company'.

 **Action points**

### Where to start looking for a name

☑ **Get friends and family together for a brainstorm**: It helps to canvass opinion, and your nearest and dearest are as good a place to start as any, according to small business insurance company More Th>n Business.

☑ **Examine what competitors are called**: Do you think the names of your competitors work? By checking them out you will know the standard you are up against, and although you can't copy any and would be ill-advised to choose a similar name, you may be inspired by good ones.

☑ **Think of good business names that stand out in your mind**: Beyond your competitors, you can also get inspiration from famous companies without directly copying them.

☑ **Use the internet, phone book, magazines and business directories to research**: You can pretty much carry out all the necessary investigation from home using handy sources of information.

☑ **Choose at least 10 names**: Then you can whittle these down to a shortlist of three or four by checking which of your prospective names are available – remember that many will already be taken. Once you have your shortlist of available names, involve friends and family in the elimination process and make sure each of the names generated stands up to the checklist you'll find later in the chapter.

## Naming a limited company or LLP

As we have seen, your name will play a huge role in promoting your new business; get it right and it will attract new customers, set you apart and convey your brand identity. Get it wrong and not only could you give the wrong impression of your business, costing you customers, you could also land yourself in hot water.

The main principles for choosing a great name apply to any business, but if you are setting up a limited company or LLP there are some specific rules you need to be aware of. Before you register your business with Companies House, make sure your name ticks all of these boxes.

*"Your name will play a huge role in promoting your new business"*

→ For starters, your business name must end with either limited (or Ltd) or limited liability partnership (or LLP), depending on which of these structures applies to your business. Also, the word 'limited' must not appear anywhere else in your name, so 'Limited Ltd' is not allowed.

→ Next, search the index of registered companies on the Companies House website to make sure your proposed name is not the 'same as' an existing limited company or LLP – unless your new business will form part of the same group as the organisation that already 'owns' the name, that is. Also, be aware that 'same as' does not necessarily mean identical to – if your name is similar enough to cause confusion, you will need to pick again.

→ If, after registering your business, your name is deemed to be 'too like' another company's, a complaint can be lodged against your business. Objections can be made within 12 months, and if upheld by the registrar you will be given 12 weeks to change your name.

→ You must also ensure that your chosen name is not too similar to a registered trade mark, and that it is not already being used by a sole trader in your local area. (See later in the chapter for more details on how to run these checks).

→ Unsurprisingly, any words or expressions deemed as offensive are a no-no. You will have to exercise your own judgement as to what such words include, but the chances are that swear words or phrases generally considered to be insulting will not be permitted. Meanwhile, there are some words and phrases that are deemed to be 'sensitive' and you will have to obtain special permission to use. These phrases can be classified into five main groups, and include words that:

- suggest your business is of national importance, such as British, Scottish, national or international;

- depict a special status or authority, such as association, chamber of commerce or council;

- describe a particular function, such as charity or trust;

- refer to a specialised activity, such as surveyor or chemist;

- give the impression that your business is connected to the government or the Royal Family.

A full list of sensitive words, along with the organisations you must seek permission from should you wish to use them, is available on the Companies House website.

**WANT TO KNOW MORE …**

Companies House
www.companies
house.gov.uk

Once you are certain that your name is available, appropriate and complies with all legalities, you must register your limited company or LLP with Companies House (see Chapter 5). You should also look at protecting your new name by registering your own trade mark. For more on this, see later in the chapter.

---

### ⟲ *Startups Tips*

**Your business name checklist**

When you choose a name for your business, make sure it:

⇢ Is not already taken.

⇢ Has no negative connotations.

⇢ Reflects what your business stands for.

⇢ Is appropriate and appealing to your audience.

⇢ Has the potential to be memorable.

⇢ Won't be able to limit your business in any way.

⇢ Has a meaning that can be transferred overseas if necessary.

⇢ Is easy to say and spell.

⇢ Can be owned and protected as your trade mark.

⇢ Can be registered as an internet URL or web address.

*(Source: More Th>n Business)*

# *Naming a sole trader business*

If you are a sole trader, you can trade under your own name or your business partner's name, should you have one. However, this is not obligatory and you can be far more creative if you wish. Should you choose to give your fledgling company a new title, selecting the right name is paramount. After all, this will form the basis of prospective customers' first impression of your offering.

"*Before you begin trading or fork out for stationery, advertising or signage, you must check that your chosen name is not already being used by someone else*"

There are certain considerations to be aware of when naming your sole trader business. Firstly, sole traders are not allowed to use the terms limited (Ltd), limited liability partnership (LLP) or public limited company (plc) in their name, as this incorrectly describes the status of their business. Again, your chosen moniker must not be offensive, nor can it contain any of the prescribed 'sensitive' words, such as those which suggest your business is of national importance (eg British or international) unless you have obtained specific permission to use them (see above for more details).

Given that many sole traders operate in the service sector, such as gardeners, plumbers, designers, hairdressers, B&Bs and builders, you may want to consider incorporating your local area and proposition into your name, for example: Queens Park Garden Services or South Coast Bikes. While this approach does not always deliver the most creative of names, it can work to your advantage in the search engines by increasing your visibility to potential customers who are seeking your offering within your locality, and can even help to boost your rankings a little (although having relevant content and keywords is the key here, and any business can 'optimise' their website for search engines – see Chapter 9, Marketing and PR, for more on this).

However, before you begin trading or fork out for stationery, advertising or signage, you must check that your chosen name is not already being used by someone else (see below for details). If a sole trader at the other end of the country is using your name, this may not be a problem. However, if another local or national company is using it you will have to go back to the drawing board.

Once you have determined that your name is available to use and complies with all the rules, the next step is to register as a sole trader. If you choose this route, you do not need to register your business with Companies House. Instead, you simply need to register as self-employed with HM Revenue & Customs (HMRC). See Chapter 5, Business structures and registering your company, for more information.

However, you may also choose to register your company with the National Business Register (NBR). This affords you more protection against any legal challenges to your name, as the NBR will perform all necessary checks on your behalf and will inform you if there are any issues with your proposed title. According to the NBR, registration also prevents others from copying your name in the future and protects your business against 'passing off' – that is, others using your name to piggyback on your success, potentially taking customers away from you in your market or trading area. Full business name searches, protection and registration for one year costs around £100.

## *Checking your name is original*

Whichever form your new company will take, it's vital that you carry out a thorough check to see if anyone else is using your name before you begin trading. The Companies House website will enable you to check if the name you have chosen is already being used by a registered company. However, as stated above, sole traders do not have to register with Companies House, so they will not show up in this search. You can also run free searches on the CheckSURE website and the National Business Register website, which contain details of millions of UK sole traders, to see what's available before choosing your business name. However, you should also check local phone books and business directories and run some internet searches on your chosen name.

**WANT TO KNOW MORE ...**

**CheckSURE**
www.checksure.biz

**The National Business Register**
www.start.biz

Crucially, you also need to make sure that your proposed name isn't the same as (or too similar to) a name that someone else has registered as a trade mark. The easiest way to do this is by running a search on the UK Trade Mark Register on the Intellectual Property Office website.

### *What to do if your chosen business name is taken*

Ideally, your checks will show that your name is completely free to use. But what if you've settled on the perfect title only to find that it's already been snapped up by someone else? Here's a look at your options:

- If your proposed name belongs to a limited company (private or public) or limited liability partnership registered at Companies House, and you are looking to incorporate a limited company or LLP, you will have to go back to the drawing board. You can't register a business with a name that is the 'same as' that of any other on the index of limited companies and LLPs ('same as' means similar enough to cause confusion among customers).

- If someone suspects a company name has been registered at Companies House opportunistically (that is, to try and sell it on to its 'rightful' owner for a profit or to prevent someone else from registering it), they can make a claim to the Company Names Tribunal at the Intellectual Property Office (IPO). However, the claimant must be able to show that they have sufficient 'goodwill' in the name and that the other company was acting in bad faith.

- As mentioned, if you plan to register as a sole trader and you find another sole trader in a different part of the country is already using your name, this shouldn't be a problem. However, if the company operates locally or nationally, or if there is any risk of confusion among customers, you should pick again. If you don't, you run the risk of being sued for 'passing off' (trading off another company's goodwill and reputation by copying their name or branding). This also applies to sole traders that start trading under the name of a pre-existing limited company, or vice versa.

- If your name is too similar to one that has been registered as a trade mark, you will definitely need to select another. You can check this by running a search on the UK Trade Mark Register on the Intellectual Property Office (IPO) website. Unlike passing off claims, the owner of a trade mark does not have to show that there was confusion among consumers or that they have goodwill associated with the mark. Registering a trade mark gives you exclusive rights to use it nationally within the relevant class.

Remember, performing these simple checks initially could save you much time, money and hassle later on. Not only could you find yourself as the defendant in a trade mark infringement or passing off claim, you may also have to absorb the cost of rebranding your business and replacing your signage, stationery, etc.

Once you have found a name that is available and ticks all the boxes, another important consideration is whether or not a suitable web domain name is also up for grabs. See the section below for more details on how to select – and register – the right domain name for your business.

*"There is no standard in the length of a domain, but the rule of thumb is the shorter the better"*

# Choosing your domain name

Today, the vast majority of companies need a website, and the name you choose for your web address is just as important as your main registered name. That's because your website should lie at the heart of your marketing strategy, and attract as many customers as possible. If it isn't doing this, you are missing out on a major online marketing opportunity, at a time when more and more people are using the internet to research the businesses they want to buy from. Of course, if your business exists solely online, your web address could be your registered company name as well, but sometimes it can be useful to have a separate registered name – in which case it's back to the start of this chapter for you.

Just like your registered name, your domain name should describe or reflect the nature of your business to create brand awareness and encourage repeat hits – that is the number of times a customer clicks onto your website – and online sales. It is the central ingredient for successful online marketing and, if appropriate to the market, your name could be spread without you even having to do anything. Names can include letters, numbers and hyphens, so there are several ways to distinguish yourself from the competition. For example, if your company is called John Smith Printers and the .com and .co.uk names are already taken, think of an alternative. This could be jsprinters.com or jsprint. com. Although johnsmithprinters.com would be the obvious choice in this case, often the shorter the web address the better, as it can be easier to remember and be keyed in more quickly, while still reflecting the company and what it does.

You don't always need a name that directly states what you do, however. Having an unrelated, catchy name can sometimes work to your advantage. Take Amazon.com, for example. The name is not directly linked to the products the company sells. However, Amazon has built a reputable brand around a totally new name that stands out from the crowd.

## What makes a successful domain name?

Before attempting to buy a domain name, you need to think about:

→ How easy is it to recall the name?

→ What about the visual appearance of the name, and how will it appear on any documentation you produce? (The name needs to be there along with your main registered name, if it's different, and all your other contact details.)

→ How will this affect your business email address, which, of course, is a key way for people to contact you?

 In my experience

Company: **Moonpig**
Owner-Manager: **Nick Jenkins**

*Choosing a memorable name*
Referrals and recommendations have been massive growth drivers for online personalised greetings card company, Moonpig. The reliance on word of mouth promotion above all else is also at the heart of the company's name.

Founder **Nick Jenkins** wanted a domain name that was easy to remember and fun enough that customers would want to tell their friends about it. 'I was looking for a two syllable dot-com domain but I couldn't find the right combination available and I didn't want to buy one from somebody else,' Nick recalls. Moonpig – Nick's school nickname – worked. At the time, if you entered it into Google nothing came up, and there was the added advantage that it lent itself well to a memorable logo – after all, it's easy enough to remember a pig in a space helmet.

As your domain name needs to make an instant impression on the customer, keep it short, recognisable and consistent with the brand you plan to establish.

If in doubt, remember the acronym RAIL:

Recall: How easy is it to recall the name?
Aesthetics: How does the name look and how will it appear on business cards and company literature?
Impressions: First impressions are crucial, so choose your name carefully
Length: Web addresses are limited to the 26 letters of the English alphabet, 10 numerals and a hyphen – 37 characters in all. When picking a name, less is more. A short name is preferable to a long one.

**Lesley Cowley**, chief executive at Nominet, the internet registry for .uk domain names, says the length of the name is crucial in customer retention. 'There is no standard in the length of a domain, but the rule of thumb is the shorter the better,' she says. Of course, you will also want your name to be easily picked out by people using search engines, as they may well be on the hunt for a business like yours. If you keep your domain name short, simple and catchy, it can be found, accessed and remembered more easily.

As briefly touched on earlier, another key consideration when selecting a name is your email address, which should be memorable and descriptive. It is a means by which you are remembered, contacted and will gain repeat hits or sales, not just a name.

## Domain names and search engine optimisation

There are companies you can pay to make your business more attractive to search engines, and they provide a service called web optimisation, or search engine optimisation. But this can be expensive and, these days, it's not really possible to fool search engines like it was in the past, so be wary of companies that offer a foolproof service, as websites that are spotted by search engines trying to use underhand means to jump up the rankings are blacklisted – a marketing catastrophe.

Many companies offer a kosher service, which will involve them helping you to track down keywords and phrases that your potential customers would use to locate your service, and then cleverly building them into the content of your site, perhaps donating a page each to the main keywords and phrases. Your domain name can help here too, as it will be a little more attractive to search engines if it is descriptive – although this is only a minor factor compared with keyword association.

Ultimately, search engines want to be sure that when someone searches for a particular service, they deliver relevant company websites. So if your website has lots of appropriate content about what you do, including advice and other relevant information, and is full of the necessary keywords, then this will help greatly.

### Choosing a domain ending

Once you have chosen a domain name you will have to think about the ending. Will it be .com, .co.uk, .org, .net or something more unusual?

This depends on many factors, including the nature of your business, whether you are national, international or both, and what is important to you and your customer base. The suffix .com is the broadest option, but as **Nick Saalfeld**, managing director of new media consultancy Wells Park Communications and former editorial director for CompuServe UK, says, if you can't register .com, then simply go elsewhere. 'You have two big choices, .com and .co.uk,' he explains. 'These are the most desirable. However, with the uptake of alternative names, such as .net and .uk, .com is slowly becoming less desirable.'

That said, the best and most highly regarded name is still .com. It is globally and universally recognised, so if you can register it, as well as .co.uk, do it sooner rather than later. Even if you don't use the UK name, by registering it you will keep others from copying your name and it will protect you from the competition. In theory, the more names you own, the better the chance you have of maintaining that brand as yours and yours alone. Unfortunately, as the web grows, shorter names are becoming scarce and fading fast. This means it's even more important to think as creatively as possible when deciding on both your main company name and that of your web address.

*"The best and most highly regarded name is still .com"*

'A British company should aim to own .co.uk and .com addresses, both of which imply a corporate entity, with .co.uk specifically identifying you as British,' says Nick.

Throughout this chapter, you will notice an emphasis on the originality of your domain name. Obviously this is to avoid confusion with other companies, and because you can't register exactly the same name as another business. However, you may find that the company that has registered the name you want doesn't actually do anything like what your business does. If that is the case, then it's probably because its function is to register and sell domain names. As more companies go online, the demand for particular words or phrases is only going to increase. And cashing in on that demand are the clever people who have already snapped up the popular domains to sell for a profit later on.

## *Registering a domain name*

Anyone can register a domain name, as long as it hasn't already been taken. Nominet encourages companies and individuals to register a domain name via a registrar (an internet service provider or registration agent) who will submit a domain name application to Nominet on your behalf. The majority of registrars are Nominet UK members.

There are many different domain name registrars to choose from, and contractual terms, charges and service levels can vary greatly, so it's worth shopping around to find the best deal. Some companies offer domain registration, while others include free web space and email addresses or more specialist options. As with every business agreement you enter into, do read the small print, and ask to see copies of the terms and conditions for domain name registration. In particular, clarify your right to move across to another provider if you are unhappy, and whether this will incur a charge. In addition, confirm that your domain name will be registered in either your name or the name of your business – and not in the name of the registrar or another third party. Look at the company's domain renewal policy too; currently, .uk domain name registrations must be renewed every two years. Nominet also recommends finding out whether the registrar has signed up to an industry code of conduct or has won any relevant industry awards or accolades.

*"As with every business agreement you enter into, do read the small print, and ask to see copies of the terms and conditions"*

Once you have decided upon which company is going to register your domain name, the process is generally swift and painless. First, you will be asked to pay a fee to secure your domain. Second, the company will send a template of your registered domain name to the network information centre (NIC). Each country has its own NIC, which is where all the details of registered domains are held. Third, if your registration is accepted, the company you have chosen will set up a domain name system (DNS) entry. Essentially, this means assigning your name to a name server that collates and keeps all registered names, so that your domain can be found on the internet. The process usually takes up to 24 hours, but could take between two and three days (depending on your provider). Once these stages are complete, you will be live on the internet and can use your name.

## Cost of registering a domain

As mentioned above, there are a variety of packages on offer when it comes to registering a domain name for your business. Some are cheaper than others and it often depends on what other services are included, such as whether you go for simple registration or choose any additional support services. Nominet's Cowley has seen a great deal of variation in the cost of domain names – from free of charge to £200 for .co.uk names – but this depends on levels of service and support. Prices will vary, depending on what your business needs, but there is an average price you will pay for single domain name registration, which is around £10.

If you ask companies how much they paid for their domain name, many will say £5, perhaps £15 or a little more. But if you thought that the name you had chosen was absolutely key to your business, perhaps because you only planned to trade online, and found that it was being sold, just how much would you be prepared to pay? Would you go as far as spending £560,000? That price tag doesn't cover the cost of creating the website, nor does it include the cost of web hosting. For a cool half million, all you get is a domain name – a highly popular one, of course, but nevertheless, just a name. And the domain name in question, according to web hosting site 123-reg.co.uk, is cruises.co.uk. Apparently, it was bought by website cruise.co.uk, and is now used to host 'the UK's largest cruise community'.

So what about the most expensive domain name ever purchased? Well poker.com has got to be up there, which allegedly went for a around US$20m, according to **Melissa Chang**, the president of Pure Incubation, a US internet incubator company based in Massachusetts. On her personal blog website, www.16thletter.com, she says: 'The domain was for sale by moniker. com at a silent auction in Amsterdam, but I can't find a confirmation of who bought it or [exactly] how much it went for. Rumours are more than $20m.' This provides an example of how prized domain names are and the lengths some companies will go to keep their purchases under wraps. And there are lots of alleged examples that similarly dwarf the official .co.uk domain name purchase record (see box), proving just how important a name can be.

**WANT TO KNOW MORE …**
www.123-reg.co.uk

---

## The world's most expensive .com domain names

| | |
|---|---|
| poker.com ($20m) | creditcheck.com ($3m) |
| sex.com ($12m) | wine.com ($2.9m) |
| porn.com ($9.5m) | creditcards.com ($2.75m) |
| business.com ($7.5m) | pizza.com ($2.6m) |
| diamond.com ($7.5m) | autos.com ($2.2m) |
| beer.com ($7m) | computer.com ($2.2m) |
| casino.com ($5.5m) | express.com ($1.8m) |
| korea.com ($5m) | seniors.com ($1.5m) |
| asseenontv.com ($5.1m) | tandberg.com ($1.5m) |
| seo.com ($5m) | cameras.com ($1.5m) |
| shop.com ($3.5m) | vip.com ($1.4m) |
| altavista.com ($3.3m) | scores.com ($1.18m) |
| loans.com ($3m) | chinese.com ($1.12m) |
| vodka.com ($3m) | invest.com ($1.015m) |

topix.com ($1m)                                 rock.com ($1m)

wallstreet.com ($1m)                      guy.com ($1m)

*(Source: www.16thletter.com)*

The most expensive non .com name is poker.de ($957,937)

The top five most expensive .co.uk domain names:

1. Cruises.co.uk (£560,000)
2. Recycle.co.uk (£150,000)
3. Ink.co.uk (£130,425)
4. Mobile.co.uk (£120,000)
5. Taste.co.uk (£110,000)

*(Source: www.brandrepublic.com)*

# *Protecting your intellectual property*

*"Failing to protect your intellectual property can mean that ideas vital to your product or service could be used by competitors"*

Once you have come up with an idea for a new business, it's important to think about protecting any original aspects of your concept that could prove invaluable to its success. This is known as your intellectual property (IP). The main reason for guarding this is to prevent others from using your key innovations and creations without your permission. Failing to protect your IP can mean that ideas vital to your product or service could be used by competitors, and this could severely affect the performance of your company in the future.

You can't protect your business idea itself; however, you can protect key aspects of your idea that set your company apart and could prove crucial to maintaining your competitive edge. Your IP could be rooted in your product, which may contain a feature that makes it different from other similar products and is vital to its appeal to your customers. This may also be the case for a particular service. Or, you may want to make sure no other company uses the original name or brand of your specific product or service.

> **WANT TO KNOW MORE …**
> **UK Intellectual Property Office**
> www.ipo.gov.uk

The UK Intellectual Property Office (IPO) can help you to identify the key elements of your business that you may need to protect, from brand names to designs and processes. It will also provide advice on how best to go about doing this, such as applying for a patent or trade mark.

Protecting your IP is also vital from an investment perspective. When starting up and as your business develops, you may well need financial backing to help your company grow. Any investor, whether a bank or private equity company, will carefully examine your business before lending any money, to make sure that the business is sound and that their investment will be safe. During this 'due diligence' process, if an investor discovers that you have not adequately protected your IP, they are unlikely to provide the required financial support. This is because, not only does this open your business to outside competition and therefore risk, it also reflects badly on you as the proprietor for not having considered protecting your IP in the first place.

*"If an investor discovers that you have not adequately protected your IP, they are unlikely to provide the required financial support"*

Further down the line when you come to selling your business, your IP can have a significant influence on its value, as well as its appeal to prospective buyers. So, as you develop the idea for your business towards a possible launch, it's important to bear in mind any potentially valuable IP that you may need to protect.

## What constitutes IP?

IP is a form of original creation that can be bought or sold. IP law is used to protect ideas or businesses, by granting the owners certain exclusive rights to various intangible assets, such as: brands, designs, songs or intellectual creation. The UK Intellectual Property Office (IPO) states that there are four principle types of IP: patents, trade marks, designs and copyright, although there are also other ways to protect your business, such as confidentiality agreements. The IPO lists a variety of ways that IP can be used to protect businesses or ideas:

- To find out whether your creation already exists.
- To identify useful technologies that could help you develop your idea.
- To license-in other outside technologies to assist in developing your idea.
- To work together with other businesses or organisations to enhance your idea's development.
- To create your own trade secret, which will protect the process, construction and formulation of your product.
- To file for a patent to protect your business from competitors.

-> To protect the originality of your business name and website.

-> To protect documents, such as brochures, from copyright infringement.

-> To ensure investors sign a confidentiality agreement.

**James Dyson**, the designer and inventor of Dyson vacuum cleaners, learnt the importance of protecting his designs the hard way. His Ballbarrow design was patented and owned by the company Kirk-Dyson, which he co-founded, and so when he was ousted by the shareholders, he left without his design. This was a mistake he vowed never to repeat again.

*"All too often others may wish to copy, and attempt to share your success"*

## What is a trade mark?

Trade marks can be words, logos, colours, shapes, or sounds that make the business, product or service you provide distinctive. 'Trade marks are powerful and valuable assets,' says **Lawrence Smith-Higgins**, from the IPO. 'Protecting your trade marks should be an important consideration whenever a new business or product is being launched.'

A good understanding of how to register your trade marks will help to prevent your intellectual property assets from infringement by others. Trade marks help both customers and other businesses identify your products and services, and the reputation and goodwill that goes with them. 'All too often others may wish to copy, and attempt to share your success,' says Lawrence. 'This may or may not have an immediate effect on turnover, but others using your name could prevent trade mark registration and the exclusivity it offers. In addition, any adverse publicity or poor reputation your rival may acquire may affect your business if customers cannot differentiate between the two names.'

Trade marks do not need to be registered. Unregistered trade marks are defined as signs which distinguish the goods and services of one trader from those of others. Providing that sufficient trading reputation and goodwill has been built up in a mark, a degree of protection is afforded by common law. However, as Lawrence points out: 'In order to succeed in an action based on an unregistered mark, it is necessary to show that one has established a reputation in the mark, and that there is confusion and harm has been done.'

Trade mark attorney **Trevor Wright** also warns that rights acquired through use are not very reliable. 'They are difficult to prove and expensive to enforce,' he says. However, registering a trade mark gives you an immediate right to stop someone using the same or similar mark, on the same or similar goods and services, without the need to prove reputation or demonstrate confusion. The owner of a trade mark would therefore always be well advised to register the mark where this is possible.

## Can you use your trade mark?

It is well worth checking that the name of your company or product is available to use before launch. 'It can be a severe psychological and financial blow to create a "new" brand and then start using this brand on a range of products, stationery, or shop signs, only to find that you are infringing an existing registered trade mark,' says Lawrence.

Before you begin, conduct searches to ensure no one has the rights to use your trade mark via the UK and European Community Trade Mark Registers. 'If someone else has obtained a registered trade mark for the same, or similar, goods or services, in the same class of registration, you could find yourself having to rebrand your goods, or re-name the company,' warns Lawrence. 'Worse still, you could find yourself being the defendant in a trade mark infringement action.'

## Registering a trade mark

There are a number of things to bear in mind when registering a trade mark. Firstly, the mark must not describe the service directly – for example, you can't register 'chocolate biscuit' for a chocolate biscuit product – nor must it mislead people about your goods or services or conflict with one already registered. You will also have to decide which classes you want to register your goods or services in – there are 45 to choose from.

The 1994 Trade Mark Act states: 'A trade mark is any sign capable of being represented graphically which is capable of distinguishing goods or services of one undertaking from those of other undertakings.' So, make your mark as original and distinctive as possible.

You may also want to think about registering your trade mark internationally. 'If your business extends to Europe, you can obtain a Community Trade Mark, which protects your mark for all EU countries,' says trade mark attorney **Trevor Wright**. 'For other countries, it is possible

*"It can be a severe blow to create a 'new' brand, only to find that you are infringing a registered trade mark"*

to obtain local national registrations or, in some instances, what is known as an International Registration (a single registration that extends to a number of countries).'

For UK applications, you will need to apply to register your trade mark at the Intellectual Property Office (IPO), who will examine it and determine whether it can be registered. You can either apply online, or download an application form from the IPO's website. If accepted, your trade mark will be shown in the Trade Marks Journal, whereupon oppositions may be filed for the next three months. If there are no objections, your trade mark can be registered and you will receive a certificate. If there are oppositions to your application, a trade mark attorney can offer you help and guidance on what to do next.

**WANT TO KNOW MORE …**
The Institute of Trade Mark Attorneys
www.itma.org.uk

Trade marks are relatively inexpensive; it costs £200 (or £170 if you file your application online) for the first or only class of the registration, and £50 for each additional class. A registered trade mark must be renewed every 10 years to keep it valid.

 **Action points**

## Trade marks: things to consider

- ☑ Always check the name of your company or product before use
- ☑ Company registration does not necessarily confer rights to trade
- ☑ Your brand/name is an asset. Consider protecting it
- ☑ You can only use ® if your trade mark is registered
- ☑ ™ can be used on registered and unregistered trade marks
- ☑ A registered UK trade mark will only give protection within the UK. If you trade outside the UK you should consider international protection
- ☑ You will need professional advice

# *Do you need a patent?*

A patent gives you the exclusive rights to a new invention, protected by law, for up to 20 years. To be worthy of patent protection, an invention has to be new, involve an inventive step, be capable of industrial application, and must not fall into an 'excluded' category, which includes literary works, scientific theories, and methods for doing business. Like any other business commodity, you can buy, sell, hire or license a patent. 'Licensing patents can lead to broader distribution, and hence market acceptance, of your technology,' says the IPO's **Lawrence Smith-Higgins**.

A patent is granted by the IPO as your intellectual property, and can be enforced in law courts to stop other people exploiting it without your permission. The application process for patenting your invention means that you describe it to the public in a written document, which details what it is and how it works.

It is crucial that you keep details of your invention to yourself until you have the patent, which means that you cannot demonstrate how it works, advertise it or publish articles about it beforehand. 'You should always be careful who you tell about your invention, and how much you reveal, before it has been patented, because it may render it invalid,' advises Lawrence. 'If you want to discuss your invention, you can talk to registered lawyers, solicitors and patent attorneys because anything you show them is legally privileged and so confidential.'

The patent system can be difficult to navigate for the newcomer, according to the Chartered Institute of Patent Attorneys (CIPA), who recommend seeking professional advice. You can find details of all the UK's chartered patent attorneys on the Institute's website (www.cipa.org.uk).

But when it works well, the system is fantastic – as it was for **Ron Hickman**, who invented the Black & Decker Workmate. As a DIY enthusiast, Hickman dreamt up his workmate when he accidentally sawed through the leg of a dining room chair he was using as a workstation. He drew up designs for a portable workbench and patented the idea, selling his invention by mail order. When he had sold 14,000, Black & Decker offered him a licensing deal which it is said earned him over £1 for each one sold. They sold 25 million worldwide.

Hickman did everything right. He had a good patent attorney, got a patent, and went on to fight infringement actions around the world. Some people argue

"It is crucial that you keep details of your invention to yourself until you have the patent"

"The patent system can be difficult to navigate for the newcomer"

that the patent system is a waste of time because it's so easy to design around it, but that's what happens when people draw up their own applications and claims. If you get it right, the patent system is wonderful – that is of course providing your invention is something for which there is a demand.

## Conducting a patent search

Whether you are applying for a patent, or merely seeking useful market information about what has already been patented, your competitors and their expanding markets, you can use the IPO's patent search service. The IPO now offers searches within a particular area of technology, by company or individual name, and searches for possible infringements of patents still in force.

Using a search in the early stages can help you obtain the best possible protection for your invention. It can also help you draw up the best possible patent application and could avoid duplication of research when someone else's results have already been published. 'A very common error is to become so single-minded about your own invention that you neglect to find out at the earliest possible moment what has been done before,' says Lawrence. 'It is intensely annoying (as well as expensive) to become aware after months of effort and investment that the protection sought is not allowable because the projected innovation has in fact been done before.'

## Applying for a patent

To apply for a patent, you need the appropriate forms from the UK IPO. Your initial application must include a request for a patent, your full name and address, a full description of your invention, any drawings and your invention claim and abstract. The description must be clear and complete, so that it can be understood by anyone who wishes to use it once the patent has expired. Once the IPO has these details, your application can be given a filing date.

You then have a 12-month period to decide what to do next. You might use the time to explore the idea's commercial value, look for finance to manufacture it or cover the cost of patenting it, and develop it further. If you do not take any further steps after 12 months, the application 'dies'.

If you pay a search fee within that 12-month period and file claims which define the invention, your application will go through to the next stage. Examiners will check your application and the office will search to see whether your invention is new. You can then go on to publish your application, together with an abstract explaining its technical features.

Action points

## Patents: things to consider

The IPO's **Lawrence Smith-Higgins** offers some pointers for those considering a patent application:

- ☑ Is your technology new? Do a patent search.
- ☑ If you make a public disclosure of your invention before filing your application will fail.
- ☑ Is your new technology worth patenting? Consider costs/revenue.
- ☑ Don't forget licensing.
- ☑ A UK patent will only give protection within the UK. If you trade outside the UK you should consider international protection.
- ☑ You will need professional advice.
- ☑ Patents could be just part of your IP strategy. You may also need to consider trade mark, design, or copyright protection.

The final stage towards getting a patent is the full examination, when your application will be examined in detail at the Office in the light of what has been uncovered at the search stage. You can then be granted a patent, once you have paid fees of £100 for a search and £70 for examination. Annual renewal fees then have to be paid, on a sliding scale of £50 in the fifth year and £400 in the 20th and last year of your patent's life. The whole process from the filing date to the granting of the patent should not take more than four and a half years.

## Patent costs

It is free to file a patent application through the IPO, but to process a patent application it will cost between £230 and £280. However, there are other costs to consider. Patent attorneys' fees, renewal fees as well as the possible cost of enforcing your patent will add significantly to this initial cost. The IPO grants patents. It does not make commercial judgements on those patents that are granted.

It could cost £31,000 to get patent protection across Europe; a simple dispute could cost over £200,000 if not resolved out of court. Any business needs to carefully consider these costs and the other options: sell the patent, or possibly license the technology.

## Using a patent agent

*"Wording is crucial on patent applications and basic errors can render the patent worthless"*

Though you can complete your patent application yourself, you are strongly advised to use a patent agent, who can steer you through the minefield of patent law and help you avoid expensive mistakes. Wording is crucial on patent applications and basic errors can render the patent worthless. But patent agents undergo rigorous training in drafting patents and intellectual property law. By law in Britain, you must use a patent agent who is on the Register of Patent Agents – you can contact them via the Chartered Institute of Patent Attorneys (CIPA).

Patent agents – sometimes called patent attorneys – can help you make your application watertight. Some offer an initial consultation for free, and they can give invaluable advice on whether an invention is worth patenting. There is little point in following the rigorous procedure to obtain a patent if it cannot be used commercially and is unlikely to make money.

**WANT TO KNOW MORE...**

The Chartered Institute of Patent Attorneys (CIPA)
www.cipa.org.uk
☎ 020 7405 9450

However, patent agents are not to be confused with invention promoters. The Intellectual Property Office now advises extreme care in dealings with invention promoters, to avoid expensive mistakes. Ask a potential invention promoter for evidence that they have the necessary expertise, and for their success rate. Check too that the firm rejects commercially unviable inventions, and take legal advice.

 ## What to do next

- Check your choice of business name against the Companies House rules before you start designing branding and logos. You don't want to have to redo all this later.

- Consider domain names when thinking of names for your business or product. If all the variations of the name have already been registered online you might need to think of a different one.

- Don't forget about trade marks. Build a successful brand and your trade mark could become your most valuable asset.

- Decide if you need to apply for a patent for your product. If you do, make sure you factor this into the costs in your business plan.

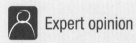

## Expert opinion

# IP strategy: what's yours?

**Nick Sutcliffe of Mewburn Ellis LLP has some tips on intellectual property strategy.**

Technical innovations, brands and designs, collectively referred to as 'intellectual property' or 'IP', are important assets for any start-up or early stage business. Whilst some start-up businesses have no dealings with IP in their early stages, others have a close involvement with IP from their very beginnings. For example, many technology businesses are started-up or spun-out around a portfolio of patent applications protecting a key technology.

Whatever its background, a clear and coherent IP strategy will help a start-up business to manage the opportunities and challenges presented by its own and other people's IP in order to maximise their potential in the marketplace.

IP adds value to a business in many ways. The existence of strong IP may help to exclude imitators from the marketplace, allowing a business to reap the full reward for the development of a successful technology or product. IP also distances the products and services of a business from those of its competitors, allowing it to build up the prestige and reputation of its brands.

For start-up businesses looking to raise funds, a strong IP portfolio may be essential in attracting investors and may even generate revenue streams in itself through out-licensing.

Some IP rights come into existence automatically. One example is copyright. Stronger, 'registered' rights, such as patents, registered trade marks and registered designs, need to be actively sought. Especially in the case of patents, it is vital that the protection is sought before the technical innovation to be protected is made public. In many cases, a business will own an IP right outright. In other cases, a business may hold a licence or other right to an IP owned by a third party.

The identification of new IP opportunities can represent a considerable management challenge, as it is easy for information to slip into the public domain before it has been assessed for possible IP rights which would be valuable to a business. Typically, a business may require its staff and collaborators to submit manuscripts and other disclosures for review before submission.

A business' IP portfolio is likely to include a combination of different types of IP, as well as intangibles, such as the technical know-how it has acquired in developing its products and processes. Key rights such as patents and registered trademarks will invariably attract most attention and the full extent of the IP which is owned by a business may not be apparent without a careful audit of the activities of the business and its employees.

Unfortunately, the stronger forms of IP protection, such as patents, come at a cost. For a start-up business, any IP strategy must strike a balance between the cost of obtaining and maintaining IP rights and the commercial value that these IP rights bring to the business. Thought needs to be given not only to what to protect and how but also to when and where protection should be sought. IP rights which no longer bring value to a business are a drain on resources and vigilance is required to keep the IP of a business aligned with its current and future commercial activities.

It must also not be forgotten that competitors may well have their own IP rights. It is important to be aware of the impact that the rights of others could have. At worst, third party IP rights could halt the activities of a business completely. Prudent businesses will have in place strategies for dealing with this. Such strategies might include watching the IP filing activity of known competitors. This may allow a business to work around competitor's patents or other rights and/or to consider whether they might be vulnerable to attack. Watching a competitor's IP filing activity can also provide useful intelligence for a business's own development work. Similarly, an awareness of the IP landscape may allow the identification of licensing opportunities to bring new technologies into the business to drive growth.

Every small business should develop an IP strategy at the earliest opportunity, as part of their overall business strategy, and update the strategy regularly as their business grows.

Nick Sutcliffe
Mewburn Ellis LLP
33 Gutter Lane
London
EC2V 8AS
Tel: 020 7776 5300
Email: nick.sutcliffe@mewburn.com
Website: www.mewburn.com

# SageOne

## Online **accounting** for small businesses **without** the **jargon**

Take control of your business finances with Sage One Accounts. Specifically developed for small business owners, it gives you greater control of your finances... and you don't need an accounting background to use it.

- Free 24/7 phone support
- Create great invoices
- Manage money in and money out

- Submit your VAT online
- Keep track of customers and suppliers
- Produce financial reports

## Sign up for a FREE 30 day trial

Visit **www.sageone.com**

Safe, simple online accounting supported by the experts

Sage UK, Sage (UK) Limited, North Park, Newcastle upon Tyne, NE13 9AA. Tel: 0845 111 6611

# Discover the Secrets of Powerful and Effective Marketing

# "Here's How You Can Avoid The Marketing Mistakes That Are Costing Businesses £1000s"

**Helen Murdoch**
*The Marketing* Champion
*for Small Business*

Dear Aspiring Business Owner,

I'd like to give you a totally free copy of my special Report about why so many business owners are failing to maximise the results of their marketing.

This FREE Report will show you how to avoid the 5 money-burning mistakes that are stopping most small business owners from achieving success in their business.

After listening to hundreds of small business owners as well as franchisees and start-ups, I've found that many of them are struggling with their marketing. They are burning time, energy and money on marketing that doesn't work.

They are busy people and they don't have time to learn all about marketing. They want short-cuts, easy-to-apply tools and techniques, and step-by-step guidance to get more customers, make more sales and generate more profit more quickly and without spending a fortune.

Does this sound like you? Then grab a copy of my FREE Report today.

Here's what you'll discover:

#1 Many people know they have to 'put the customer first' but have no idea how to do it – I'll show you how.

#2 Afraid to narrow your focus? This is the #1 reason why so many fail to maximise their sales!

#3 The 2 words that you must use to really make your marketing message fly.

#4 Poor response from your advert, website, email? Check out Mistake #4 and what you can do to avoid burning money.

#5 This mistake is the biggest of them all – skip this important step and your business will never really take off.

If you've struggled to make your marketing work and want to turn it around right now, the "5 Biggest Marketing Mistakes" by Helen Murdoch (value £27.00) is just what you've been looking for.

To claim your FREE REPORT visit:
**www.HelenMurdochMarketing.com NOW!**

I wish you the very best of success with your marketing.

*Helen*

**Helen Murdoch**

# Visit www.HelenMurdochMarketing.com NOW!

# Starting a new business...

Missed calls damage your business. Few people leave voicemails. You're busy, you can't always answer. We have the solution...

## ...you Need More Time!

Need More Time Ltd has been supporting start-up and small businesses like yours for a decade. Our small, professionally trained teams will answer your calls in your business name and send messages to you by email or SMS, or speak to you on your mobile and offer to put each call through to you. Your callers will be impressed!

| telephone answering | virtual pa administration | business address | telephone numbers |

We provide a seamless telephone answering solution which has helped thousands of small businesses. As our customers grow, they further benefit from our flexible approach and our ability to assist with much of their day to day administration, like appointment booking. It's like having your own PA, but in our office, not yours – a truly "virtual" service.

## Special offer!

### FREE setup + FREE city number + £50 credit

In addition to telephone answering and virtual PA services, we offer a prestigious business mailing address, and can supply local and national telephone numbers for your business. You could save a fortune on premises and admin staff, and have more time to concentrate on your work. Call us today and we'll help you get started.

**needmoretime**
supporting small businesses

**www.needmoretime.co.uk**
**020 3303 3303** - quote **syob12**

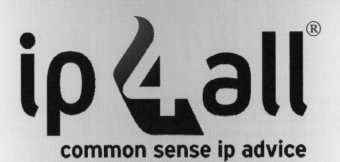

common sense ip advice

**Intellectual Property (IP) refers to creations of the mind:**
*Inventions,*
*literary and artistic works, and*
*symbols, names, images and designs used in commerce.*

Regardless of the size of your business, the nature of the goods it supplies or the services it provides, your business will create and as a consequence, it will own some forms of IP. *ip4all* knows that when dealing with IP issues, the two main barriers micro, small and medium sized enterprises face are a lack of time, and the financial cost.

*ip4all* was established to help. It provides:-

• a source of practical, relevant and accessible information; and

• credible, reliable, and affordable IP advice and assistance

tailored to the particular needs of micro, small and medium sized enterprises.

**Contact *ip4all* at:-**
**3-5 Wormalds Yard, off King Street, Huddersfield HD1 2QR**

| | |
|---|---|
| **Mobile:** | **07800545089** |
| **Huddersfield:** | **0148 481 7770** |
| **Leeds:** | **0113 278 9974** |
| **Manchester:** | **0161 939 0141** |

**e-Mail: roger.lowe@ip4all.co.uk**

**www.ip4all.co.uk**

*"Intellectual property is the oil of the 21st century. Look at the richest men a hundred years ago, they all made their money extracting natural resources or moving them around. All today's richest men have made money out of intellectual property."*

(Mark Getty – Chairman of Getty Images)

# Invest in Coventry & Warwickshire

## ...supporting your business

Coventry and Warwickshire is the perfect place for your business and we are here to help

Invest in Coventry & Warwickshire provides the following services for your business...

- Property & site search
- Economic & demographic data
- Environmental & ICT business advice
- Staff recruitment & training
- Business networking opportunities
- Free & confidential service

Modern, cost-effective and flexible business space ideal for new businesses and growing SMEs...

- High quality offices at the award-winning Eliot Park Innovation Centre
- Light industrial space at Centenary Business Centre & Sir Frank Whittle Business Centre
- Flexible hot desk facilities at The Hub Innovation Centre

Contact us now – call: 01926 412140 or email: wips@warwickshire.gov.uk

# ARE YOU GETTING THE MOST OUT OF YOUR INCOMING SALES CALLS?

*Robin James of Planet Numbers makes sure you're fully up to speed...*

## THE NUMBERS GAME

Planet Numbers is one of Britain's leading suppliers of specialist business phone numbers. Their M.D, Robin James, explains how the very latest call management technology lets you take your phone number with you whenever you move office and handle your incoming calls with state-of-the-art 'virtual receptionist' services.

*"There are a whole raft of numbers now: the traditional free-to-call 0800 and 0808, where the business pays for the calls it receives, and 0845s, 0844s and the newer 0333s which are now free-to-call in many consumer call packages. 0844s are an increasingly popular choice for businesses as they are free to receive, too."*

These 'non-geographic numbers' (NGNs) as they're known also let you move the location of your business around with your clients and customers being none the wiser. So if your main business number for incoming sales calls and enquiries is an 0844, when you move office you simply change the destination number the calls are routed to.

Robin explains how it works...

*"When you buy an NGN we simply divert your incoming calls on that number to one of your existing phone numbers. The phone can still get calls on its original number and you can use it to make outgoing calls in the normal way. All the clever stuff is done at our end. This also means we can add what we call 'virtual receptionist' services to your number, like call queuing, automatic out of hours diversion to another number, routing to different departments and so on."*

**A free 0844 number for Start Your Own Business readers**

There's normally a set-up charge of £49 but Planet Numbers are offering an exclusive deal for readers of "Start Your Own Business" — an 0844 number for your company, completely free.

**To find out more, call customer support on 0333 370 0014 and quote STAR 11.**

## planetnumbers

www.planet-numbers.co.uk

# ⤴ CHAPTER 5

## Business structures and registering your company

 **What's in this chapter?**

→ Company structures

→ Sole traders

→ Business partnerships

→ Limited companies

→ Community Interest Companies

As we have just seen, when selecting the perfect name for your business, a key consideration is what legal structure your new venture will take. You've basically got three choices: you can register as self-employed and become a sole trader; team up to form a partnership; or register a new limited company.

Naturally, each one has its upsides and downsides, as well as varying degrees of ongoing administrative duties. This chapter will go through each legal structure in turn, looking at the pros and cons of each and how you go about registering the business, to help you determine which one is right for you.

## Company structures

There are several different legal structures a new business can take – which one is right for your start-up will depend on a number of factors, such as whether you are going into business alone or with a co-founder, whether you plan to raise external finance, and whether you wish to allocate shares in your company. Record-keeping and administrative duties, tax considerations and your future plans for the business should also enter into the equation.

For start-ups, it basically boils down to whether you want to register as self-employed and become a sole trader (or form a partnership, should you have one or more co-founders) or whether you wish to incorporate your business at Companies House to create a new limited company (or a new limited liability partnership, if you have at least one co-founder).

That said, if you plan to set up a social enterprise, you might want to think about registering your new business as a Community Interest Company (CIC). This is a special type of limited company which includes features to ensure that the primary interest of the company is – and always will be – to benefit the community, rather than to make money for shareholders.

This chapter will explore each company structure in detail, looking at what each involves, any eligibility requirements, the pros and cons that go along with each form and what ongoing legal and administrative duties each entails, to help you decide on the most appropriate form for your business.

It's worth noting here that there are two different types of limited company: those that are publicly traded on the stock market (known as a public limited company or 'plc') and those that are privately owned (identified by the abbreviation 'Ltd' at the end of their name). Start-ups don't tend to start life on the stock exchange, so this chapter will focus on limited companies which are privately owned.

## Sole traders

Sole trading is defined as when an individual is the only owner of the business and has complete control over the way it is run. The law makes no distinction between the business and a sole trader: this unlimited liability means that any business debt can be met from the owner's personal wealth if the business fails, and the business usually ceases on the owner's retirement or death.

A sole trading business is usually small in size, with a low turnover, and few, if any, employees. If you want to literally go it alone in business, remember you won't actually be alone! A massive 73% of all private UK businesses have no employees, according to Department for Business, Innovation and Skills (BIS) figures. There are an estimated 4.5 million private businesses in the UK, according to the latest government statistics, and nearly 3.3 million of these are class zero businesses – that is without employees. So you could say that sole traders pretty much drive the UK economy.

The popularity of this type of business reflects the ease with which you can start sole trading: registration is straightforward, record keeping is simple and you get to keep all the profits after tax. Starting small by sole trading is a way to test your chosen market, and many companies are born this way. Most sole traders operate in service sectors, with popular areas including: photography, plumbing, hairdressing, real estate agencies, construction, business-related services and bed and breakfast hotels.

*"Starting small by sole trading is a way to test your chosen market, and many companies are born this way"*

## Getting down to business

You need to fulfil certain legal requirements before you can open for business. If you are going to trade under a name different from your own personal name, you must display the business name or names of the owners and an address where documents can be served on all business stationery and at your premises. So you will need to design letterheads, business cards and signage accordingly.

## Naming your business

The previous chapter offered detailed advice on choosing the right name for your business and the legal issues concerning business names. As a sole trader, it is not compulsory to register a business name, but you can do so with the National Business Register.

Remember that you need to be careful about choosing a name. In particular, your business name cannot be the same or too similar to that of a registered trade mark, or another company in the same market or geographical location. If it does conflict, you could face legal action from its owner. While you can perform your own checks online, in phone books, trade journals and magazines to ensure against clashes (see Chapter 4 for more details), to be absolutely sure that you can use a name, contact a solicitor to perform the checks or register your name with the National

Business Register, which will then do the checks for you and ensure that no one copies it in the future or passes it off as their own.

## Registering with HMRC

Anyone who becomes self-employed must register for income tax and National Insurance contributions with HM Revenue & Customs (HMRC). This can be done either online, by phone or by post, however it is far quicker and more convenient to sign up online. When registering you will need to provide your National Insurance number – if you don't have one, contact Jobcentre Plus.

You must register as self-employed within three months of starting up or you will have to pay a fine. The three-month limit starts from the last day of your first month of trading. Upon registration, you'll need to provide the following information:

- Name
- Address
- National Insurance number
- Date of birth
- Telephone number
- Email address
- The nature of your business
- Start date of self-employment
- Business address
- Business telephone number
- Your Unique Tax Reference (UTR) – only if you were within self-assessment previously
- The business' UTR – if you're joining an existing partnership
- If relevant, the full name and date of birth of any business partners

## Legal issues

A sole trader business is simple to set up legally, although certain trades may need a licence. These include nightclubs, taxi and car hire, restaurants, pet shops, indoor sports venues, adult shops, street trading, hotels, pet kennels, nursing homes, waste management, weapons sales and money lending. You can get a licence from the relevant local authority for most of these.

There are also some key areas of the law that you need to be aware of:

⇢ The Trade Descriptions Act 1972 – it is a criminal offence to knowingly make false or misleading claims – verbal or written – about goods or services you offer. This covers areas such as ingredients, place of manufacture and customer testimonials, as well as associating yourself with a brand without being entitled to.

⇢ The Sale of Goods Act 1979 – this dictates that the goods you sell must be of satisfactory quality, match your promises of performance and be as you describe them.

⇢ The Supply of Goods and Services Act 1982 – this commits you to undertake the services you offer with reasonable care, skill, time and cost.

⇢ The Data Protection Act 1984 – this directs you to register the source, nature and purpose of any personal data you keep about individuals, except data used for internal administration such as the payroll. Registration forms are available at post offices.

⇢ The Consumer Protection Act 1987 – this holds you liable if you supply a faulty product causing damage or injury, unless you can show that not enough was known about its dangers at the time of supply. To protect yourself under this Act, offer an estimate first and a written quote only when you have properly assessed costs.

⇢ The Price Marking Order 1991 – this makes it compulsory to put the price of goods offered for sale in writing.

**WANT TO KNOW MORE …**

National Business Register
www.start.biz/home
☎0800 069 9090

The Department for Business, Innovation and Skills (BIS)
www.bis.gov.uk

You should also consider any legislation relating to environmental and health and safety requirements, as well as checking the planning and building regulations relating to your premises. Local authorities and the Department for Business, Innovation and Skills (BIS) should be the first ports of call for this.

## Tax and sole traders

As a sole trader, your profits are taxed like any other income by HMRC, and as you are self-employed, your tax will be self-assessed. The amount you

"As a self-employed person, many of your business expenses can be deducted from your taxable income"

owe is calculated after business expenses and personal allowances have been deducted. Your income will fall under tax Schedule D, and as you will be paying income tax twice a year, it makes sense to put money aside. As a self-employed person, many of your business expenses can be deducted from your taxable income, such as overheads on your premises, travel, delivery costs and trade association subscriptions, but you will have to pay capital gains tax if you sell or give away any assets. You will also be paying National Insurance contributions (NICs).

## Who is an e-trader?

You are an e-trader if you:

- Sell goods that were bought with the intention of re-selling them.
- Sell items you made yourself for a profit.
- Sell or buy on behalf of others for financial gain.
- Receive payment for a service.

If you do any of the above, then you must register as self-employed with HMRC within the three-month deadline mentioned earlier. With regards to eBay, it is extremely unwise to delay registering, as HMRC carries out checks on online auction sites to root out members who process a high number of transactions.

If your income rises above a certain level (currently £73,000) you will have to apply for value-added tax (VAT) registration. This means you will be collecting VAT from your customers and paying it to HMRC less the VAT you have paid out in the course of conducting your business. You can talk to your local HMRC offices for advice. Make an appointment and explain the details of your business plan, and then ask them exactly what you need to do. They will provide you with advice, relevant leaflets and a selection of forms – such as VAT registration – which you should complete before beginning trading. This is vitally important. If you start off with all the necessary information, it will make the bookkeeping process much easier. It also helps to have a contact within the local offices who you can call should you run into any difficulties. Bookkeeping is covered in more detail in Chapter 8.

The increase in popularity of online businesses has led to a growing number of people setting up part-time businesses for additional income to their main job. As a result, many are unsure what they have to declare for tax purposes and at what point they should register as self-employed. The rules stipulate that all e-traders must be registered with HMRC, so that their income can be taxed.

 *Action points*

### Key things to do after setting up as a sole trader

*Once you've set up as a sole trader, there are a few other things to consider that will help you and your new business:*

☑ **Banking:** *You can operate your sole trading business from your personal bank account. You must, however, be able to distinguish your personal spending from that of your business for tax purposes. You can also run separate bank accounts and major banks are keen to get you on board for the future custom you may bring. Shop around for a bank that best suits your needs.*

☑ **Insurance:** *Ensure your business will keep working even when you are not by insuring it. As a sole trader, unless you employ staff or make alternative arrangements, your business will come to a standstill if you fall ill, have an accident or go on holiday. So shop around for health and medical insurance tailored to small businesses with self-employed owners. Check to see if subsidised insurance schemes are offered by your trade association or local chamber of commerce. You should also consider taking out disability insurance to cover you for time off through illness or injury. But check the qualifying period — some policies with lower premiums won't pay out until after an excess period of three months.*

☑ **Pensions:** *Although putting aside money for the future may be hard for you right now, a pension plan is well worth considering. And not just for the financial security it will offer you in retirement — investing in a pension scheme can be tax-beneficial too. Everyone in the UK can get a basic state pension if they have built up a record of NICs for a quarter of their working life. But only those with a record of NICs for nine-tenths of their working lives are entitled to a full state pension, so self-employed people need to make further arrangements. Sole traders should also contribute to a private pension scheme. Many pension schemes on the market are designed for the* self-employed, and several of these allow you to pay a lump sum, take a break from payments for a year or even make withdrawals.

☑ **Taking on staff**: As a sole trader you might want to take on employees to help with your growing business. There are no restrictions on staff numbers, but you will have to deduct pay-as-you-earn (PAYE) tax from wages and pay it to HMRC each month. You will also need to make some summaries for employees and HMRC annually, as well as when a staff member leaves your employment. As a sole trading employer you will be responsible for your employees' Class I NICs and your employer contributions. These are calculated as a percentage of an employee's wage (see Chapter 8 for more details on this). You will also need to consider statutory sick pay, equal opportunities and health and safety conditions, as well as employment terms and contracts. And remember that if you have taken over a business, you must uphold employees' existing terms of employment.

## *Business partnerships*

*"One of the fundamental issues is to draw up a partnership agreement"*

Collaboratively owned or acquired firms are probably more successful and grow faster, and in certain important sectors, such as hi-tech, collaborative ventures may actually predominate. This is when two or more people combine to form a business unit. Each partner receives a percentage of the return of the business, depending on how much they invested.

In a standard partnership, as with sole traders, all partners are also responsible for all the debts owed by the business. This doesn't only apply to debts you have incurred as a partner but to those of any partner. This means in a partnership you need to pay particular care to the conduct of your fellow partners, because creditors will take your personal assets to pay off debts incurred by any of the others if necessary.

However, should you choose to form a limited liability partnership (LLP), this is not the case. An LLP is perhaps more similar to a limited company than a standard partnership – although there are some key distinctions. An LLP needs to be incorporated at Companies House in the same way as a limited company (see later in the chapter), and LLP partners also have limited liability, meaning the LLP itself is liable for debts run up by the business, rather than the individual partners. As with a limited company, members in an LLP cannot lose more than they invest (assuming no fraud or illegal activity has taken place). Meanwhile, partners have responsibilities as directors but are not personally liable for each other's actions.

There are more ongoing administrative and filing duties involved with running an LLP compared with a standard partnership, and like a limited company, the LLP has a continuing legal existence independent of its members, unlike a standard partnership.

However, where tax is concerned an LLP is more similar to a standard partnership – that is, the LLP itself pays no UK tax but its members do in relation to the income or gains they make through the LLP. In other words, profits are shared among members of an LLP (each must register as self-employed), and individual members pay income tax on their share of these profits. Unlike limited companies, LLPs don't pay corporation tax.

Whether you are thinking about setting up a standard partnership or LLP, when considering what format the business should take, partnerships need extra attention. One of the most fundamental issues is to draw up a partnership agreement. 'We require all business partnerships to visit a solicitor (through our pro bono legal advice set up) and have a legal partnership agreement in place before we can finalise funding,' says **Elaine Thatcher**, business support manager for the Prince's Trust in London.

**WANT TO KNOW MORE …**

Prince's Trust
www.princes-trust.
org.uk

Such an agreement forces partners to think about issues such as the structure and roles of each person involved, as well as the likely exit routes for the partners, according to **Thelma Quince**, who conducted a study into 390 businesses in East Anglia. This can ensure that there is a mechanism for valuing and buying one partner's shares. 'It is a bit like a marriage and divorce. No one wants to think about the fact that it could go wrong,' says Thelma. But partners can address the issues in less confrontational ways by asking what each partner wants to do when they are bored of the business.

## *The causes of conflict*

One of the common factors with collaborations that weren't successful in Thelma's study was mutual respect. 'If you lose confidence in the competence of your partner and start to worry about whether they can do the job, that can be fatal,' she warns. A number of threads ran through the accounts co-owners in the study gave as to why collaboration had failed (see box over the page). Thelma found that mostly the collaboration failed when personal, individualistic or selfish goals started to take precedence over the collaborative, shared goals. 'One partner attempted to take control and focused on personal gain rather than long-term growth of the business,' was one comment.

*"If you lose confidence in the competence of your partner and start to worry about whether they can do the job, that can be fatal"*

According to Thelma, partnerships can be highly successful, but a high proportion of co-owning teams are likely to experience conflict leading to the departure of one or more of the original partners. When this happens it can have severe effects not only on the business, but on partners' personal lives. Thelma's research revealed that in 42% of the firms founded collaboratively by people who were not related or married to each other, the original owning team had fragmented, leaving only one of the original co-owners. Meanwhile, 41% of the 106 co-owners taking part in the study reported that they had prior experience of an unsuccessful collaborative relationship.

## Why some partnerships fail

**The reasons why collaborations don't work include:**

- Differences in personal values.
- Differences in personal objectives.
- Differences in objectives and visions for the firm.
- Loss of respect for the competence of the other.
- Failure to communicate effectively.
- Failure to reward effort justly.
- Loss of trust in the other.
- The price of conflict.

In their accounts of failed relationships the co-owners described three main adverse effects of the conflict. Only three claimed the conflict had not adversely affected themselves or their business, with just two of these feeling that, in the long term, the outcome of the conflict had actually been beneficial. Most, however, told a very different story. For nearly 40%, partner conflict had hit their businesses badly in a number of ways, including: lost revenue, which in eight cases sank the firm; poor morale among employees; suspicion and lack of cooperation between co-owners; and even personal effects on partners, such as financial loss, a lack of self-worth and marriage break-ups.

So although many partnerships work, they can be prone to conflict, which anyone thinking of starting up this kind of business must bear in mind. Meanwhile, a carefully constructed partnership agreement can help increase the chances of a harmonious and successful long-term relationship between partners.

As further evidence of the need to approach partnerships with caution, here are personal comments on the fallout from partner disharmony by a number of people who contributed to **Thelma Quince's** study of 390 businesses in East Anglia:

- ⇢ 'Disharmony at board level led to unnecessary risk and confusion of direction.'
- ⇢ 'Challenged my reason to go on.'
- ⇢ 'Staff morale declined.'
- ⇢ 'The board was unable to make decisions about things that mattered – views were too diverse. Performance suffered through inertia and the company became loss-making. The team collapsed and this came close to causing the collapse of the company.'
- ⇢ 'It caused an early sale of the company at the wrong time and at a disadvantageous price.'
- ⇢ 'The additional financial commitment was difficult to sustain.'
- ⇢ 'My marriage broke up shortly after the break-up of the company.'

## Pros and cons of partnerships

These are the advantages and disadvantages of collaboration cited by almost all of the 106 co-owners in **Thelma Quince's** East Anglian study:

### Why you should collaborate ...

- Being able to share the burden.
- Having access to more skills, knowledge and experience.
- Better, more effective decision-making.
- Being able to look at problems from different perspectives.

### And why you shouldn't ...

- Less autonomy and not always getting your own way.
- Differences in personal aims and objectives for the firm.
- Decision-making can be slower.
- Collaboration often means a loss of spontaneity.

From the owners who had once collaborated, but now found themselves in sole ownership, came other stories of attempted suicides, nervous breakdowns, divorce, attempted assaults and one sad case of attempted murder.

---

 **Startups Tips**

**For a successful partnership, co-owners need to:**

⇾ Have the same shared visions, aspirations and objectives for their firm.

⇾ Have similar or compatible personal values.

⇾ Have clearly defined responsibilities and roles.

⇾ Have complementary skills and knowledge.

⇾ Have mutual respect for the other's competence.

⇾ Have mutual trust in the other and for the other's honesty.

⇾ Be good at working as a team.

⇾ Be tolerant of the other's weaknesses.

---

*"In a limited company or LLP, it is the business itself that shoulders the liability as opposed to the individuals who run it"*

# Limited companies

A limited company is very different from a sole trader business. Registering and running a limited company requires more legal administration than a sole trader business or a standard partnership. However, if you are a sole trader or partner, you can be held personally liable for your business, which means that any outstanding debts can be met from your personal assets. In a limited company or LLP, it is the business itself that shoulders the liability as opposed to the individuals who run it. This is because a limited company is a separate legal entity to the company directors (discussed below). Profits and losses belong to the company, and the business can continue regardless of the death, resignation or bankruptcy of the shareholders or people who run it.

Limited companies pay corporation tax on their profits and company directors are taxed as employees in the same way as any other people who work for the company. Your personal financial risk is restricted to how much you have invested in the company and any guarantees you gave when raising finance for the business. However, if the company fails and you have not carried out your duties as a company director, you could be liable for debts, as well as being disqualified from acting as a director in another company.

A limited company can be limited by shares or by guarantee. A company limited by guarantee has no share capital or shareholders – instead, members act as guarantors, who agree to pay a nominal amount (often £1) in the event of the winding up of the company. This structure is mostly used by not-for-profit organisations, charities and membership organisations, such as students' unions and sports clubs.

| | Advantages | Disadvantages |
| --- | --- | --- |
| **Sole trader** | Easy to set up<br>Simple to run<br>Minimal ongoing filing | Full personal liability<br>Harder to raise finance |
| **Standard partnership** | Quite simple to set up<br>Minimal ongoing filing<br>Different skill-sets and perspectives | Full personal liability, including for debts incurred by fellow partners<br>Harder to raise finance<br>Risk of conflicts |
| **Limited company** | Limited liability<br>Easier to raise finance<br>Can pay less tax | Ongoing filing burden<br>Need to disclose information<br>Directors have obligations<br>May have to pay more tax |
| **Limited liability partnership** | Limited liability<br>Different skill-sets and perspectives | Ongoing filing burden<br>Need to disclose information<br>Directors have obligations<br>Risk of conflicts |

Before you can start trading, you need to officially register your limited company, decide on the company officers and choose a name for your business. Then, once you've filed the correct documents with Companies House, you are ready to start trading. Here's a guide to each step.

**WANT TO KNOW MORE …**
Companies House
www.companieshouse.gov.uk

## *Registering your company*

Although you can register a limited company yourself, unless you've done it before you may need to engage the services of a solicitor, accountant, chartered secretary or a company formation agent. Formation agents, such as the National Business Register, use their own software that works directly with the Companies House systems. If you want to register your company electronically (most are registered this way) you will need to have the specific Companies House electronic interface – hence the need for a formation agent. However, you can still deliver the physical documents directly to Companies House without the need of a formation agent or specific electronic interface.

A key advantage of using a formation agent is the advice they can give you on the compiling of the necessary documents and the right structure for your business. Companies House does not provide this service when registering, so if you are unfamiliar with the process it's advisable to get help to avoid errors. Going through the registration process yourself can be time-consuming, especially if you make a mistake. In addition, Companies House staff will not advise you about specific matters, such as the content of the required memorandum and articles (more about these later).

These days, many company formation agents operate online (see below). However, the level of support and personal service you will receive can vary greatly, so it's worth spending some time assessing the options available.

Finally, you can buy an 'off-the-shelf' company, receiving a ready-made limited company that has designated company officers listed on the paperwork. You simply transfer your name, and the names of any other company directors, to the company once you receive your documentation. The process can be completed on the same day, and many accountancy firms have several ready-made limited companies that they can sell to you.

## Recent developments in the registration process

It has never been easier to register a limited company due to recent key developments, according to **Simon Harrison** at Complete Formations, one of the UK's leading online company registration agents. 'While accountants and solicitors still play a role in registering companies, particularly for their corporate clients, their involvement in incorporations for individuals has undoubtedly reduced,' he explains. 'A typical modern scenario might be where a private individual uses an accountant for advice on what type of company to incorporate, based on an assessment of tax position and plans for the future. The individual might then go away to form the company themselves through a formation agent and save themselves money in the process.'

The costs of incorporating a company have also reduced, due in part to greater competition between formation agents and their development of more efficient internal systems, which have automated some of the manual tasks. 'Examples of this include batch printing of incorporation documents and providing more controls and guidance over what customers can and should enter on the online registration forms,' says Simon. 'This, in turn, results in less support costs dealing with repetitive issues. It is now possible to purchase an electronic company formation for as little as £24.99 plus VAT.'

Another significant change in the way in which companies are registered today is the manner in which the eventual directors, secretary (if the option is taken to have one) and the subscribers are appointed. 'Previously, accountants, solicitors and company formation agents typically used nominees to act as the shareholder and company officers at the time a company was incorporated,' says Simon. 'Once the company was successfully formed, the purchaser's officers would be appointed and the nominees would resign. This practice often caused issues when the purchasers then went to open a company bank account and the nominees were still shown on the Companies House register, which might not have been updated to reflect the new ownership and management appointments.

'With the exception of ready-made companies, where the use of nominees is still commonplace, the expectation for most companies incorporated today is that the first appointees will be those which the purchaser requests. This does mean that more time must be spent by the purchaser at the pre-formation stage, entering details of their directors and shareholders. Once the company has been set up, however, there is not then the requirement for this task to be undertaken in order to take ownership of the business.'

## The necessary documents

If you get professional help to register your company, which will save time and avoid errors, you are unlikely to be dealing directly with these documents; however, it's still useful to know them. When registering a limited company, three documents must be provided to Companies House. These are described below.

### 1. Memorandum of Association

The Memorandum of Association is a statement made by each subscriber confirming their intention to form a company and become a member of that company. If the company is to have a share capital on formation, each member also agrees to take at least one share.

*"When registering a limited company, three documents must be provided to Companies House"*

As of October 2009, it is no longer necessary to set out the company's name, where the company's registered office is located in England, Wales or Scotland and what the company will do in the memorandum, as this information is now included in form IN01. You can download a pro-forma memorandum for a company limited by shares or by guarantee from the Companies House website.

## 2. Articles of Association

In this document you set out the rules for running your company. You must state how shares will be allocated and transferred and how the directors, the secretary (should you choose to appoint one) and your meetings will be governed. The standard document used is Table A of the Companies Regulations, which is available on the Companies House website. However, if you choose an amended version of Table A, you must submit this version when registering. Once your company is incorporated you can only make changes if the holders of 75% of the voting rights in your company agree, so it pays to get this right at the outset.

## 3. Form IN01

This document (which replaced forms 10 and 12 in October 2009) gives details of the director(s), company secretary (if applicable) and the address of the registered office. Company directors must give their name, address, date of birth and occupation. It also contains the details of any shareholders and the statement of share capital (if it is a company limited by shares), and the statutory declaration of compliance with all the legal requirements of the incorporation of a company (namely compliance with the Companies Act 2006). The form must be signed by each of the company officers (the directors and secretary, if you have one).

To register a limited liability partnership, use form LL IN01. Both forms can be downloaded from the Companies House website.

## Cost of submitting the documents

The standard fee to register a limited company is £20, but a same-day service costs £50. If the registration documents are filed using the Companies House software filing service, the fee is £15 for a standard and £30 for same-day registration. However, to file electronically you must either purchase the suitable software, develop your own or go through an agent.

## Company officers

If you set up a private limited company, you appoint company officers, who are simply the formally named directors and company secretary, as stated in the Articles of Association described previously. Usually, as the founder of the company, you would be one of the directors, along with the people with whom you may have launched the company. One of the directors could also be appointed as company secretary, although this could be someone who is not a director. Following the implementation of the Companies Act 2006, having a company secretary is no longer a legal requirement, although you may wish to appoint one. It is a legal requirement for company officers to be in place at all times and for their names and current addresses to be written on the registration documents. If there is a change in company officers, you must inform Companies House immediately. All private limited companies must have at least one director. The following sections provide a rundown of the official roles of your company officers.

"Having a company secretary is no longer a legal requirement, although you may wish to appoint one"

## Directors

Company directors must manage the company's affairs in accordance with its Articles of Association and the law. At least one director must be a natural person (an individual). The post does not require any formal qualifications, but you cannot become a company director if:

→ You are an undischarged bankrupt or disqualified by a court from holding a directorship.

→ You are under 16.

Company directors have a responsibility to make sure that certain documents reach the registrar at Companies House. These are:

→ Accounts.

→ Annual returns.

→ Notice of change of directors or secretaries.

→ Notice of change of registered office.

Directors who fail to deliver these documents on time can be prosecuted and are subject to fines of up to £5,000 for each offence. An average 1,000 directors are prosecuted each year for failing to deliver accounts and returns to the registrar on time. So unless you are particularly knowledgeable about company facts and figures, it's a good idea to appoint an accountant to help you prepare these documents. Your accountant will also advise you on the necessary information you need to keep hold of and prepare, such as invoices, receipts, etc.

## Company secretary

The duties of a company secretary are not specified by law, but are usually contained within an employment contract. For private limited companies, the secretary is not required to have any special qualifications, but this is not the case if you decide to change your company to a public limited company. The main duties of a company secretary are to:

- Maintain the statutory registers, which means updating the details on the business held at Companies House when necessary. For example, if you relocate or appoint or lose a director.
- Ensure statutory forms are filed promptly.
- Provide members and auditors with notice of meetings.
- Send the registrar copies of resolutions and agreements.
- Send a copy of the accounts to every member of the company.
- Keep or arrange minutes of meetings.

With limited companies now no longer needing to appoint a company secretary by law, few will probably do so when launching, with the administrative duties being covered by the directors. These do not take up much time at all. In fact, once your company has launched, there is unlikely to be much to do on this front for a couple of years at least, barring submitting accounts and annual returns and recording the content of director meetings, unless you relocate or change directors over this period. Your accountant will help with accounts and returns, and can also offer general advice on the official roles of company officers, as can your solicitor.

*"CICs are a new type of limited company, designed specifically for those wishing to operate businesses for the benefit of the community"*

# Community Interest Companies (CICs)

The community interest company (CIC) model is becoming increasingly attractive to a growing number of social entrepreneurs looking to use their business acumen to bring about sustainable social change. CICs are a new type of limited company, designed specifically for those wishing to operate businesses for the benefit of the community, rather than to maximise profits for company owners. CICs can be limited by shares or by guarantee, and are subject to regulation by both an independent CIC

Regulator and Companies House. All CICs must be registered limited companies; they cannot be charities.

This structure gives CICs access to a range of financing options, which can be used to scale the business – and potentially deliver a wider social impact. However, CICs must follow strict rules in order to limit the return to investors and ensure the social mission remains the top priority, for example:

- ⇢ CICs must have an 'asset lock' to ensure that the assets and profits are used for the benefit of the community, and assets cannot be transferred or distributed for less than their full market value, except as permitted by legislation

- ⇢ CICs limited by shares can issue shares to investors, but the dividend payable is capped at a rate set by the independent CIC Regulator. This is currently 20% of each share.

When registering a CIC you will need to provide additional documentation, including a community interest statement outlining your social purpose. You can find detailed guidance on the registration process and requirements on the CIC Regulator's website.

The CIC Regulator must approve your application, which will be subjected to a 'community interest test'. Together with the asset lock, this ensures that the CIC is established for the benefit of the community and its assets and profits are dedicated to this purpose. The regulator then plays an ongoing monitoring and enforcement role with CICs, and you will be assessed each year to ensure that you are honouring your social commitments.

**WANT TO KNOW MORE ...**
Community Interest Companies Regulator
www.cicregulator.gov.uk

---

 **What to do next**

- Consider the legal structure of your business carefully and make sure you're aware of the associated pros and cons of each option.

- If you decide to register your business as a limited company, make sure you get the appropriate help if needed to avoid errors when registering.

- If you're starting a social enterprise, considering registering it as a Community Interest Company (CIC).

- Don't forget to register with HRMC too. You face a fine if you don't do this on time.

- Some businesses require additional licences or to be registered with various authorities. If you run a business in one of these sectors, make sure you've got all the necessary licences.

# ⤺ CHAPTER 6

## *Raising finance and business banking*

##  What's in this chapter?

-→ *Funding your start-up*
-→ *Banking on success*
-→ *Business loans*
-→ *Asset-based lending*
-→ *Leasing*
-→ *Equity finance*

If, like many entrepreneurs, self-funding your idea isn't an option – or if your business model puts the brakes on organic growth – you may need to raise external finance to get your venture off the ground. There are a number of different options available, so be sure to arm yourself with plenty of information before you decide on the best route to take.

Chapter 6 is a good start. From business loans to angel investment, we look at the funding options available to start-ups, as well as offering useful advice on what different investors and lenders are looking for in the businesses they back. We'll also look at how to find the right business bank account, and the importance of maintaining a good relationship with your bank manager – through the bad times and the good.

# Funding your start-up

The issue of funding is a hot topic among entrepreneurs and business owners at the best of times, but throw a recession and a credit crunch into the mix and the discussion intensifies to searing temperatures. When you come up with a business idea, the next step is usually to work out how you're going to fund it. There are plenty of options out there for getting your business off the ground, it's just a question of picking the right one for your venture. Here's our list of the top 10 ways of funding your business idea. Some of these options will be explored in more detail later in the chapter.

## 1. Savings

Got some money in the bank? With interest rates at an all-time low, it's not doing much for you sitting in an account. Or perhaps you've been made redundant, and have a large chunk of cash burning a hole in your pocket? The great thing about using your own money to start up is you don't have to go cap in hand to anyone else. Plus, there's the added bonus of not starting out in debt, or giving away equity at an early stage. There are other advantages too – if you want to pump more cash into the business later on, investors often like to see you're committed to a venture enough to put your own financial weight behind it.

## 2. Friends and family

If you're serious about starting a business you'll need all the encouragement and moral support you can get from your nearest and dearest. But sometimes they're also in a position to help you out with cash. You can negotiate more favourable lending terms with your loved ones, and often they'll be eager to help for a slice of the pie rather than a straight loan or donation. Be careful though. A financial transaction gone sour can result in the breakdown of the relationship and things can get sticky when borrowing money from those closest to you. It's important to agree the terms of the loan or investment upfront, making sure everyone knows where they stand – whether the business is a roaring success or a bit of a dud.

## 3. Business angels

You've seen *Dragons' Den*, but business angels aren't all as scary as the fire-breathing five on BBC2. A business angel can be an acquaintance, a former employer or someone you've found through a funding network. There's no hard rule other than that this kind of funding involves an individual or group that offers cash in exchange for a share of the business. Sometimes they take an active role in the venture and sometimes they act as silent partners. It really does depend on the individual circumstances and it's up to you to decide on the kind of angel investor you want involved.

## 4. Banks/loans

If anecdotal evidence is to be believed, small business loans are hard to come by these days. That's not to say they're non-existent however. There is still money out there and the banks haven't closed shop completely. You'll need a solid business plan and a clear idea of when and how your revenue will come in before a bank will even sit down with you though. If you haven't got the assets behind you to guarantee the loan yourself, make sure you ask your bank about the Enterprise Finance Guarantee (EFG) scheme, which the government introduced to help small businesses secure finance.

*"There is still money out there and the banks haven't closed shop completely"*

## 5. Grants

There are literally thousands of different types of business grants available. The hard part is finding them, and getting through the application process, which can be long and arduous. However, if you or your business qualifies, they can provide the financial impetus your idea needs to either get off the ground or grow into something bigger and better.

## 6. Asset-based finance

Essentially, this involves borrowing against assets you already own. It could be equipment and inventory or something less tangible like an invoice. If you've billed a customer but haven't received payment yet, you can borrow cash against that invoice or even sell the debt on. It can work wonders for your cashflow if you're growing fast but your clients have lengthy payment terms. You'll need to pick the company you work with carefully though to make sure they uphold the reputation of your business if they're chasing clients for unpaid invoices.

*"If you've billed a customer but haven't received payment yet, you can borrow cash against that invoice"*

## 7. Private equity and venture capital

You'll be hard pressed to find a venture capital or private equity company willing to invest if you're pre-revenue or very early stage these days. They're also not really interested in small amounts of cash – you've got to be looking for several million before they start to take notice. However, if you've got big plans and a viable exit strategy it doesn't hurt to get out there and meet a few VCs if you get the chance.

## 8. Corporate venturing

If you've got a great idea but want a helping hand getting it off the ground in terms of finances and other resources then you might want to consider being incubated by a larger company. It's not for everyone, especially if you're not willing to give up a degree of direction and control, but if you find the right partner you could find start-up funds, office space, marketing and even human resources provided for you.

## 9. Credit cards

"It's not the ideal way to start your business, but many entrepreneurs have successfully funded the early stages of their venture with plastic"

It's not the ideal way to start your business, but many entrepreneurs have successfully funded the early stages of their venture with plastic. You'll need to be strict though. Low rates or even completely interest free periods are common but you need to be able to pay it back quickly because the monthly charges won't be cheap once they start. Approach this funding method with extreme caution but there's no need to rule it out completely if you need a relatively low sum of money for a short period.

## 10. No money – organic growth

Starting a consultancy from home? Got an idea for a website you can build and code yourself? There have been plenty of successful ventures over the years that started with no, or negligible amounts of cash. This kind of funding method works well if you're offering a product or service where you receive payment before you have to buy any stock or actually deliver the goods. The revenue received can then be used to plough back into growing the business. It's certainly the most risk averse way to start a business, and while it may not be the quickest route to a multimillion pound turnover, there's nothing stopping you getting there eventually.

# Banking on success

Whichever route you take to fund your start-up – and whether you decide to be a sole trader, set up a partnership or run a private limited company –

you will need a good relationship with your bank. And although it has never been easier to switch banks, taking time to decide on the right one (and bank manager) for you at the outset can save problems later that could adversely affect your business. If you are a sole trader you can keep a personal account, but you need to make it clear what incomings and outgoings relate to your business. If you launch a partnership or limited company, you will need to set up business bank accounts.

*"You need a manager who will understand your business and one whom you can trust"*

There are many factors to consider when choosing a bank. Interest rates and charges will obviously play their part, but it's also essential to look at the quality of service you will receive from your bank manager. After all, this is the person who you will deal with on a regular basis and the person you will need to approach for funding. So you need a manager who will understand your business and one whom you can trust.

When looking at banks, don't hesitate to ask to speak to the manager who will be dealing with your account, and when you do, make sure your needs are met.

To help you find the right bank manager, Allied Irish Bank (GB) has put together a list of questions that you should be asking:

⇢ **Do you really understand my business and industry?**

Every industry has slightly different needs and you want to be sure your bank understands what's important in your industry.

⇢ **How long have you been in your job?**

Ideally, you don't want to keep having to build relationships with different bank managers; continuity is key.

⇢ **Can I reach you whenever I need to? Or will I speak to someone working in a call centre whom I have never met?**

There is no substitute for having a contact who intimately understands your business and what you want to achieve – not so easy to do over the telephone.

⇢ **Are you able to make a quick decision when I need one?**

We all know that if you really need to extend your overdraft for a short period you need a quick decision. Having to jump through lots of 'hoops' just eats up your valuable time, and few businesses can afford that.

⇢ Will I have one point of contact who knows who I am, and crucially, understands my business?

The Model-T Ford approach to service is no longer good enough – one colour does not suit everyone.

⇢ Can I speak to companies you currently work with in a similar industry for a reference?

There is no substitute for third-party endorsement. All banks say they deliver great service, but do they really? You need to find out.

⇢ Will you provide more general business advice when I need it?

Getting the basics such as a bank account, credit card, etc is simple, but businesses require far more. They want a bank that will deliver much more value.

⇢ How are you rated in the industry?

Have they won any awards recently, for instance? Again, third-party endorsement can be a powerful method with which to judge the success of an organisation.

⇢ Do you have the name of a company in your patch that you helped to grow?

Most businesses have similar aspirations – to grow and to improve profitability. Banks play a major role in helping to turn ambition into reality. You need to know that the bank you select can help you achieve your business objectives.

Remember, when it comes to choosing a bank, the more questions you ask, the more likely it is that you will enjoy a long and fruitful relationship.

## What banks offer businesses

Before you start comparing different business bank accounts, it's worth knowing what products and services they may offer, what these involve, and deciding on the ones that are most critical to your business.

## Bank facilities

⇢ Deposits: paying in cash and cheques.

⇢ Withdrawals: taking out cash through an ATM or at a branch.

- ⇢ Payment by cheque: use of a business chequebook, which can sometimes be personalised with your company logo.

- ⇢ Online banking: for monitoring and managing your accounts. Check what functionality is on offer.

- ⇢ Automatic money transfers: direct debits and direct credits. The UK Payments Council wants to see cheques phased out by 2018, and more and more businesses are opting to pay their suppliers and bills electronically.

- ⇢ Night safe: for depositing money when the bank is closed.

- ⇢ Balance enquiry and statements: for keeping track of your finances, record-keeping and reconciliations.

- ⇢ Company debit card: this will debit an amount immediately from your business account. In most cases the transactions are free and there is no annual fee.

- ⇢ Company credit card: a charge card (such as Barclaycard or MasterCard) that can be issued to key members of staff. Repayment is made monthly from your business current account. Interest could be charged if you do not clear the balance in full each month. In addition, there is usually an annual fee per card.

- ⇢ Overdraft and loan facilities: short-term financing, subject to an application procedure. May also provide access to the government-backed Enterprise Finance Guarantee (EFG) scheme.

- ⇢ Introductory offers: most banks offer free business banking for start-ups (for the first 12-24 months). However, check whether this is conditional (often you will need to operate your account in credit or within agreed limits), what the penalties are for breaching account limits, and crucially, what the charges will be once this period has expired.

- ⇢ Asset finance: leasing and hire purchase facilities to enable you to buy equipment.

- ⇢ Factoring and invoice discounting: short-term borrowing against the value of unpaid invoices.

→ Commercial mortgage: funding to help buy a business. Often up to 80% of the purchase can be financed by the bank.

## Other features

→ Deposit accounts: a lot of banks have business deposit accounts with higher interest than a current account for any reserve funds your business may have.

→ Merchant services: if you want to accept credit and debit card payments from customers, you will need a merchant account. This is provided by a bank but to get one you will often need two years' trading history and audited accounts. Once set up, you will be charged an annual fee plus a percentage of every transaction.

→ Insurance: larger banks often offer their customers insurance cover for business interruption, health, loan repayment and more.

→ Support: most of the larger banks offer resources and support to help you run your business. For example, you may be assigned a relationship manager who will offer business advice. The bank may also provide seminars, educational literature, or bookkeeping software.

**WANT TO KNOW MORE ...**

British Bankers' Association
www.bba.org.uk

The British Bankers' Association's Business Account Finder offers independent advice on what various banks offer small businesses.

## Dealing with banks in a downturn

It was less than careful lending by banks and other financial institutions that caused the credit crunch and the ensuing economic downturn in 2008, so it's logical that they will now be a lot more cautious when handling their customers, whether they are individuals or businesses.

Before the boom finally collapsed in 2008 and the recession began, banks couldn't lend enough money, and that included overdraft facilities for new businesses. But the credit crunch sent shockwaves through the finance industry that haven't been seen since the Great Depression of the 1930s. With some of the more established institutions going out of business or having to be propped up by the state, fear has gripped the banking community, resulting in a highly risk averse approach. In the wake of such a massive turnaround, it's no surprise that businesses' relationships with their banks have been affected.

*"A well–thought out business plan and professional approach are more important than ever"*

Many companies have found that their banks have become more stringent with respect to existing overdraft and loan arrangements. In some instances agreements have been tightened, putting additional financial pressure on companies, and in extreme cases overdraft facilities have been withdrawn and loans called in. This has resulted in a number of businesses simply not having the cash reserves to continue trading – and it's the younger and smaller operations that have been hit the hardest.

If you are starting up, of course, you probably don't have an existing relationship with a bank. What this means for you is that banks will require stronger assurances than previously of the viability of your business simply to secure a business bank account, never mind a loan. So a well-thought out business plan and professional approach are more important than ever.

You may also find it difficult to secure as large an overdraft as previously, while bank loans are likely to be far more difficult to come by. However, if you are offered a bank account with an overdraft facility, you can be confident that your business idea has a good chance of success and that you have put together a strong business plan, which will stand you in good stead when looking for more finance, should you need it. Banks and other lenders are still open for business, but are only tending to invest in those businesses that they consider to have an excellent chance of success.

As banks are still actively looking for new business customers, it remains crucial for you to shop around and find the one with the best offer for your company. Then, to get the most out of your relationship, it's more important than ever to handle your bank manager with care and respect, as described in the following action points.

Action points

## Managing your bank manager

Although it is important to ensure you have a bank and a bank manager capable of giving you what you want, it is a two-way relationship and there are a number of things you can do to get the most out of it, as **Christopher Jenkins**, co-founder and senior partner of Wingrave Yeats, a leading London accountancy and management consultancy firm, points out.

☑ **Keep business and personal accounts apart**: It's not always a good idea to keep your business account at the same bank as your personal account. Resist the temptation of the one-stop borrowing concept. You don't invest without spreading risk, so don't borrow without doing the same.

☑ **Keep your bank regularly informed**: Don't go and see the bank only when you need something – no one likes to be constantly confronted with tales of doom and gloom, or even worse, thinly veiled gestures of optimism. Get in contact or make an appointment to visit when you have good news and when you don't need to borrow more money. Get them excited about your business, enthuse about it and go away without asking them for more cash. Equally, if you are having any problems that could affect your ability to make a loan payment or stay within your overdraft limit, give your bank manager plenty of warning. You will find your bank far more receptive and willing to help you out of your predicament if you let them know of any issues as far in advance as possible.

☑ **Be professional**: Make sure any figures or information you present are correct and consistent with the story you told last month. Remember that everything goes on file and will come up again – often when you least expect it. Don't let your accountants/financial advisers do it all for you, but don't go anywhere without them. Bankers can spot a report that has been written by a professional but signed off in your name. They want to know that you as the borrower understand and believe what you are telling them. However, don't try to forecast for the bank without professional help. A profits and losses forecast and cashflow estimate that hasn't been reconciled to a balance sheet and which would show negative debtors in year two will not go down well with a banker.

☑ **Consider what the bank wants to see**: If you don't feed your bank regular information, it can only resort to what can be gleaned from your account. Bankers examine average balance calculations from your statements and also highs and lows on the account. 'Hardcore borrowing' (where the account is constantly up against the limit) makes them twitchy, but they appreciate wide swings from full utilisation of the facility to occasional credit balances. They also compare your company statistics with comparable industry standards. So look at the trend of your own account before you present it to them, and have prepared answers in your mind to the questions they are bound to ask.

☑ **Monitor lending agreements**: Lending usually comes with covenants, which are certain financial limits that your company must adhere to. For example, not allowing particular balance sheet items or ratios to fall below or go over an agreed figure. It is easy to monitor these covenants and rather than letting the bank do so, include a calculation in the monthly management accounts that you send to the bank.

☑ **Manage your total borrowings**: Be careful with your capital expenditure. Try out asset finance, leasing and rental deals rather than outright purchases of equipment and technology goods. While they may look expensive, they are 'off-balance sheet financing', which does wonders for your covenant calculations. Also consider other forms of maintaining cashflow, such as using a factoring company to collect and manage your invoices (see later in the chapter).

☑ **Don't over-promise**: At all times, try to minimise the bank's perception of risk in lending to you, and increase its confidence and enthusiasm to lend by promising no more than you know you can achieve. Understand what they can and can't offer and then structure your request so that it's watertight in banking terms.

## *Business loans*

Although many small companies are now financed by the founders themselves, when people think about raising money their first port of call is generally the bank, from which a loan is the most typical form of debt financing. When applying for a business loan, you will need to clearly state how much money you need and why, based on the business plan you are presenting. Generally, the loan has to be repaid at an agreed interest rate and within a specified period of time. The interest rate can either be variable or fixed.

*"You will have to show how the money will be repaid, and details from your business plan should help"*

Typically the loan is secured against an asset. This means that if the business fails to repay the loan, the lender has the right to claim the asset. An asset could be a house or other premises, or some equipment owned

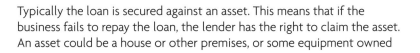

by the business. If you are unwilling to put personal possessions like your house on the line and your company has insufficient assets, a bank is unlikely to lend you money.

*"A bank loan locks companies into a payment schedule, which may cause cashflow problems for small businesses"*

Often a bank will also expect some financial commitment from you personally, such as a percentage of the amount you are requesting. As the loan is secured, the cost is usually less than other more risky types of borrowing. However, a bank loan also locks companies into a payment schedule, which may cause cashflow problems for small businesses. You will have to show how the money will be repaid, and details from your business plan should help.

The straightjacket of making a set payment at what may be a fixed interest rate can also cause a lot of problems for fast-growing companies that consume capital very fast. For these reasons, loans are more suited to tried-and-tested business models that offer good prospects for profitability.

## What the banks are looking for

If you want to use a bank loan to finance your start-up, you will need to present the bank with a detailed business plan. The British Bankers' Association offers this list of key factors that a bank manager will be looking for:

**Character:** Is the customer trustworthy with a clean credit record?

**Ability:** What experience does the customer have in this line of business? Has market research been done? How good is this product?

**Margin:** How risky is the proposal and what interest rate would reflect this risk?

**Purpose:** What will the money be used for? Would a different type of finance be appropriate? Are there any government schemes to help?

**Amount:** Does the amount seem too much or too little? How much is the proprietor putting in themselves?

**Repayment:** Will the business be able to generate enough money to repay the loan and interest?

**Insurance:** If it all goes wrong, is there an alternative source of repayment?

Following the credit crunch, banks have become very risk averse, making securing finance from them more difficult, particularly if you are launching a start-up and have no track record of running a company. That's not to say however that it isn't available. Banks are still providing finance, but the terms are likely to be tougher, such as higher interest rates. This makes it more important than ever to shop around for the best deal, as it could save you money in the long term.

You can also use a financial broker to suggest the best terms on offer for the type of finance that your business needs. This can save you time and money, and can also increase your chances of getting a loan by presenting your proposal in the best way to the most appropriate lenders. Before enlisting the help of a broker however, find out what they are going to charge you.

With loans harder to come by, there could be a tendency to be so relieved you've secured one that you rush into it. However, try to negotiate the best terms you can, as this can have a direct impact on the health of your business once you launch. Aside from discussing obvious issues, such as the due date of the loan and the interest rate, you also need to establish the amount of the loan fees.

It's important to make sure that you will have the flexibility to pay off your loan earlier than the due date and, if possible, try to avoid any penalty for early settlement. Try to negotiate a grace period for your payment schedule and check to make sure that late payment charges are fair. Make sure you have scrutinised the small print before you put pen to paper. It can help to ask an expert, such as a solicitor, to review the terms.

## *The Enterprise Finance Guarantee (EFG) scheme*

The global economic crisis that shook the banks so fiercely in 2008 was bad news for small businesses seeking loans. However, in an effort to get banks lending again, the government introduced a number of measures, most notably the Enterprise Finance Guarantee (EFG) scheme. In effect, the scheme is a reworking of the old Small Firms Loan Guarantee scheme.

*"While the banks have faced criticism for failing to promote the EFG, the good news is that many high street lenders have signed up to the scheme"*

The EFG was originally established to support up to £1.3bn of new lending to economically viable small businesses that need some funding help. In the 2010 Emergency Budget, the EFG scheme was extended by £200m and made available until 31 March 2011. However, in the 2011 Budget, the coalition government pledged to continue the EFG scheme until 2014–15, providing up to £600m of additional lending to around 6,000 small and medium-sized businesses in 2011–12 and, subject to demand, more than £2bn in total over the next four years. What's more, a processing target of

20 working days is being introduced for all major lenders participating in the EFG, which the government hopes will provide certainty for businesses over how long it will take to receive a decision.

The EFG scheme is open to businesses with an annual turnover of no more than £25m that are seeking loans of between £1,000 and £1m, repayable over 10 years. The cash for the loans still comes from the bank, but the difference is the government will underwrite 75% of the loan, which in theory means you have a chance at debt finance even if you don't have the collateral to back it up. The EFG covers new loans, refinancing of existing loans or the conversion of part or all of an existing overdraft into a loan.

The scheme is open to businesses in all sectors with the exception of companies in the agricultural, coal and steel sectors, which are bound by

**WANT TO KNOW MORE …**

Department for Business, Innovation and Skills (BIS)
www.bis.gov.uk

## In my experience

**Company: tastecard**
**Owner-managers: Jamie Milner and Matthew Turner**

*A tasty proposition*
On average, the British public eat out at least twice a week and the recession has done little to damage the frequency of restaurant dining. What it has done however, is create a boom in the diner discount industry. One of the most successful ventures in the sector is undoubtedly tastecard (formerly tastelondon), the 'pay to save' service which provides customers with a discount card offering up to 50% off in more than 4,750 outlets in return for an annual fee.

Launched in 2006 by founders **Jamie Milner** and **Matthew Turner**, who adapted the idea behind American company Entertainment Book, tastecard now has more than 250,000 members, while turnover in 2010 was £3m – of which £2m was profit.

While getting London's restaurants on board with a new concept was initially a big struggle (the venture launched with 100 outlets, the result of several months of hammering phones from Jamie and Matthew's Huddersfield base), funding was a lot easier to secure, thanks to the founders' comprehensive business plan.

Jamie and Matthew put together a three year plan which clearly set out their revenue strategy. First they'd tap the consumer market and then move on to corporate sales, which now provide a quarter of total revenue. With the help of the government's former Small Firms Loan Guarantee scheme (which was replaced by the Enterprise Finance Guarantee), they secured bank funding from the very first pitch as well as a grant from Yorkshire Forward. Jamie attributes the funding success to their 'sensible' business plan which showed them losing money for the first 18 months.

Jamie believes his and Matthew's previous experience combined also created the perfect foundation for the business' success. Matthew had run a bar and restaurant while Jamie was a sales director for a database marketing company in Leeds.

Today, restaurateurs approach the company on a daily basis. The plan is to double revenue year-on-year while continuing to expand coverage outside of London – hence the recent rebrand. 'There's a Taste restaurant on every corner in London and we want to replicate that nationally,' says Jamie.

state aid rules. While the banks have faced criticism for failing to promote the EFG adequately to business customers, the good news is that many high street lenders have signed up to the scheme, so it is well worth asking your bank for more information. Loan applications should be made directly to the bank in the usual way.

## *Other debt finance options*

As shown in the box on the next page, there is a vast range of different debt financing tools and each business should find the one that is right for them. So, if your business needs some working capital, but the amount fluctuates, an overdraft is probably best for you. The interest rate is agreed in advance and you only pay interest for the time and amount that you are overdrawn. But if your business needs longer-term finance, in particular for a specific purchase or planned expenditure, you should look to take a loan that can be repaid over a set period.

There are many reasons why debt finance could suit your business – it is accessible, flexible and tailored. Debt finance will be the first option for most small businesses, and whether it is loans, overdrafts, leasing or invoice discounting, the company is borrowing against reserves rather than giving someone ownership of shares. One key reason that most businesses will borrow money rather than sell shares in their business is that debt finance is

## Different types of debt finance

Debt finance can also take the form of an overdraft, term loan, leasing, factoring and invoice discounting.

- An overdraft is generally used to fund working cashflow rather than capital expenditure, and is repayable on demand, while exceeding the agreed limits can be expensive.
- Increasingly banks are offering term loans to small businesses as an alternative to using an overdraft facility. In particular, it allows the banks to impose a regular repayment schedule over a fixed period of time and to see the amount of credit gradually reducing.
- Leasing, which is a way of borrowing to buy specific equipment or machinery, is also gaining in popularity.
- Factoring and invoice discounting is where the small business borrows against sales as a means of freeing up cash. Invoice discounting involves a company loaning you a large percentage of the money for each invoice as soon as it is raised, which is then repaid plus a commission fee when payment is received from your customer within a specified time period. Under factoring, the company will also chase the debt for you, for a slightly larger commission payment.
- Each method provides a way around cashflow problems for new or small companies, and they can prove particularly useful for those businesses that have a large outlay for each job or if they use a lot of suppliers.

usually available from organisations in smaller amounts than equity, and unless the company is very large it will be too small for institutional equity funding.

## *Asset-based lending*

**WANT TO KNOW MORE ...**
National Association of Commercial Finance Brokers
www.nacfb.org

With traditional bank loans being particularly difficult to come by at the moment, offering the assets of your business as security may help to persuade reluctant lenders. This is called asset-based lending, and has been slowly growing in popularity for some time now – and certainly long before the recession hit. Under the system, a financier will lend on items with high sell-on values, such as stock, machinery, premises, invoices – even brands or trade marks. The borrower usually has access to a revolving credit facility, where there's an upper limit, and the amount loaned changes as it does with an overdraft. Lenders retain security over the assets for the length of the contract.

To get the most from asset-based lending, it helps if your business is asset-rich, which could cause problems for start-ups. However, if you have machinery or property to use as assets you can expect advances of up to 80% of their value. For stock and raw materials, this reduces to 30%–70%. Typically, the annual cost of borrowing on a revolving credit facility is around 1.75%–3% above the Bank of England base rate, plus an annual and/or closing fee of around 0.5%–1.5% of the total borrowed.

Before agreeing to an asset-based loan, which could take up to six weeks to secure, a lender may consult a specialist valuer. As part of the assessment process, an in-depth evaluation of your business will be carried out, in which your proposed assets will be valued and cashflow and budget projections reviewed.

## *Factoring*

All too often small businesses get carried away with securing that 'next big order', without considering if they've got the cash to meet it. Factoring won't completely solve the problem, but it'll get pretty close. Factoring is a flexible form of loan, which advances money to a company as it issues new invoices.

*"All too often small businesses get carried away with securing that 'next big order', without considering if they've got the cash to meet it"*

There are two major advantages of factoring compared to overdrafts or other loans. Firstly, factoring is flexible, in that the amount a company can borrow grows with sales. This is often essential to enable companies to fund that growth, since they must usually pay for supplies before they receive payment from customers. The second advantage factoring offers is that no other assets are needed to secure the funding.

A factoring company will lend a company a certain percentage of each invoice that it issues; it will then collect the invoice when it becomes due and pay the balance back to the issuing company. The factoring company charges a fee, usually a very small percentage of the value of each invoice, and interest on the amount of money borrowed.

A company must notify all its customers of the new arrangement, and hand over the task of collecting debts to the factoring company. Often at the start of a new factoring relationship, the factor will take on existing debtors, which can involve a very substantial payment being made right at the start.

Setting up a factoring deal can be done far more quickly than most other forms of finance. Factoring can work for most companies which sell to customers on credit, and is especially well-suited to companies which are growing rapidly.

Typically, factors will lend up to 80% of an invoice value. The words 'up to' are all-important there. Much depends on the terms of sale your company operates and the credit-worthiness of your customers. There are two elements to the cost: a 'service charge' and interest payments. The service charge is calculated as a percentage of turnover.

Having a third party collect your debts does mean that you have less control over the manner in which customer relations are managed than if your own company was handling everything. Today, though, most good factoring companies will let you affect the style in which different customers are handled and chased.

*"To qualify for invoice discounting, companies would normally need to be profitable"*

## Invoice discounting

Invoice discounting is a variation on factoring where the client company collects its own debts, but the lender still advances money against them. One advantage of this is that the fee charged is far smaller, though there is still a fixed percentage of turnover charged for processing. It is usually confidential, so that none of your customers need know that you are borrowing in this way, which appeals to some people. It does however mean that you are entirely responsible for collecting your own debts.

Factoring and discounting companies take the view that they have far less control and security with invoice discounting than with factoring, so they are much more stringent about the type of companies they deem eligible for it. To qualify for invoice discounting, companies would normally need to be profitable, established for several years with audited accounts, and have an established and strong credit control function. It is not unreasonable for lenders to wish to be sure that the debts they lend against are real and will be collected efficiently.

# Leasing

Leasing is a way of purchasing equipment, machinery or other assets without having to pay the full amount upfront. There are various different structures that can be used and the attraction of each one will vary according to your requirements and, perhaps, according to tax changes made by the government.

In essence, a lease is an agreement between you (the lessee) and the finance company (the lessor). You will pay a periodic fee, usually monthly, for the use and possibly ownership of equipment. The range of equipment that can be bought under a lease is expanding rapidly – from the most basic purchase, such as office computers or company cars, to more specialised equipment, such as a forklift truck or a safe. This is partly due to the fact that the number of companies providing this service has expanded rapidly. Not only do most banks and a number of specialised finance houses offer this service, but there have also been a growing number of equipment manufacturers entering the market. It is now possible to lease your office computer direct from Dell, Compaq and IBM among others.

In fact, the Finance and Leasing Association (FLA) estimates that some 15% of office equipment is financed through a lease. The FLA also expects the market to continue growing gradually but notes that the business is always dependent upon the latest tax and accounting changes.

## *Equity finance*

Equity finance involves giving up a stake in your business in return for money. Many small businesses actually use equity finance without even realising it. As Bank of England figures show, some 61% of businesses are launched with either personal capital or that of friends and relatives. That can be an equity arrangement, where friends and family take a stake in the business in return for their funds.

The big advantage of equity finance is that it never has to be repaid and there is no interest rate paid on the money. Equity investments are true 'risk capital', as there is no guarantee of the investor getting their money back. The investment is not tied to any particular assets that can be redeemed from the business and, should the business fail, an equity investor is less likely to get their original investment back than other investors.

The return from an equity investment can be generated either through a sale of the shares once the company has grown or through dividends, a discretionary payout to shareholders if the business does well. However, the reason that investors will give you cash in this form is that they will take a share of the business in return, therefore gaining some influence over it. Formal equity finance is available through a number of different sources, such as business angels, venture capitalists (see box) or the stock markets. Each varies in the amount of money available and the process of completing the deal.

*"The big advantage of equity finance is that it never has to be repaid and there is no interest rate paid on the money"*

> ## Business angels and venture capitalists
>
> Business angels are usually individuals who invest in companies they think have the potential to make them money, and are typically looking to invest between £10,000 and £750,000, according to the British Business Angels Association (BBAA). Venture capital (VC) firms are organisations set up to invest in companies, and typically prefer to deal in figures higher than business angels.

*"Typically, business angels have already made their fortune through other business ventures, possibly their own start-up"*

## *Business angels*

Business angels are wealthy individuals who invest in start-up and growth businesses in return for equity in the company. The investment can involve both time and money, depending upon the investor.

Typically, business angels have already made their fortune through other business ventures, possibly their own start-up or a career in business. Most are men aged between 45 and 65. However, investors can be younger – particularly in the technology sector. Business angels can operate independently, but many work as a syndicate. This is because the majority of angel investments make a loss. Research by the National Endowment for Science, Technology and the Arts (NESTA) and the British Business Angels Association (BBAA), which reviewed 1,080 angel investments, found that angels lost money in 56% of deals. To avoid losing a lot of money on one big deal, an investor needs to make a number of investments and spread the risk.

More than half of the investments in the study were directed at very early stage, pre-revenue start-ups – 'the riskiest time of a company's life', says NESTA. However, the higher risk associated with investing in early-stage businesses can potentially be rewarded with far greater returns if the business takes off and its valuation soars. According to the research, 9% of the deals generated more than 10 times the capital invested. Meanwhile, the average rate of return for successful deals was 22%.

The BBAA estimates that business angels invest roughly £800m every year. BBAA research has also indicated that business angels invest more in early-stage businesses than formal venture capital (VC) funds.

## What can business angels offer?

Business angels are a vital tool used to fill the gap between venture capital and debt finance – particularly for start-up and early-stage companies. They also provide a useful source of equity finance for relatively small amounts that would not otherwise be available through venture capital.

According to the BBAA, angels typically invest between £10,000 and £750,000 in a company. On average, business angels in the UK invest £42,000, and each investor makes around six investments. Where larger amounts are invested in a business, this usually takes place through a syndicate of angels organised through the entrepreneur's personal contacts or a business angel network. The BBAA/NESTA research found that co-investments were the preference for investing in start-ups, with on average five angels co-investing in any one round. Most syndicates will have a lead investor, who is often referred to as the 'archangel'. In addition to a first investment, business angels often follow up with later rounds of financing for the same company.

As well as cash, business angels can offer years of experience in the business world, not to mention useful contacts to help you grow your business, which can add real value to your company. Although some prefer to become a sleeping partner, others will get actively involved in your business, offering help with anything from writing a marketing plan to taking the company through a flotation on the stock market. Indeed, the BBAA/NESTA report recommends that angels invest in their area of expertise and stay connected with the business, preferably at board level, as a way of improving the success rate of angel deals.

## Who do business angels invest in?

Unlike venture capitalists, whose business it is to invest in privately-held companies, business angels do not have to invest their cash. This means that they are selective about which companies they will fund. More than 90% of businesses applying for angel funding are rejected in the initial stages.

*"As well as cash, business angels can offer years of experience in the business world"*

Business angels often invest in local companies, generally within a 100-mile radius from their home, and tend to favour sector-specific investments. This is particularly true of the IT and biotech sectors. Most importantly, business angels invest in growing companies. You may not be able to tempt a business angel unless you can show growth potential of at least 20%.

First and foremost, business angels will expect to take a percentage of the ownership of your company. This is typically a minority stake, as they recognise that entrepreneurs are best left in control of their own businesses. However, this is not likely to be an insignificant amount of equity either. The rule of thumb is that one third is given to each of the following:

- → The idea.
- → The management.
- → The investors.

Business angels will want to know how they will get their money back, so be prepared to justify your business plan. They will also want to see a financial commitment from the founders. However, while some business angels are purely interested in a financial return, others are simply hoping to protect their cash and get involved in a going concern. Many want to take an active part in a new business in a sector that interests them.

There are big tax breaks on offer to business angels through the Enterprise Investment Scheme (EIS), although the rules can be complex.

*"Start with all of your family and friends – you may find an investor from your own personal contacts"*

## Finding a business angel

The big problem with business angels is that they are hard to find. They tend to guard their identity so that they are not inundated with applications from companies.

Start with all of your family and friends – you may find an investor from your own personal contacts. Draw up a list of business contacts including bankers, accountants, lawyers or other advisers who might have access to potential investors. Occasionally, advertisements or cold calling known business angels can work. Remember to also target potential investors from the industry you are in, and to make use of any networking opportunities that you can.

There are many angel networks across the country. Networks operate as an introduction agency, matching businesses looking for finance with potential investors. If your business fits the criteria for investment, you may get the opportunity to present your case at an investor forum, where business angels are invited to listen to the presentations of a number of companies. However, even if you get to this stage there is no guarantee of success.

You can find lots more information on angel investment, along with a directory of UK angel networks, on the British Business Angels Association (BBAA) website.

**WANT TO KNOW MORE ...**

British Business Angels Association (BBAA)
www.bbaa.org.uk

## *Making an investment deal*

The first and most important thing is to get your business plan right. Business angels can be inundated with proposals, so try to get your message across while keeping the proposal short and simple. Don't try to bluff your way through. Business angels are experienced in business and will see through any hyperbole. Make sure it is easy to find basic information on:

→ The product.

→ The market.

→ The management team.

→ The current shareholding structure.

→ The current financial status; and the options available to the investor.

In particular, the business plan should spell out the likely exit routes to an investor. Make it explicit as to what is on offer, what the investor will get for their money and how they will get it back. If the business plan is well written and the investment is attractive, you may get a meeting with a business angel. In fact, you should expect to meet with a potential investor two or three times before any offer is made.

Be prepared for the due diligence process. A business angel will want to check all sorts of details about your company. This may include personal references about you and your management team, detailed financial projections about your business and the industry sector, as well as talking to clients and suppliers. However, the due diligence process of a business angel may take less time than a venture capitalist. Research shows that on average venture capitalists took nearly 20 weeks to complete, compared with under 15 weeks for business angels.

*"The business plan should spell out the likely exit routes to an investor"*

If an offer is made, you will need to determine whether this is acceptable. If you are offered £100,000 for a 50% stake in the business, this implies a total valuation of £200,000 for your business. You need to know whether this is a fair price. Look at your competitors or similar companies to try and get a better idea of how your company should be valued.

Once the outline has been agreed and is acceptable to both parties, it might be worthwhile drawing up an agreement called 'heads of terms'. This will set out the main terms and will form the basis of any legal agreement later on, although it is not, in itself, legally binding. It may include confirmation of the terms, the price, any conditions that need to be met before the deal is done and any confidentiality or exclusivity arrangements.

You may also find that the offer comes with a subscription agreement. This can cover a number of things, but it is essentially a form of protection for the investor. A subscription agreement will typically impose a series of negative controls on the business. For example, it could impose limitations on issuing additional shares that could dilute the percentage held by a minority shareholder. Instead, business angels may want to stipulate that they have the right to buy additional shares to maintain their overall share. It may also cover the salaries of directors or regulate the role of the investor.

Depending upon the structure of the deal, you may also want to include a shareholders' agreement. If you are issuing the same types of shares to the investor as held by existing shareholders, an agreement is not necessary. However, if your deal is creating different classes of shares, such as ordinary shares and preference shares, then you may find it beneficial.

 ### Action points

### How to pitch to an angel

Michael Weaver, chief executive of business investment agency Beer & Partners, offers his top 10 tips on delivering a winning investment pitch.

1. Elevator pitch — Business owners should be able to pitch their products or services in any circumstances, even when they have a very limited amount of time. An elevator pitch is a quick, yet comprehensive, overview of a business short enough to be delivered in the time span of an elevator ride.

2. Prepare — As Mark Twain said: 'It takes more than three weeks to prepare a good impromptu speech.' Pitching to a potential business angel could

dramatically change the future of a business. Preparation is key to take advantage of this opportunity.

3. Setting the stage — If possible, it's always ideal to prepare the room of the meeting well in advance. This is especially important if the pitch includes a product demonstration or the use of multimedia aids.

4. Look your best — Wearing a suit is usually preferred as it shows a level of respect for a potential investor. A general rule of thumb is that you can never overdress.

5. Know your numbers — When looking for investment, small business owners should know their accounts inside-out and be able to discuss them with investors in detail. Commit key figures to memory and prepare a one-side 'crib sheet' to avoid forgetting crucial information due to nerves.

6. Have a clear strategy in place — A solid business plan that identifies the strategy is crucial. The plan must contain a commercial idea which will provide an eventual profit for investors or, as a minimum, sufficient profit to repay the interest and the principal on a loan.

7. Product vs. people — Investors are interested in not only the product, but also the marketplace, the competition, the management team, the eventual exit strategy and of course the entrepreneurs themselves. Business angels are investing in people as much as companies, as they plan to work together over the long term. Establishing a rapport with the potential investor is key to a successful partnership.

8. Care — Business angels invest their own money and they would expect to see business owners putting themselves on the line for their project. If an entrepreneur doesn't show commitment to what he/she is doing, why should investors?

9. Be honest, even about tricky subjects — A question that angel investors frequently ask is 'what are the risks in this business?' Small business owners must be prepared to discuss contingency plans and potential difficulties the business could face. Angel investors will appreciate a realistic assessment and honest responses as opposed to a rose-tinted view.

10. Feedback — Regardless of the outcome of the pitch and whether funding gets secured, receiving feedback from potential investors is invaluable. Entrepreneurs should be prepared to receive negative feedback and take it on board to refine their business ideas.

## Venture capital

Before giving a business or prospective business an injection of venture capital, entrepreneurs need to assess their current and future situation. A company is suitable for venture capital investment if it exhibits high growth prospects, has a product or service with a competitive edge or unique selling point and has a strong management team. Managers must exhibit an understanding of their market, their own unique position and how to grab market share. Many small companies are lifestyle businesses whose main purpose is to provide a good standard of living and job satisfaction for their owners. These businesses are not generally suitable for venture capital investment, as they are unlikely to provide the high financial return for investors.

### What is venture capital?

Simply put, venture capital provides long-term, committed share capital to help private companies grow and succeed. Obtaining venture capital is very different from raising a loan. Lenders have a legal right to interest on a loan and repayment of the capital, irrespective of your success or failure. Venture capital is invested in exchange for a stake in your company and, as shareholders, the investors' returns are dependent upon the growth and profitability of your business.

There are now hundreds of active venture capital firms in the UK, which provide several billion pounds each year to unquoted companies mostly located in the UK. The venture capital firm is an equity business partner and is rewarded by the company's success, generally achieving its principal return through an exit. An exit may include selling shares back to management, selling shares to another investor, a trade sale – where the whole company is sold to another – or a stock market listing. Generally, venture capital firms look to retain their investment in between three to seven years and during that time, they also look to generate at least a 20% return per annum.

### How to find VC investment

The most effective way of raising venture capital is to select just a few firms to target with your business proposition. The stage your company is in, the industry sector in which your business operates, the amount of finance needed and the geographical location of your business all factor in the mix.

To find the right investor a good place to start is the British Venture Capital Association (BVCA), which has a full list of members on its website, along with details of what they're looking for in businesses. A bit of research will be appreciated by venture capital firms, as it shows them that you have thought carefully about the type of investment partner you want and are not only seeking a cash infusion.

To allow a business concept to be developed, the production of a business plan to be completed, prototypes to be made or additional research conducted, a company may seek seed capital. Seed capital is usually a smaller amount and is often supplied by business angels. For companies that are beyond the product development stage and want to initiate early stage commercial manufacturing and sales, or expand a business, a substantially larger investment may be needed. Early-stage financing can be around £500,000; expansion financing around £1m and management buy-outs and buy-ins around £5m.

The process for investment, however, is similar. Whether the amount sought is £100,000 or £10m, the amount of time and effort venture capital firms have to spend in appraising the business proposal prior to investment is the same. For this reason, medium-sized to larger investments are more attractive for venture capital investment, as the total size of the return, rather than the percentage, is likely to be greater than with smaller investments.

Professional advisers – such as accountants or solicitors – are often used to give guidance in developing business plans and approaching investors. Advisers' fees can vary greatly depending on the complexity of the transaction, but typically this charge will be around 5% of the money being raised.

## Pitching for investment

When the business plan has been prepared and it has received input from a financial adviser, the next step is to put it in front of venture capital firms. At this point, it is worth considering only sending a copy of the executive summary. This has the advantage of saving costs and increasing the chances of receiving attention.

You may want to also include a confidentiality letter for the venture capital firm to sign, but generally a confidentiality letter is only sent

*"This due diligence process is used to sift out any skeletons or fundamental problems that may exist"*

after an investor requests to see the full business plan. You can obtain a standard confidentiality letter from the BVCA. It bears noting, however, that BVCA members are bound by a code of conduct, which states that they will respect confidential information supplied to them by companies looking for funding.

While receiving the actual funds can take three to six months, you could receive a response from a venture capital firm on a business plan within a week or so. If the answer is no, you should find out the reasons why and then consider incorporating those ideas into a revised business plan, changing/strengthening the management team or carrying out further market research before approaching other potential investors.

If the venture capital firm commissions external advisers to look over a plan, don't be alarmed. It usually means that the investors are seriously considering investing in the business. This due diligence process is used to sift out any skeletons or fundamental problems that may exist.

## Valuing your business

In order to receive funding, you should be aware of how valuable your company is. Calculate the value of the company in comparison with similar companies on the stock market.

**WANT TO KNOW MORE ...**

British Venture Capital Association (BVCA)

www.bvca.co.uk

The key to calculation is to establish an appropriate price/earnings (p/e) ratio for your company. The p/e ratio is the multiple of profits after tax attributed to a company to establish its capital value. The calculated value of a company will give the venture capital firm their required rate of return over the period they anticipate being shareholders. For their part, venture capital firms think in terms of a target overall return from their investments.

Generally return refers to the annual internal rate of return (IRR), and is calculated over the life of the investment. The returns required would depend upon several factors, such as the perceived risk, length of time the money will be tied up, how easily the investment will be realised and how many other venture capital firms are interested in the deal. As a rough guide, the average rate of return will exceed 20% per annum.

For your part, you must have already invested or be prepared to invest some of your own capital in the company to demonstrate a personal financial commitment to the venture.

## Life after funding

After you have received the funding from an investor, the relationship with the venture capital firm has not ended. Venture capital firms can offer fledgling companies much more than funding, and the non-financial input by the venture capital firm is a very important contributor in the growth and success of companies.

Of the venture-backed companies analysed in a survey conducted on behalf of the BVCA and Coopers & Lybrand, 88% said they had benefited from their venture capital backers providing more than just money. Often venture capital executives have a depth of experience and professional contacts that can assist you.

Levels of support from venture capital firms vary from hands-on to hands-off. Hands-on investors will aim to be a business partner, advising on strategy and development as well as offering helpful ideas and discussion. Often hands-on investors will expect to participate through a seat on a company's board and may be suitable for companies embarking on rapid expansion. Usually, they will leave day-to-day management alone.

Hands-off investors will have a less active role in the business. Essentially, these investors will leave management to run the business until it is time to exit, but they will expect to receive regular financial information. If a company defaults on payments, does not meet agreed targets or runs into other types of difficulties, a hands-off investor is likely to turn into a hands-on one.

In reality, however, most venture capitalists operate somewhere in between the two, and many believe start-ups in particular should use the experience of a venture capital firm.

*"Venture capital firms can offer fledgling companies much more than funding"*

### What to do next

- Consider funding options carefully and assess whether you actually need outside investment or not. Some businesses grow organically so it's not essential to attract investment. It really depends on the individual business

- Decide whether you want to go down the debt or equity finance route. If you're not willing to give up shares in your company you'll need debt finance

- Make sure your business plan is rock solid, and you know it inside out, before you start pitching for finance

- Don't take rejection personally. Ask for feedback and try to apply this to your next pitch. Sometimes the bank manager or a business angel can identify weaknesses in your plan which you should address

## ↪ CHAPTER 7

*People, premises and suppliers*

 What's in this chapter?

- → Do you need premises?
- → Determining what you need
- → Equipping your office
- → Taking on staff
- → The recruitment process
- → Your obligations as an employer
- → Finding and dealing with suppliers
- → Insuring your business

Once you've put your idea through its paces, crafted a killer business plan, chosen the perfect name and structure for your venture and worked out how you will fund it, you are almost ready to start trading. Before you do, there are some other key areas that you may well need to address.

This chapter will help you get everything in place for a successful launch, from finding the right premises for your business to working out your recruitment needs, hiring the right staff and understanding your obligations as a new employer.

Your new business may also need stock. Read on for advice on how to find wholesalers – often an elusive bunch – and get the best deals, along with key information on insuring your business.

# Do you need premises?

Finding the appropriate home for your business can be time consuming and, once you've found the right place, it can be a key expense for your company. It can however cost you very little if you can simply rent a desk in another company's office, or if you decide to work from home. So before you do anything else, decide on the kind of premises you will need to launch your business – or indeed, whether you need dedicated premises at all.

For some people, the chance to move into commercial premises provides a more professional outlook, greater scope for expansion and the room to accommodate permanent staff. However, many businesses may find that this is more than they can afford, and this may not even suit the nature of their company.

Furthermore, the nature of modern business means that home-working is an increasingly feasible option for early-stage entrepreneurs, and many start-up businesses begin life in their founders' homes. Of course, this will not be appropriate for every type of business, but if you can make it work it can be an effective way to keep your start-up costs down while you get your venture off the ground and build up your client base.

So, if running your business from home is an option, it's crucial that you make an informed decision on whether – or when – to move into a dedicated office (or other commercial premises). To help you make that decision, here are 10 key questions to ask yourself before committing to office space.

## 1. Do I need an employee?

This might seem basic, but it's a crucial consideration. If you've reached the stage where you need someone to work alongside or beneath you, it's probably wise to start looking for office space. The people you live with are unlikely to enjoy having to share their home with an outsider, and things could get very cramped!

## 2. Do I hold lots of meetings?

No matter how nice your home is, it's generally good practice to hold meetings in an office, rather than your front room. If you have lots of clients who demand face-to-face meetings, it's probably prudent to invest in office space as soon as possible.

## 3. Do my clients need to come and see me?

For some businesses, such as lawyers, accountants and physios, most clients either want, or need, to come in for face-to-face appointments. Other businesses, such as advertising firms, may be able to service their clients while hardly ever meeting them in the flesh. If you're constantly receiving clients, it's probably best you invest in an office; but if not, you may well be ok running your business from home.

## 4. What sort of image do I want to convey?

If your business is based on a quaint, homely image, it may be disastrous for your profile if you move into an office; conversely, if everything you do is sleek, grandiose and cutting-edge, people might not take you seriously if you work from home. Remember that your office is a tangible part of your marketing and brand; you need to think about the image you want to convey, and work out what sort of premises would support that image.

## 5. Do I have retained customers?

A steady stream of repeat customers gives you the regular, reliable income you need to pay rent, bills and other office overheads. On the other hand, if your business veers from feast to famine, it is almost impossible to tell how much money you'll be bringing in each month – and you could end up sweating over keeping up with your office payments.

## 6. Can I maximise my potential?

It's not just about the possibility of failure – you also need to consider what will happen if things go well. If your business suddenly improves dramatically, will you be able to service the demand from your home base? If you can't cash in from home, you may be hampering your long-term chances by staying there.

## 7. Am I getting distracted?

If you keep being distracted by the temptations of radio, television or other household appliances, it's probably best you get out of there! Moving into an office could significantly reduce the distractions you face, and encourage a professional attitude with little time-wasting.

### 8. Have I become complacent?

When it comes to doing business, it's easy to go from a routine into a rut; you become too familiar with your customer base, and the demands of your company, and you stop going the extra mile to make your company the best it can be. If you think you're stuck in a rut, and complacency is setting in, it may well be time to take your business up a notch. Moving into an office can be a great way of doing this.

### 9. Can I afford the market rate?

The cost of renting an office will vary wildly, depending on where you live. If you live in a particularly affluent area, it may be hard to afford the rental prices on local commercial premises. If you think you're going to struggle, it's best to stay where you are.

### 10. Am I in it for the long haul?

For some people, running their own business is a lifetime plan. For others, such as freelancers in between permanent jobs, or ex-students who have just finished uni and are looking for some quick cash, it's only a fleeting venture. If you don't think you want to be your own boss long-term, don't shell out for office space.

## *Determining what you need*

*"One overriding factor dominates the priorities of start-up businesses looking for premises, and that's cost"*

If your business dictates that you are going to need dedicated premises to operate from, knowing the type of property you need – office, workshop, shop, etc – is merely the beginning. You also need to consider the location and available transport links, and then ask yourself questions such as how important common areas are to you and what standard of facilities you need, such as bathroom, storage, meeting room, kitchen, delivery access and so on.

One overriding factor dominates the priorities of start-up businesses looking for premises, and that's cost. There is usually an overwhelming temptation to go for the cheapest property, but this is often a mistake that can take decades to rectify – and even bring a promising business to its knees. Ironically, some people swing too far in the other direction, committing themselves to a heavy initial outlay because they believe image is vital – and image doesn't come cheap. So finding the right premises is the real secret. That can, and will, vary enormously according to the type of business. But there are some general rules that apply to any operation.

## Location

Location is an important consideration for all new businesses. A key factor when deciding where to locate your business is whether you need passing trade, or whether customers will come looking for you. Rents fall quickly within yards of main roads. Offices are even more flexible, particularly if most business is done on the phone. Manufacturing and storage relies heavily on access, so think about how vans and lorries will deliver and collect goods. Nearby parking can be important, but as traffic restrictions tighten, public transport may be even more so.

If you are starting up a retail shop, it's crucial to get the location right, as it will determine your business activity, and can also define your image. Should you head straight for the high street and aim to directly attract customers as they walk past, or should you locate on the edge of town or just off the main shopping avenue, because there are better parking facilities? Alternatively, should you head out of town altogether and follow the larger stores into a retail park, but pay more rent?

When deciding, consider what sort of shop you are and the kind of customers you are going to be targeting, then research possible locations in terms of how accessible it is to your target market, how much competition exists there and how much it will cost you. For example, if you run a sandwich bar or café, are the customers in the high street the ones who will buy takeaway snacks? Will they be able to afford your prices? What is the footfall or number of passers-by that will walk in or past your shop? How visible is your store compared to those of your competitors, and how easy is your business to get to?

## Size

Size is another crucial factor. Health and safety laws provide basic guidance on how much space is needed per office desk or manufacturing process, but it will pay to allow for growth. After all, the whole point of business is to expand, so try to be flexible. Although you may think this will cost more, bear in mind that today's outgoings must be balanced against the prospects of tomorrow's earnings.

## Growth

Almost every small business aims to become a big business, but this
prospect can be choked from birth if the wrong decisions are made. Building
in flexibility at the start can be important. Can a building be physically
altered internally, by knocking down walls, extending outwards or upwards?
Is there spare land next door for expansion? It can be important to make
agreements with landlords from the outset about what will be allowed
and how much extra will be charged on top of the cost of rebuilding or
alteration.

Demand for office space has declined during the downturn, which should
give you some room to negotiate with the landlord over what alterations
you can make and any additional fees. Planning rules must also be
considered, as local authorities are not always open to discussion about
the future of premises. They may have rigid rules about increasing density
of development, or buildings may be in a conservation area or near housing,
in which case it will be much more difficult to consider changes.

## Use of premises

You must also consider restrictions on potential alterations in how
premises may be used – even where no physical changes to the premises
are required. Lease conditions and planning rules are usually quite specific
about what goes on within a building. For example, you can't change a shop
into an office, or vice versa, without permission from the local authority
and landlord. Even switching from one type of shop to another can
sometimes fall foul of planning restrictions. So you will need to assess all
the options and regulations before signing on the dotted line.

Most leases overflow with restrictions on how buildings can be used. This
is partly to protect the landlord's investment by, for instance, preventing
dangerous or noisy activities. There may also be covenants from the original
ground landlord on types of business activity, as well as local planning
restrictions. Sub-letting is commonly denied without the permission of the
landlord. If a lease contains too many of these caveats, it can restrict your
ability to pass on the lease to another tenant when you want to move on.

## Redecoration and repair

Designating when, where, and how often redecoration and repair should
take place, and who should do it, can be a crucial factor, particularly for

older premises, where hefty costs may be involved. Furthermore, many modern leases load most of these onto tenants, and landlords usually demand power to carry out the work at your expense if it is not done on time and to a required standard. Tenants also face what are called dilapidations schedules at the end of their lease term, where the landlord can demand payment where premises haven't been kept in good condition.

## Length of lease

A tradition has grown up in the UK for long leases. At one time, these ran for as long as a century, but the term has gradually been eroded to between 10 and 15 years. These generally apply to new buildings or those in high-demand city centres. Much shorter terms can be found – or negotiated – nowadays, as landlords are adjusting to conditions where tenants are unwilling to commit themselves for such long periods. Three to five years is generally considered a good compromise between a landlord seeking security of investment and small businesses unsure of their future.

For financial reasons, a landlord may prefer to maintain the lease length at 10 years, but allow a break clause. This effectively means the tenant can leave after, say, three or five years. On the other hand, it also means that the landlord can demand this break even when a tenant does not want to move, causing expense and disruption.

## Security of tenure

Many businesses may feel more secure with longer leases. They are usually assured of this by the 1954 Landlord and Tenant Act, which gives them the right to a new lease when the existing one expires. But sometimes these conditions do not apply. Serviced premises are one example, along with a sub-lease situation or older buildings in temporary use pending redevelopment. Others may seek the freedom to get out of their commitment. Watch out for restrictions on sub-letting or assigning a lease, which are common, as landlords usually like to keep control of who is using their buildings. Be aware that this may involve you paying someone a premium to take on the responsibility for a lease. One crucial factor when taking on an assignment, which means paying a fee to the existing leaseholder to take over their lease, is whether that lease is subject to an archaic rule called 'privity of contract'. Until the law was changed in 1996, a tenant remained responsible for rent and other charges even after assignment of the lease to a new tenant.

## *Alternatives*

There are options outside renting premises through a traditional lease:

- ⇢ Serviced offices – these are becoming commonplace as more investors plough into this growing sector. This involves a contract rather than a lease, running for terms ranging from a few hours to several months. The charges may appear high compared with usual rents, but include all services such as heating, lighting, security and business rates. Offices sometimes come complete with furniture and carpets.

- ⇢ Serviced industry – this sector is growing as landlords find it more difficult to attract tenants to older industrial space. The same terms apply as serviced offices, with an all-in monthly charge for rent and services.

## *Before you start the search*

*"The current economic climate means landlords are far more open to negotiating rates than they have been for a number of years, so be prepared to haggle"*

Having decided on the building details, there are a few things to bear in mind before you start your search. Although landlords used to give few choices, today's business environment is less certain and the market has responded by providing a range of options to suit small firms. Consider your business' financial model, and decide on your growth plans and the amount of money you want to spend. This will give you guidance on the services you want the landlord to include in the package, those you wish to pay for and the length of the lease term that suits you best.

So, before you start your research, calculate your budget, including one-off costs for items such as furniture and IT equipment, as well as ongoing costs such as rates and service charges. Remember again that the current economic climate means that landlords are far more open to negotiating rates than they have been for a number of years, so be prepared to haggle as it could save your business valuable funds both now and in the future.

There are many ways to find potentially appropriate units – through commercial agents, online searches, local newspapers and even just walking around. Then comes the really important stage – the viewings. At this stage try and think about questions that go beyond the obvious:

- ⇢ Can you control the room's temperature?

- ⇢ Is the building well maintained and watertight?

Once you've found a property that meets all your criteria (including, of course, your budget), remember the following:

- ⇢ Check out the landlord before you agree to take the space
- ⇢ Talk to other tenants in the building to establish their reputation, and ask for a copy of their 'customer service charter', as you need to know how responsive they will be if anything goes wrong. If they don't have one, take that as a warning sign!
- ⇢ Clarify what the monthly payment covers (for example rent only, or are some utilities included?).
- ⇢ Confirm what services the landlord is contractually obliged to give.

Before signing the first offer that you are presented with, try to negotiate, because you may be able to achieve a rent-free period, for example. Lastly, rethink the whole process to help you finally decide if this is the right space for your business and for your customers. This will be your last chance to change your mind without it potentially costing you money, so ask yourself these key questions:

- ⇢ Are you sure you can afford both the direct and indirect costs?
- ⇢ Are you happy with the landlord?
- ⇢ Do you understand the deal and what you are committing to?

Once you've done your homework and you feel confident that you are getting a fair deal, you should move to secure the space.

## Getting the right help

The cost and plethora of potential problems means buying, leasing and selling property can absorb huge amounts of your time, and at worst, lead to bankruptcy before you are even off the ground. So it's advisable to take specialist advice from a chartered surveyor or a valuer. Just as lawyers know the law, surveyors know bricks and mortar. There are different types of surveyor and valuer who can help:

- ⇢ One group are effectively agents and know all about availability, rents and prices. It may be worth employing one to find the right space.

Building surveyors specialise in the nitty-gritty of construction. They can organise a new-build or inspect existing buildings for potential faults. Another skill lies in analysing the average 40-page lease a landlord will expect. Or they can take over negotiations on rent reviews, rating appeals and planning applications. Use an expert with letters after their name. Professional organisations award these, such as the Royal Institution of Chartered Surveyors (RICS). Ask in advance how much it will all cost. Then, after taking a deep breath, consider how quickly such fees will be saved in making the right choice or winning a cut in the asking price.

**WANT TO KNOW MORE ...**
Royal Institution of Chartered Surveyors (RICS)
www.rics.org.uk

## *Equipping your office*

*"Office or workspace-making can be as rewarding as home-making, but it can also be just as stressful"*

Once you've chosen your premises and completed the formalities, the next step will be preparing your workspace for business, making sure that it has the necessary equipment to allow you to run your company. It's also important to think carefully about the layout, as this will directly affect your ability to operate. Office or workspace-making can be as rewarding as home-making, but you are likely to have only a limited amount of time to do this as you will start paying rent from the moment you've signed the contract, so it can also be just as stressful.

If you are manufacturing a product, then your workspace is likely to be your workshop, so you will need to get all the necessary equipment installed and make sure that you adhere to statutory health and safety guidelines. Your industry association should point you in the right direction for your specific requirements.

**WANT TO KNOW MORE ...**
Health and Safety Executive
www.hse.gov.uk

If you simply have an office – if you have a workshop you may also have an area set aside for this purpose – think carefully about the equipment you will need to keep your business running smoothly, from technology such as telephones and IT to desks and chairs. Health and safety should also be a priority, particularly if you are employing people, and the Health and Safety Executive will be able to provide you with the necessary guidelines. The last thing you want in the early stages of starting your business is to find yourself liable for damages following a workplace accident involving one of your staff (or customers for that matter). Guidance on insuring your business is covered later in this chapter.

If you will be dealing with customers face-to-face, it's vital to make sure that your office reflects the values of your business and doesn't deter customers. So put some careful thought into décor – having spent time and effort thinking about the vision and values of your company for your business plan, your premises should reflect them. Of course, if you are opening a shop or a restaurant, for example, this is one of the most important facets of your business. This also involves key elements such as signage, which must be consistent with your brand image and logo, and must complement your marketing materials. Positioning is also vital here, particularly if you are looking to attract custom to your premises.

You may do some of the décor preparation yourself, as well as installing some of the equipment. However, to ensure your premises look pro-fessional, it could well be worth using decorators, builders and office installation companies. If you will be doing this, plan well in advance, as you will not only pay for the work, but also for any delay in getting your business up and running. Recommendations from friends and other businesses, and reputable trade federations, are a good way of sourcing the best companies in your area.

To prevent overspending or misjudging the equipment you will need, think carefully about this well in advance and make a comprehensive list of the items you require. Then consider the best places to source them. Be as economical as you can, but go for quality as well. Decide for which items you need to go for the 'Rolls Royce' option, because, say, they directly determine the quality of product or service you offer, and for which you can choose the 'Volkswagen' – reliable. Always look for good value and never be tempted to go for poor quality, as this is likely to end up being a false economy, with an item letting you down at a crucial time. Check out what can be bought second-hand and whether there are special online markets or exchanges for your particular sector.

*"Check out what can be bought second-hand and whether there are special online markets or exchanges for your sector"*

Security is an area you shouldn't look to cut back on. If your premises don't look impenetrable, it'll just attract thieves. For recommendations on what precautions to take, call your local police station. The police will usually come and survey your premises, and will probably also recommend a good local security company to do the work for you – and testimonials don't come better than that.

Finally, although it may sound obvious, don't overlook utilities, such as heating, lighting and water. Effective air conditioning, for example, can help make your working environment more pleasant throughout the year.

# *Taking on staff*

As well as finding the right premises, staffing is another key area for small businesses. You may feel that you can start and run a small business all by yourself. But there will usually be some areas you can't handle – we're not all salespeople, for example. The first thing to do is identify what skills and experience your company needs to grow and make it a success. Then you can start to work out who you need to recruit for a successful launch and what your requirements will be in the short and long term.

## Guidelines on equal opportunities legislation

Throughout the recruitment process, you should be fully aware of equal opportunities legislation (primarily the Equality Act 2010, which consolidated and replaced existing anti-discrimination legislation such as the Race Relations Act and the Disability Discrimination Act).

This means understanding how discrimination can occur – even unintentionally – throughout the recruitment process. For instance, in 2006 anti-ageism legislation made it illegal to overlook job candidates because of their age. Be aware that some job advertisements may discourage particular groups from even applying for the vacancy. For example, an advertisement calling for 'vibrant' or 'thrusting' personnel is implicitly ageist as it will deter older candidates who will associate these words with youthfulness. Also, untrained interviewers can form very subjective opinions on the basis of entirely irrelevant criteria – such as background or appearance.

*Unlawful discrimination*
You are not allowed to express a preference in terms of the gender, age or race of the candidate (or regarding any 'protected characteristics' in the Equality Act – the others are: disability, religion or belief, sexual orientation, gender reassignment, marriage and civil partnership, and pregnancy and maternity), as this is discrimination.

*Genuine occupational requirement*
You are only allowed to state a preference for a man or woman, for instance, if you can produce a genuine occupational requirement (GOR) saying why it must be a man or woman, for example, if you need a man for cleaning male toilets. The same applies where any of the above protected characteristics are concerned, although in most cases this would be extremely hard to justify.

To be on the safe side and to protect yourself against potential discrimination claims, the Department for Business, Innovation and Skills (BIS) recommends seeking legal advice before advertising the job if you believe there is a GOR.

Ideally, as your company grows, you should monitor the applications received to make sure that you are attracting applicants from a cross-section of society, with sufficient numbers from diverse groups and sections. Also, the entire selection process should be monitored to ensure that selection occurs on the basis of objective criteria related to the job requirements – and nothing else.

Of course, you also need to honestly assess what you can reasonably manage without the expertise of others by relying on your own resources. This is something you should have addressed in your business plan (see Chapter 3), along with defining the exact nature of your product or service and its marketplace, and how to recognise the problems of that market. All of this will help you to decide what additional people and skills you may require. It will also show you where your own strengths lie.

It's vital to be strictly honest about your strengths and weaknesses, and this should be an ongoing process: continuous improvement comes through continuous monitoring. Practically speaking, you can learn to market your own product – after all you are the expert on it – and you can run the office and develop new custom. But if, for example, on top of this you are spending far too much time struggling to balance the books, it's probably time to pay someone else to do this, most likely on a part-time basis.

*"It's vital to be honest about your strengths and weaknesses"*

## The recruitment process

If you get the recruitment process right, you virtually eliminate the risk of hiring the wrong person for the job. On the other hand, getting the process wrong means you won't attract applications from suitable candidates and will be much less able to spot them during the selection process. Recruitment is not just about meeting immediate vacancies, but should be seen as part of an overall organisational strategy for sourcing personnel. Once you fill one vacancy, you should be left with a list of candidates who you would consider for the same or other vacancies in the future. This makes the process much easier the next time around.

A recruitment exercise exposes your company to a wide section of the public. These people could be current or potential clients, customers

*"Recruitment shouldn't just cover immediate vacancies, but should be seen as part of an overall organisational strategy for sourcing personnel"*

or suppliers. What's more, people talk. If a job applicant has had an unfavourable experience with your company, you can be sure that they will tell others about it. Hence it's vital that the recruitment process creates a positive impression of your company while at the same time enabling you to find the right person to launch your business effectively.

## The job profile

Define the role (job profile) and the person required (person specification) as accurately as you can in order to attract the right people. It also helps if you have a clear idea of the kind of person you need and the actual work involved. When listing skill requirements, only mention those actually related to the position. Similarly, when stating prior experience needs, think about how much is strictly necessary for the candidate to do the job well. You may ideally want your new employee to be an office whizz and highly trained in all things, but consider the competencies they actually need for the position offered.

## The advertisement

Once you have prepared a profile, draw up a clear but brief recruitment advertisement. This should include:

- → The job requirements.
- → The criteria for applicants.
- → The salary package.
- → The length of the contract.
- → A short description of your organisation.
- → The job location.
- → The application procedure (do people apply in writing, by phone, or fill in an application form?).

Where you advertise will depend on the type of position offered. Surveys show that specialist and trade publications work best for managerial and professional posts. Meanwhile, advertisements for skilled workers give best results when placed in the local press. The internet as a recruitment tool is also becoming more and more popular, and can be very cost-effective, so it will pay for you to research the online options available. Some trade magazines, for example, will offer to put your vacancy online as part of their recruitment advertisement package. There is more on where to place your advertisement later in this chapter.

## Where to look for staff

Once you've drawn up the profile of the person you are looking for and written a draft of the advertisement, there are four main routes to making contact. Each has its pros and cons.

### Local newspaper

Everyone looking for a job knows the day the job pages come out. It's the one day that is guaranteed to be a big seller for a local paper, as everyone from national to one-man-band companies vie to attract new staff. It isn't the cheapest form of recruitment, but you are guaranteed to get a sizeable response. Most locals told startups.co.uk that smaller companies didn't need to put an advertisement in for more than one week to get a more than adequate choice of applicants.

Prices vary from region to region, but the procedure is largely the same. You fax or email through the text of your advert (over the phone there is too much risk of misspelling), and the recruitment classified desk will call you back to discuss options. If you've never placed an advertisement before, don't worry, they will go through with you how big the advertisement should be and how long it should appear to attract a certain response, and then calculate the cost.

The simplest advertisements might be charged by lineage, for example £17 per line plus VAT, where each line will fit three or four words. You wouldn't be able to say a great deal or have a company logo, but it would get the message across. So typically, a small advertisement in a local paper will cost in the region of £300. Many local papers are part of a wider syndicate, so you might also be able to get your advertisement in more than one paper. For example, some local papers have a more business-orientated journal, which can be helpful if you are looking to reach that market. This is again something the classified department will be able to help you with.

**Pros**: This is possibly the best way to access your region, as the local paper on job day is still the first port of call for many people.

**Cons**: This is not a very targeted approach, as the paper goes to everyone and unless you make your advertisement specific, you might have to wade through lots of unsuitable applicants.

Check with your local newsagent which paper people buy for jobs in your area and which day is job day – it's usually Thursday.

### Jobcentre Plus

Jobcentre Plus has more than 1,000 Jobcentres nationwide that can help you find recruits for a whole range of positions and sectors, either locally or nationwide in some cases. It doesn't cost anything to post a vacancy, and you can benefit from support both before and after the position is filled.

Services offered by Jobcentre Plus include advice on recruitment methods and procedures, information about the local labour market such as employment levels, availability of candidates and wage rates, and advice on any difficulties or barriers to filling your vacancies.

When posting a job, you will need to provide full details of the vacancy, including location, wages, hours and any qualifications you expect candidates to have. It is also important to file any other details such as whether a driving licence will be required. This will help to avoid wasting your and your candidate's time later on.

The details of the job are entered into a computer system that jobseekers can either access themselves or through a consultant at the Jobcentre, and posted on the http://jobseekers.direct.gov.uk website.

**WANT TO KNOW MORE …**
Employer Direct Online
www.businesslink.gov.uk

You can now post, view and update your jobs yourself through Employer Direct online. You can also email your vacancies at any time to employerdirect-vacancies@jobcentreplus.gsi.gov.uk.

**Pros**: You can use the Jobcentre as a base for interviews and the consultants are always on hand to help. It is also free.

**Cons**: It can be a time-consuming process as you are relying on people coming into the Jobcentre to see your adverts, or searching on the Directgov website.

### Online recruitment

You don't have to be an online company to think about recruiting via the web. Often if you place a newspaper advertisement with a local paper, they will have a package to post your advertisement on an affiliated website. But there are also dedicated websites: Monster.co.uk, Stepstone and easyJobs are some of the ones available, where both potential employees and employers can search online. The idea is that you save time by cutting out the middleman, using the website instead. With Monster, for example, you can potentially deal with the whole process online. You log on, post your vacancy and pay for it using your credit card. For a small business, you will probably choose the one-off option, which costs £360 and will post your advertisement for up to 60 days.

**Pros:** Once you are registered you can control the job advertisements yourself, taking them down when you have enough applicants. There is also the added bonus of a team on hand to help you out with any problems. Moreover, you can reach a much wider audience, nationally and possibly Europe-wide, without going through agents.

**Cons:** People are unlikely to see the job as easily as they might in a newspaper when scanning the advertisements. Websites rely on people searching.

## *Recruitment agencies*

There are a lot of recognisable high-street recruitment agencies, including Select, Travail, Manpower, Hays and Reed, which can provide you with both part-time and permanent staff. In theory, they all deal with every level of company, from small operations to national businesses. There are also many industry-specific recruitment agencies. With most agencies you can choose how to contact them initially – by phone, email or in person at your local branch. You will then need to provide details of what type of staff you are looking for and the kind of salary you plan to pay. Agency staff will advise you on the current employment rates if you are not sure, or indeed if your estimate is over or under the odds. It is also likely that you will have to undergo some kind of credit check so the agency knows you can pay the bill.

If you don't have premises, you can hold your interviews at the agency, but they will need to come and view your offices to check they are suitable for the potential employee. It also helps for them to see the culture of your company, the people and environment to help match the applicants. Once you have agreed exactly what the job description is and what the conditions and the salary are, you will have to sign an agreement. This just ensures that the candidate is getting the job they have applied for. But it is important from your point of view that you have the position clearly defined at this stage to avoid difficulties later. This is also important when

**WANT TO KNOW MORE ...**

**Jobsite**
www.jobsite.co.uk

**Monster**
www.monster.co.uk

**Stepstone**
www.stepstone.co.uk

**easyJobs**
www.easyjobs.com

**WANT TO KNOW MORE ...**

**Hays**
www.hays.co.uk

**Manpower**
www.manpower.co.uk

**Reed**
www.reed.co.uk

**Select Appointments**
www.select.co.uk

**Travail Employment Group**
www.travail.co.uk

the agency fee is set. They may take a percentage of the candidate's annual salary, say 20%. However, the amount will vary according to the level the person is coming in at and how hard they were to find.

After you have recruited someone, there will probably be a period during which the fee is refundable – but only a few months. So it is in your interests not only to choose carefully but also to work with the agency to ensure you and your new staff member are happy in the first three months. That way, it will be money well spent not wasted.

**Pros:** If the agency wants your fee, it is in their interests to find you someone good, therefore you should receive decent support and guidance.

**Cons:** As part of the process your finances and premises will be investigated and questioned if not up to standard.

## Action points

### Make sure you have the people and the skills to launch successfully

☑ **Identify the skills your company needs to succeed:** Carefully look at the various functions required for the successful running of your business from administration to sales and marketing.

☑ **Assess which of these you and your existing workforce can realistically cover:** If you already have staff on board, honestly assess who can handle the various functions and the skills necessary.

☑ **Work out the skills gaps:** Make a list of the remaining functions to gauge where help is needed.

☑ **Decide on how many people you will need to take on:** Look at the functions and skills needed and assess how many people will be required to plug the gaps and whether they'll be recruited on a freelance, part-time or full-time basis.

☑ **Kick-off the recruitment process:** Draw up the necessary job descriptions and decide how to reach the people you need.

## The response

All applications to job advertisements should be replied to. Remember they could well be or know clients. The sooner the response, the better, as this shows your company is efficient and interacts well with the public. Remember too that all applications – even unsolicited ones – are confidential.

## The criteria

Even if the response to your advertisement is overwhelming, don't eliminate candidates on the basis of certain self-selected criteria such as geographical proximity to your office. You could easily miss the application from your ideal employee. Instead, use a checklist of *essential criteria*, based on the job profile and person specifications you compiled earlier. It's surprisingly easy to let personal prejudice slip in, so it's best to be aware of this possibility at all times.

Stay objective. You could try using a points system to screen applications based on every core skill requirement spotted. This lends a broad and more objective method to the process.

# *Your obligations as an employer*

Part of the process of building your team is recognising your responsibilities as an employer. This involves making sure that you are up to speed with all the relevant employer legislation, so that you avoid any legal problems – which can be quite severe – and treat your staff fairly. Gaining a reputation for being a good employer will pay dividends in the long run as it will help you attract the best talent. Here are some pointers (for more details, contact the Department for Business, Innovation and Skills).

*"Gaining a reputation for being a good employer will pay dividends in the long run as it will help you attract the best talent"*

## Equal opportunities

Just as when you are recruiting, your workforce should be treated equally, regardless of race, nationality, gender, sexual orientation, religious belief, age or marital status. Also, you shouldn't discriminate against a disabled person because of their disability, either directly or by failing to make 'reasonable adjustments' to working conditions. For free information about equality at work, contact the ACAS Equality Direct helpline, a confidential equality advice service for small businesses (see contacts below).

## Terms and conditions of employment

All employees should be given a written contract so that the terms of employment are clear. By law, an employer must at least provide a written statement of particulars to an employee within two months of them starting work, even if employment ends beforehand. In practice, most employers choose to include this statement with the main contract of employment when a new member of staff joins. This statement should include:

- Names of the employer and employee.
- The employee's start date.
- The date on which continuous employment began.
- Job title and a brief job description.
- The place(s) of work and employer's address.
- The scale or rate of remuneration and intervals at which it is paid.
- Hours of work.
- Holiday entitlement.
- Sickness entitlement.
- Details of pension scheme.
- Length of notice which the employee must give or is entitled to receive.
- Where employment is not permanent, the period it is expected to last or the date on which it is to end.
- Details of disciplinary and grievance procedures.

## Transfer of undertakings (protection of employment) regulations (TUPE)

Employees' terms and conditions are preserved when a business (or part of one) transfers to a new employer.

## Fair and unfair dismissal

If an employee has at least one year's service, they have the right to complain of general unfair dismissal.

## Unions

Employees have the right to belong or not belong to a union, and the right not to be refused employment on the grounds of trade union membership or non-membership.

---

### Period of notice

- For continuous employment of more than one month, but less than two years, one week's notice of termination of employment must be given unless a longer period is stated in the employment contract.
- After two years or more, at least two weeks' notice must be given.
- After two years' employment, one additional week's notice for each further complete year is required.
- After 12 years' continuous employment, a minimum of 12 weeks' notice is required.
- An employee is required to give his or her employer at least one week's notice that they are leaving if employed continuously for one month.
- This minimum is unaffected by longer service, but you may ask for longer in their contract.

---

## Illegal workers

You can face a criminal prosecution if you employ illegal workers and haven't made certain checks on new employees, such as seeing a P45, P60 or payslip showing a National Insurance (NI) number – or one of a range of other specified documents. Copies need to be retained in most cases.

## National Minimum Wage

All employers must adhere to the UK National Minimum Wage, which is £6.08 an hour (£4.98 an hour for 18–20 year olds) as of 1 October 2011.

## Pay and tax

You must inform Her Majesty's Revenue & Customs (HMRC) when you take on your first employee. HMRC will set up a PAYE (pay as you earn) scheme and send you a new employer's starter pack. You should complete a P45 form for each employee or complete a P46, making the necessary tax deductions and sending them in monthly. All employees must be given itemised pay statements showing deductions. National Insurance is payable for employees aged 16 or over earning more than £102 per week (as of April 2011).

In the coalition's Emergency Budget, on 22 June 2010, it was announced that start-ups outside of London, the South East and the East of England will be exempted from NI contributions for their first 10 employees hired during their first year of business, as part of a three-year scheme to boost enterprise in other UK regions.

## Statutory sick pay

If an employee is sick for less than four consecutive days, no action is needed. If the employee is sick for more than four days, and is entitled to statutory sick pay (SSP), you are obliged to pay it in the same way as wages and keep records of payments made and dates of sickness absence. An employee is entitled to SSP if they have average weekly earnings of at least £102. The standard weekly rate for SSP is currently £81.60. If the employee is sick for more than four days, and not entitled to SSP, the employee may claim state incapacity benefit instead.

You can ask your employee to provide some form of medical evidence, such as a 'fit note' from their doctor, after their seventh calendar day of sickness. The fit note (which has replaced the traditional sick note) enables doctors to provide more details about how your employee's condition affects their ability to work. Doctors can now advise whether someone is 'not fit for work' or 'may be fit for work' with some support. They can also suggest ways to help your employee return to work, for example through a gradual return, altered hours or amended duties.

## Statutory maternity leave and pay

Employees have the right to 26 weeks of ordinary maternity leave and 26 weeks' additional leave, making one year of statutory maternity leave in total. Provided your employee gives you the correct notice, they can take statutory maternity leave no matter how long they have worked for you, how many hours they work or how much they are paid. Statutory adoption leave follows the same pattern as statutory maternity leave – however, an employee will qualify if they have worked with you for at least 26 weeks before the beginning of the week they are matched with a child.

Likewise, employees can claim statutory maternity pay (SMP) if on the 15th week before their baby is due (or for statutory adoption pay, the week they are told they have been matched with a child for adoption) they have been employed by you for more than 26 weeks. They must also be earning at least the lower earnings limit for National Insurance, which is £102 a week for the 2011–12 tax year.

Employees can choose to take SMP from the 11th week before the baby is born. They must tell you at least 28 days before they intend to stop work, and you should get them to make this request in writing. They must also provide you with evidence of when their baby is due. This is normally on the maternity certificate MATB1. You should receive this no later than three weeks after the date their SMP begins.

Meanwhile, new fathers are entitled to two weeks' ordinary paternity leave and pay (assuming they have completed 26 weeks' service by the specified time). However, following recent changes to the law, fathers of babies due on or after 3 April 2011 (or notified that they and their partner have been matched with a child for adoption on or after this date) may be entitled to take up to 26 weeks' additional paternity leave if their partner returns to work. The leave can be taken between 20 weeks and one year after their child is born or placed for adoption, and they may also be entitled to receive additional statutory paternity pay.

## Hours

Working hours are limited to an average of 48 hours a week, although workers can choose to work more if they want to (by opting out of the European Working Time Directive). Night-workers' hours are limited to an average of eight hours' work in a 24-hour period, and they have a right to receive free health assessments. All employees have a right to 11 hours' rest a day, a day off each week, and an in-work rest break if the working day is longer than six hours.

## Insurance

If you employ staff you must take out Employers' Liability Insurance and display the necessary certificate. (For more on insuring your business, see later in the chapter.)

**WANT TO KNOW MORE …**

**Department for Business, Innovation and Skills**
www.bis.gov.uk

**ACAS Equality Direct**
☎0845 600 3444

**Health and Safety Executive**
www.hse.gov.uk

### Health and safety

You must register your business with either the Health and Safety Executive (most factories, workshops, etc) or the local authority (most offices, shops and catering businesses).

# Finding and dealing with suppliers

Many businesses are built around selling goods, and as such are reliant on getting these items at the best possible prices, so that they can make more profit on a sale. This is where suppliers or wholesalers come in. If you've never dealt with these kinds of businesses before, you could be surprised as sometimes it can even be difficult to track down the right one. However, this is a relationship that is worth nurturing, as it is key to the success of your new business.

### Finding wholesalers

*"For the modern small business the lack of wholesaling presence on the internet is a cause of great frustration"*

It's not just large firms who make use of wholesalers, but how do you find them in the first place? Thumbing through your *Yellow Pages* or calling a directory service might yield results, but for the modern small business the lack of wholesaling presence on the internet is a cause of great frustration. Wholesalers tend to stick to traditional tried and tested methods – and this includes attitudes, or a lack of them, towards technology such as the web and email.

Relationships between wholesalers and their customer base are often built up over years of loyal service, so suppliers often rely on word of mouth and local knowledge to attract new clients. You are unlikely to come across attention-grabbing advertising from wholesalers in comparison with large retailers. 'It can be very hard for people new to trading to find wholesaler contact information and thus it makes it hard to shop around,' admits wholesaling specialist **Richard Grady**. 'One of the reasons for this is that very few UK wholesalers have decent websites and even fewer have taken any time to ensure their sites are ranked well in internet search engines. This means that if you are looking for suppliers on the internet, it will take ages and you probably won't have much luck,' he warns.

Luckily, this gap in the market has been belatedly acknowledged with several websites and books that point you in the direction of your nearest wholesalers. However, entrepreneurs will still have to do most of the legwork in researching the quality of wholesale products and getting the best value for money. Richard has compiled an online resource to accompany his sought-after e-book, *UK-Trader's UK Wholesale Guide*. Visitors to his website (see contact box) can get details on over 700 wholesalers and gain other relevant information. Alternatively, www.thewholesaler.co.uk has a large wholesale directory, with details on products ranging from fireworks to toiletries.

As websites like these may charge you for membership and access, it can be worth sticking to print publications when looking for your wholesalers. Therefore, a quick flick through *The Trader* magazine (monthly at most newsagents) will reveal plenty of wholesale advertisements, as well as a list of contacts.

**WANT TO KNOW MORE …**

**The UK-Trader**
www.theuktrader.co.uk

**The Trader**
www.thetrader.co.uk

## *Sourcing overseas suppliers*

Many companies look abroad to source cheaper products or raw materials. This approach is definitely worth considering, particularly at the moment when every penny counts. The breaking down of global trade barriers also means that this may be necessary to stay competitive.

If you find a willing supplier selling the product you need at the cheapest possible price, you have to consider the following: how far away the country is; whether there might be compromise on levels of regulation and protection; and how well you will be able to communicate with your chosen supplier should any problems arise. Issues of creditworthiness and reliability are even more important when your supplier is based abroad.

As a general rule, developed countries are easier to trade with than developing ones. If your supplier is from a country in the European Union, for instance, many key regulations and standards will be similar to those in the UK. If a country has high volumes of existing trade with the UK, it probably means other businesses have been successful in establishing relationships with traders there. If this is the case, enquire after good suppliers in your target country from other traders in your sector, go on an overseas trade visit, or attend some foreign-focused trade exhibitions.

In fact, trade shows and expos are among the best places to find new suppliers, but make sure that the event is relevant to your needs, as they can be time-consuming and expensive. To find the appropriate fairs and expos, check out the trade publications associated with your sector, and look online. Websites such as www.exhibitions.co.uk, www.tradeshows.

co.uk, www.biztradeshows.com and www.expocentral.com will point you in the right direction. For international tradeshow listings, visit www.FITA.org.

For an overview on international trade, visit the Business Link website, while for information on potential suppliers, your local UK Trade and Investment (UKTI) team should be your first port of call. The UKTI website also includes an online test to see whether your company is ready to trade with businesses abroad and tips from international trade advisers. It's also worth trying your supplier country's embassy in the UK – you will find contact details on the Foreign & Commonwealth Office website. Furthermore, contact information for your target country's chambers of commerce can be found on the British Chambers of Commerce (BCC) website. Trade associations for your sector will most likely have information regarding suppliers for your industry too. You should be able to find details of trade associations for your industry sector on the Trade Association Forum website.

**WANT TO KNOW MORE …**

Business Link
www.businesslink.gov.uk

UK Trade and Investment
www.uktradeinvest.gov.uk

Foreign & Commonwealth Office website
www.fco.gov.uk

British Chambers of Commerce (BCC) website
www.britishchambers.org.uk

Trade Association Forum
www.taforum.org

Once you find your supplier, make sure you research their reliability. Speak with experienced UK importers or trade associations in your sector so that you have an idea of what to expect. Find out if your supplier has any UK references they can provide and try to visit them, so that you can check out their work and their production systems first-hand.

Make sure you carry out financial checks too. If your supplier cannot furnish you with a credit history, your bank's international trade team may be able to carry out a 'status query', which will investigate the company's financial standing for you. But no matter how clean your supplier's bill of financial health, don't sign a long-term contract straight off or agree to any advance payments until you have built up a relationship of trust.

## Approaching wholesalers

As long as you have proof of trading, which can be as little as a letterhead or business card, you are entitled to deal with a wholesaler. Suppliers need business just as much as you do, so there's little chance you will be turned away. So be confident when approaching them and focus your concerns on getting a good deal for your business. It is important that you actually visit the wholesaler in person because as mentioned above, wholesalers are quite traditional in their practices, and the chances of getting hold of an email address to contact them are slim.

There is, similarly, a limited amount you can do over the telephone. Your supplier will be happy to send you a list of stock and the relevant prices, but to gain a proper understanding of what you are ploughing your wholesaling budget into, it is vital you have a face-to-face meeting.

The time that you actually visit is up to you, but be aware that the busiest time for a wholesaler will be around midday, when shop owners converge to purchase stock for their stores. If you arrive around 4pm, you will have a less frantic search for your goods, as this is the wholesaler's quietest period. You will also benefit from more attention from the wholesale staff, as they will have fewer customers to deal with. The downside is that stock you have turned up to buy may have already gone, so, again, it is vital that you call ahead to check on what stock is still available. Striking the right balance is important, so don't be put off if it takes a few visits before you get it right.

## Phone before you go

Do phone ahead before your visit to save yourself from a wasted journey, as it is best to find out in advance if your wholesaler has the goods you require. Stock changes every day at a wholesaler, so lists you receive a week in advance will be out of date by the time you turn up to purchase the items that you need. Many wholesalers also like to assign certain visiting times for customers to look at stock – this is particularly the case with larger and more popular suppliers. Wholesalers with valuable items that require supervised visits will also need you to call ahead. Policies vary according to the supplier, so check out their procedures before you turn up.

## *Choosing a good wholesaler*

As is common when you are starting up a business, for all the calculations and careful planning, sometimes a good or bad gut instinct can serve you best of all. 'Most people will get a feel for whether they are comfortable with an individual quite quickly and this is often very accurate,' explains wholesaling specialist **Richard Grady**. 'I would tend to be happier dealing with a large wholesaler with pleasant premises and a friendly atmosphere, although, that said, I have also traded with some very good suppliers that have operated from very unpleasant lock-up units on rough industrial estates!'

*"A good wholesaler will take the time to talk to you and listen to your needs"*

Generally speaking, a good wholesaler will take the time to talk to you and listen to your needs. The more they are prepared to do for you suggests that they are reliable and their stock will not let you down – customer service, after all, is essential to wholesalers who rely heavily on repeated visits from shop owners and small firms. On the other side of the coin, if you turn up to a derelict garage and are confronted by a nervous looking 'wholesaler' who thrusts a box of pickles into your hands before snatching your money and speeding off in his GTi to the sound of wailing police sirens, you should maybe consider looking elsewhere for your supplies in the future. So trust your first impressions. If you are not happy you can always change your wholesaler until you find someone you are comfortable dealing with.

## How much should you spend on stock?

*"There is nothing worse than being stuck with a large quantity of stock that you can't sell"*

Before you set off to visit your wholesaler, make sure you have worked out a budget to suit your business' needs and means. Although the need to budget carefully is essential in all aspects of business start-ups, it is particularly important when it comes to buying stock. Working out how much you need of a certain product and how much money to set aside can be a tricky balance to strike. Purchasing too few supplies to satisfy customer demand or keep your business running smoothly means you could end up losing out financially. Buying too much stock means not only will you have a room full of unsold items, you could end up putting your cashflow at risk.

It's also wise to keep some money back, because if you don't, you might miss a bargain or neglect other essential areas of your business. Of the two scenarios, over-spending is the least preferable, as you won't be able to correct your order next time if your firm suffers serious financial damage. So, when working out your budget, err on the side of caution.

'How much you buy in one go depends on what you are purchasing the stock for,' says Richard. 'If you have a large high-street outlet, then you are going to need to buy far more stock than an individual trading part-time from home. Most wholesalers have fairly low minimum orders, say from £50 to £300, and this means that traders can buy in small quantities initially. This is recommended so that you can check that you can actually sell the products. There is nothing worse than being stuck with a large quantity of stock that you can't sell, especially if you have invested all of your capital into it.

'Wholesalers will expect payment with order unless you have a credit account with them. It is not usually appropriate to finance stock purchases with other finance deals or instalments as the purchases would normally be too regular – every couple of weeks or monthly.'

## Wholesaler credit accounts

As a new start-up you shouldn't expect a wholesaler to offer you a credit account with them. You will probably have to make some straightforward purchases with them first. This is generally what wholesalers will expect from you. It may be cheaper to set up a credit account, when you've established yourself with suppliers, than get involved in any finance deals with your bank, and it is best to avoid getting into a never-ending circle of loans and deals to fund your stock purchases.

## *Don't forget about VAT*

Unfortunately, we all have to pay VAT and wholesalers are no different – in fact it is the most common tax you will come across when dealing with your wholesaler. VAT is charged by suppliers of goods and services, and wholesalers certainly fall into the former category. As they are not entitled to any exemptions or a reduced VAT level, wholesalers will charge the standard rate on your purchase, which is currently 20%. What you must be aware of is that many wholesalers price their goods without VAT, so you may be under the impression that you have a brilliant deal when, in fact, you will have a 20% charge slapped on top of it. So the four widescreen televisions you buy for just £1,000 will in fact set you back £1,200.

**WANT TO KNOW MORE …**
For the most up-to-date figure on VAT visit: www.hmrc.gov.uk

'From my experience, it's fair to say that many new traders do forget that the prices displayed by wholesalers won't include VAT,' says wholesaling specialist **Richard Grady**. 'I know of a couple of people that got very excited at the incredibly low deals on offer and got a shock when they got to the till and found another 20% added to the cost.' Although you are obliged to pay the VAT on these, and indeed any other goods, you are entitled to claim the money back if your firm is VAT registered. Input tax (the VAT you pay on raw goods) can be claimed back as part of the legitimate expenses that your business runs up – if you regularly pay more VAT than you collect you can claim this money back on a monthly basis by filling in a return.

To become VAT registered, your firm's turnover must exceed £73,000 a year, although this figure has risen considerably in the past few years.

These increases have been aimed at helping new businesses that cannot deal with the burden of filling out continual VAT forms. However, although small firms often grumble about VAT, you can often save money by registering for it and many businesses voluntarily put their name forward even if they are under the threshold. So, if you are VAT registered and you keep in mind the charge when purchasing, you will be able to shape your budget accordingly to ensure that your cashflow is unaffected.

## Are you guaranteed?

There are no specific guarantees that wholesalers use, although the goods you buy will usually have a manufacturer's warranty, which will be passed to you from the supplier once the transaction is made. A wholesaler should be happy to replace faulty stock, although, legally, they are not bound to do so, unlike high-street stores. Significantly, the regulations that amended the Sale of Goods Act in 2002 did not cover wholesalers. This means that although shops are duty-bound to give refunds or exchanges for faulty goods, wholesalers are not. 'The regulations only cover business-to-consumer transactions, so wholesalers wouldn't be relevant,' says **Martyn Rapley** of the Department for Business, Innovation and Skills. 'However, the main requirements of the Sale of Goods Act . . . are certainly relevant.'

So it's not all bad news if you have, for example, bought 100 solar-powered torches. The original Sale of Goods Act makes it clear that all products sold should be of satisfactory quality and serve the purpose for which they are intended. Most reputable wholesalers offer exchanges or refunds for faulty items, so just because the law now only recognises this right in retailers, this shouldn't damage your chances of getting your money back or getting a decent replacement.

However, a word of warning: the regulations shifted the onus of proving the goods were faulty at the time of purchase to the seller – but only in regard to shops. Wholesalers will still be able to demand that you prove the products were inadequate when you first bought them. Also, if you buy untested goods from a clearance warehouse, they will have no warranty at all and you will run the risk of having a damaged bank balance as well as damaged stock.

## Buying online

As befits their traditional image, wholesalers generally prefer to do their trading on the floor of a warehouse rather than in cyberspace.

Consequently, there are few UK websites dedicated to wholesaling, and even fewer for individual suppliers themselves. However, this is slowly beginning to change and several websites have been created to allow you to purchase goods online, the most common being sites dedicated to selling pallets of items at knockdown prices. 'When buying online, make sure you know exactly what you are purchasing – read the description thoroughly and study any pictures,' says wholesaling specialist **Richard Grady**. 'If you are not sure, contact the supplier for additional information. Nothing beats a visit to the supplier so that you can see the products before making a purchase. Also, use a credit card to make your payment, that way you have a right of recourse via the credit card company if things go wrong.'

Buying batches or pallets of goods online from wholesalers is different from buying on Amazon, for example, as you may not be entirely sure what you are being sold due to the varied goods on offer in a single purchase. Make sure you have a detailed list of what is on offer and contact the wholesaler if you have any queries. Although it is wise to exercise caution when purchasing online, you can make big savings as internet sales can often be much cheaper, due to lower overheads, than traditional warehouse buying.

*"When buying online, make sure you know exactly what you are purchasing"*

## Making a profit

There are several simple steps you can take to make a profit on your wholesale stock:

### Cash payments

Simple cash payments may be the most beneficial for your business, as many wholesalers give discounts (see more on this below) to customers who pay upfront in this way. This method of payment, however, depends greatly on the cashflow situation of your company, and it is important not to risk over-stretching your business by making large cash purchases early on. Try to build up the amount of stock from a low level to begin with, to ensure you can sell all of it on and to save valuable funds for the future.

### Price matching

Once you have a firm idea of the amount of stock your business can sell on, you can 'price match' wholesalers against each other on large orders. Don't be afraid to ask your supplier to compare prices with someone else for you – wholesalers are generally, contrary to their image, approachable and happy to see your business flourish (as well as keen to keep your custom), and will often knock down their prices to a competitor's level.

## Getting discounts

Discounts are given roughly in proportion to the amount of money you spend, much like many other trades that offer such incentives to encourage you to place large orders. Therefore, orders under £200 are generally not going to attract discounts from wholesalers. But don't forget that if you buy goods for the sake of a discount and are left with excess stock and a big hole in your budget you could end up in trouble. So make sure you strike the right balance, meeting your customers' needs without buying too much stock.

## Give it time

Don't be frustrated if you don't see instant profits on your wholesale goods. If you continue to stick to an appropriate budget, shop around for value and strike up a good working relationship with your wholesaler, you should start to see results within a few months. Of course, much of this depends on the size and circumstances of your business, but by sticking to this formula you will be on course to meet the potentially large profits that buying wholesale goods provides.

---

### Startups Tips

**Dealing with wholesalers**

- Get to know the wholesalers that you deal with – this will help you find out when new products are in stock and get the best deals on price.
- Don't be afraid to ask one wholesaler to 'price match' another, especially if you are placing a particularly large order.
- Don't expect huge discounts unless you are buying in huge quantities.
- Start-ups are unlikely to get an instant credit account. Pay cash upfront for a couple of months before requesting credit.
- Don't be intimidated – as most suppliers will be more than happy to help you as much as they possibly can.

# *Insuring your business*

Making sure your company is protected against as many disasters as possible could ultimately save it and protect all the time and effort you are likely to put in to making it a success. However, finding the right business insurance can be a difficult and complex process. There is a certain amount of jargon associated with the area, which can put off many small firms. As an entrepreneur you might see your insurance as one of those unavoidable costs – you don't much like it but you will go along with it. However, for many firms it ends up being their life support. You never know if disaster is lurking around the corner, but it is too late to get cover after the incident has happened.

Insurance is also not an area where one size fits all, so don't buy a policy unless you really need to. However, don't fall into the trap of scrimping on costs, as you might find out that you are not covered when the worst happens. Essentially, it is important to understand your own risks, know what the insurance market has to offer and to thoroughly read and understand any policy before committing to it.

## *Why you need insurance*

Aside from legal requirements and demands from customers to have a certain level of liability, you might well think that there is little point to your insurance policy. However, there are many examples of businesses going to the wall following a disaster for which they weren't covered. Similarly, there are many instances when a company has bounced back after it looked like it had passed the point of no return, all because it was insured to the very hilt.

You might consider the risks that your business faces to be small or even affordable, but if this is the case, then you are probably underestimating them. The chances of your business being hit by a flood or destroyed by a fire might seem low, but disruption to your work can come from many quarters. For example, a crime in your street could lead the police to cordon off the area for a period of time. Despite not being able to trade, you will still have to pay your staff, rent and other costs, and you could lose a very significant amount of business or incur heavy costs while attempting to maintain it. However, all of this could be prevented with a business continuity insurance deal.

As mentioned earlier, some of your clients might ask about your insurance details before they are prepared to do business with you. Public liability is important for many clients, particularly in the public sector. In a business-to-business setting, an insurance policy acts almost like a credential. By having a high level of cover, you are demonstrating that you are a respectable business, which takes health and safety very seriously, and that you fully understand your own responsibilities. So paying for insurance is far from just dead money, but a way of accessing opportunities that you wouldn't otherwise be able to gain.

## Essential cover

There is some insurance that you must have, and this is covered below.

## Employers' liability insurance

Nearly all businesses need some level of liability insurance, and employers' liability insurance is the most common one. If you are about to take on staff then you should ensure you have this first. Also, if you are thinking of setting up a limited company then it is a legal requirement, as technically the company is the employer. If any member of your staff is taken ill, suffers injury or dies and this is deemed to be as a result of their work, then you are potentially liable. Therefore, the law states that you must have cover in order to cope with this eventuality. By law, employers must have at least £5m of liability, although many policies offer £10m. There are just under 400 deaths and nearly 30,000 major injuries at work each year in the UK, so you are well advised not to make any savings in this area.

### Motor insurance

As any driver knows, motor insurance is a legal requirement, but many come unstuck when using vehicles for work-related activities. You might think that your current insurance covers you, but unless your policy includes work use then you are mistaken. The good news is, however, that this isn't usually expensive and some insurers offer it for free. If you are employing someone who is using their own vehicle for work purposes other than travelling to work, then you have a responsibility to ensure they are fully covered. A work purpose could be as innocent as dropping you off at a meeting – it doesn't matter how minor this seems, they still require business insurance. It is also highly advisable to check with the Driver and Vehicle Licensing Agency (DVLA) that your staff are legally able to drive and take copies of their insurance and MOT documents, as well as their driving licences.

**WANT TO KNOW MORE ...**

DVLA
www.dvla.gov.uk

## *Public liability*

Public liability insurance, though not compulsory, is something only the most cavalier business would cut back on. It covers you for damage against property or persons that you might encounter during your work. Many clients won't deal with you or can't legally work with you unless you have it, so you might consider it to be obligatory.

---

 **What to do next**

- Think carefully before securing premises. Make sure you assess exactly what your business needs. Too little or too much space could cost you in the long-run.

- Don't go overboard on equipment if you don't need it. Consider leasing instead of buying if you're worried about cashflow.

- Assess your own shortcomings before recruiting. See where you're lacking in skills and add people with these skills to the team.

- Put together a full job description for everyone you recruit so you know exactly how they fit into the business and where the resources are most needed.

- Remember that you can negotiate with your suppliers on an ongoing basis. The first deal doesn't have to be a permanent one. You can renegotiate terms as you build up trust.

- Don't forget to make your sure your business is adequately insured. It's crucial that you're adequately protected.

---

# CHAPTER 8

*Tax and accounts*

## 📖 What's in this chapter?

→ Bookkeeping
→ Self-employed accounts
→ Registered company accounts
→ Corporation tax
→ VAT
→ Credit control
→ Tackling late payment
→ Hiring an accountant
→ Paying yourself

So, after months of preparation, the time has finally come to open your new company for business.

Key to your early success will be setting up effective processes for invoicing and payment collection – both are crucial for effective cashflow management. You also need to think about setting yourself a realistic salary, not to mention making sure you are meeting all of your tax and filing obligations.

This chapter will look at how to stay on top of your accounts, whether you are a sole trader or have registered your company at Companies House, as well as offering key advice on how to manage your debtors and tackle late-paying clients. Read on to learn why hiring an accountant can be a sound investment – even for start-ups – and what to look for in your number cruncher.

# Bookkeeping

One of the most daunting things about giving up full-time employment to start your own business is the prospect of looking after the company accounts. For an ex-employee who is used to having his or her tax and National Insurance contributions (NICs) deducted at source via PAYE (pay as you earn), the prospect of dealing with the vast, looming shadow that is HM Revenue & Customs (HMRC) can be quite unnerving.

It's tempting to say that there's no need to worry and that the entire bookkeeping process is child's play, but that wouldn't be strictly true. If it were, accountants wouldn't be paid so well. But HMRC is not – perhaps contrary to popular belief – a bullying, authoritarian organisation. On the contrary, its aim is to help businesses manage their accounts as effectively as possible. To this end it publishes regular newsletters and leaflets giving tips and guidance on bookkeeping, and has teams of advisers on hand to help out over the phone should you run into difficulties.

# Self-employed accounts

If you are setting up as a sole trader with no employees, then your bookkeeping work can be kept to a minimum. There's the added advantage that sole traders pay less tax than any other class of working people, although you have to be careful that you don't fall foul of the IR35 regulation. This rule, which quite simply states that if you look like an employee, you are an employee, was introduced to prevent contractors working on site for single clients for long periods of time, effectively acting as employees, but invoicing as sole traders or single-employee limited companies.

As a sole trader, you have to keep track of monthly income and expenditure, which means holding on to all invoices and business-related receipts. You could manage your accounts by hand, but it's easier to do it using a computer. A spreadsheet will suffice, containing columns for income, expenditure and VAT (if you are VAT registered). This means keeping track of all invoices (along with the dates they were issued and paid) and all receipts for work-related transactions, including any ground rent, telephone bills, heating and electricity costs and so on. If you work from home, some of your household expenditure may be tax deductible.

This is all the information you will need to fill in the tax return form each year. However, if you have been an employee for any part of the tax year, which may well apply in your first year of business and will of course be the case if you are setting up a business while still in part-time or full-time employment, you will also need your P60 form from your employer to take into account the tax you have already paid that year through the PAYE system.

It's actually all quite straightforward, and managing your accounts shouldn't take more than a couple of hours each month. Setting up as a sole trader, or freelancer, is by far the easiest and quickest way to start a business. It's fairly light on paperwork and doesn't require paying a registration fee, however it's paramount that you register as self-employed within three months of working or starting to trade. Failure to do so may result in a penalty of up to £100, plus interest on any taxes due. Below is a round-up of your ongoing tax and administrative obligations as a sole trader. (For details on how to register with HMRC, see Chapter 5.)

## *Self-assessment*

As a self-employed sole trader, you'll have to complete a self-assessment tax return to HMRC. This involves filling in a tax return form, either online or paper, in which you inform HMRC of your income and capital gains, or in which you may claim tax allowances or reliefs. Usually, HMRC will send you your self-assessment tax return in April. However, if yours doesn't arrive by the end of April, contact your tax office.

If this is the first tax return you've completed, you'll need to fill in a self-assessment registration form first. Make sure you have your National Insurance number to hand when doing this. This involves completing a CWF1 form to inform HMRC about your business, and this will also register you for self-assessment.

Once this is done, HMRC will set up tax records for you and will send you a Unique Taxpayer Reference (UTR).

## *Self-assessment deadlines*

After the tax year has ended (in April) you must complete a self-assessment tax return, either online or on paper. The deadline for submitting paper returns is midnight on 31 October, while online returns must be submitted by midnight on 31 January the following year. This is also the payment deadline (whether you file online or on paper).

You will need to pay one or both of the following:

- The balancing payment (the balance of tax you owe for the previous year).
- The first of two 'payments on account' (advance payments for the current tax year).

You should receive a self-assessment statement that shows the amount due, however if you don't receive this before payment is due, you'll need to work out the tax due yourself by using your tax calculation and previous statements or by registering for self-assessment online and using the 'view account' option.

If you're asked to make payments on account, your deadline for making your second payment is July 31.

It's essential that you file your return and make payments on time, as penalties for missing the deadlines can be steep.

## Registering for VAT

If you expect to have a turnover of more than £73,000 a year, VAT is applied to your earnings, which also involves contacting HMRC to register for VAT (more on this later).

## Maintaining records

It is important that you set up a financial record-keeping system, which includes maintaining all records that show your business income and expenses. This is vital for tax purposes but is also beneficial to help you stay on top of your finances. Details of the specific records you need to keep are listed in the box below:

You should retain your records for at least three years after the end of the tax year that they're for. You'll be required to make them available, should HMRC ask to see them. In general, you should retain all your business records that are relevant for VAT for at least six years (see later in the chapter).

## National Insurance contributions

If you're self-employed you must pay Class 2 and Class 4 National Insurance contributions (NICs). Class 2 NICs are paid at a flat rate of £2.50 a week,

## Business records you need to keep:

- Annual accounts, including profit and loss accounts.
- Bank statements and paying-in slips.
- Cash books and other account books.
- Orders and delivery notes.
- Purchase and sales books.
- Records of all the goods and services you buy or sell.
- Copies of all sales invoices you issue.
- All supplier invoices / receipts for items you buy.
- All credit notes you issue or receive.
- Records of daily takings such as till rolls.
- Relevant business correspondence.

while Class 4 NICs are paid as a percentage of your annual taxable profits, which is 9% on profits between £7,225 and £42,475 (for tax year 2011–2012), and a further 2% on profits over that amount. However, if your profits are expected to be less than £5,315 per year you may not have to pay Class 2 NICs. Class 2 NICs can be paid either monthly by direct debit or by quarterly bill. You will pay Class 4 NICs when you pay your income tax.

All this may seem quite daunting at first, but if managed properly it's really not as overwhelming as it seems. The best thing you can do is stay organised, maintain your paperwork and flag up any tax or self-assessment deadlines in your diary well in advance so you have adequate time to prepare for them.

## *Registered company accounts*

Things get a little more complex once you start employing people, because you will have to look after their salaries as well as the general company accounts. You will have to manage the deduction of their tax at source, payment of employer and employee NICs, plus any pension schemes, bonus arrangements and non-salary expenses (this also applies if you decide to take on staff as a sole trader of course). The process is far quicker and simpler than it ever was thanks to bookkeeping software packages, which also let you plot graphs of profit and loss or income and expenditure, and track overdue payments (both incoming and outgoing), while the more advanced tools can even automate the submission of the relevant forms to HMRC.

*"When it comes to doing your company accounts, you will be better off finding a good accountant"*

241

Options available include QuickBooks, Mind Your Own Business (MYOB), Sage Instant Accounting/Payroll and Liquid Accounts (online accounting software), which can all be used for companies of up to 20 employees – and don't be put off by the relatively low cost of these packages. Most of these packages are powerful accounting tools that can double as business assessment and stock control systems, giving you a real feel for which areas of your business are doing well and which are failing. For the sake of convenience, it's best to ask your accountant which software package he or she prefers to use and then buy that one for internal use.

When it comes to doing your company accounts, you will be better off finding a good accountant. Note that they won't do the donkey work of everyday data input for you, unless you are prepared to pay extra – a lot extra. What they will do is take the figures you have provided for the year and plug those into various forms to tell you the amount of money you have to pay for each class of tax. (See later in this chapter for more on accountants and finding the right one.)

## Keeping on top of tax and accounts

In your first year of operation it will seem as though there's an endless array of forms to be completed and taxes to be paid, whereas in fact there aren't really so many. Although your accountant will guide you through the process, it pays to understand the tax and accounting demands on your business, and if you bear in mind the following basics, you won't go far wrong.

### During the tax year you must:

- Deduct the correct amount of PAYE from your employees' pay
- Work out the amount of NICs that you and your employees have to pay
- Keep a record of your employees' pay and PAYE and NICs due
- Make monthly or quarterly payments of the total PAYE and NICs due to the Accounts Office
- Manage VAT return completion and payment on a quarterly basis

### At the end of the tax year you must:

- Send a Return (form P35) and an End of Year Summary (form P14) showing details of each employee's total pay and the PAYE and NICs due, to your HMRC office

- Send details to HMRC about expenses you have paid to employees or benefits you have provided (forms P11D and P9D)

- Give each employee (who has paid PAYE or NICs and is still working for you at the end of the tax year) a certificate showing their pay, PAYE and NICs details (form P60)

- Give each employee a copy of the information you have given your HMRC office about their expenses payments and benefits provided (duplicate of form P11D)

*At the end of your company's accounting year you must:*

- Submit full statutory accounts and a company tax return to HMRC

- Submit statutory accounts and an annual return to Companies House. Small and medium-sized companies (with a turnover of less than £5.6m) can submit an abbreviated version of their accounts

- You should receive copies of the Employer's Bulletin from HMRC along with the Employer's Annual Pack. Request the copies if you haven't received them within a month or so of starting your business, as these provide useful tips on the above duties, plus contacts and advice for business owners

The percentage of companies audited each year by HMRC is quite small, but the organisation has effective ways of tracking suspicious returns. The auditing process is thorough and time-consuming, since all receipts and invoices must be checked against the returns and shown to the investigating accountant. Also, the Statute of Limitations is biased in the auditors' favour, so you may have to dig out paperwork going back many years. This means that you may want to take out auditing insurance with your accountant. The work involved during an audit is considerable – allow for three days at the very least.

## Corporation tax

Corporation tax is a tax on the profits of limited companies and certain other organisations. If your company is based in the UK, you will have to pay corporation tax on all of your taxable profits – wherever in the world they came from.

"If your limited company is turning a profit, you must inform HMRC that you are liable for corporation tax"

If your limited company is turning a profit, you must inform HMRC that you are liable for corporation tax. You must also ensure that you pay the right amount on time, as well as filing your company tax return and supporting documents by the relevant deadline. There are different deadlines for these two requirements, and failing to meet them could result in your business being charged interest and/or penalties.

Unlike other taxes, such as income tax or VAT — where the filing and payment deadlines are usually identical — this is not the case with corporation tax. Generally, you must pay your corporation tax within nine months of the end of your corporation tax accounting period, and file within 12 months of this period. For example, if your company's financial year runs from 1 April 2010 to 31 March 2011, and your corporation tax accounting period is the same, you must pay your corporation tax for that period by 1 January 2012 and file your company tax return for the same period by 1 April 2012.

## Accounting periods

Your company's corporation tax accounting period will typically be 12 months. The accounting period will usually match your company's financial year, which begins and ends on the dates covered by your annual report and accounts, as submitted to Companies House.

However, there are some instances where your accounting period will not be the same as your financial year: for example, if your start-up is preparing its first set of accounts to cover a period of more than 12 months. While a corporation tax accounting period can be shorter than 12 months, it cannot be longer. So, if your company accounts cover a period that is longer than a calendar year, you must file two tax returns (even though you only need to file one set of accounts at Companies House).

The first accounting period covers the first 12 months; the second covers the rest. For instance, if your company has its accounts prepared for 15 months from 1 January 2010 to 31 March 2011, your corporation tax accounting periods will be: 1 January 2010 to 31 December 2010 (12 months) and 1 January 2011 to 31 March 2011 (three months).

## Self-assessment

It's up to you (not HMRC) to work out how much corporation tax your company owes for each accounting period. In other words, you self-assess your corporation tax, by filling in a company tax return. You can choose to deal with HMRC directly, or appoint an agent to do this on your behalf. The pre-tax profit figure shown in your company's year-end accounts is only the starting point for your tax calculation, and you will need to make various adjustments and deductions in order to work out your taxable profits and your tax liability. Full details on how to complete your tax return can be found on the HMRC website.

## Corporation tax rate

The chancellor sets the rates of corporation tax and any allowances, reliefs or credits in the Budget each year. There are currently two rates of corporation tax, and in the Emergency Budget in June 2010, chancellor George Osborne announced plans to lower both. How much you pay will depend on how much profit your business is making:

⇢ Small profits rate: This applies to companies with taxable profits of less than £300,000. This will be 20% as of 1 April 2011 (down from 21%).

⇢ Main rate: This applies to companies with taxable profits which exceed £1.5m. The headline rate will be 26% as of 1 April 2011 (down from 28%). The main rate will fall again to 25% in April 2012.

If your company's profits fall in between these two thresholds, there is a sliding scale between the two rates, known as 'marginal relief'.

## Online filing

From 1 April 2011, you must pay your corporation tax electronically, for any accounting period. As of the same date, you must also file your company tax return online – including supporting documentation – for any accounting period ending after 31 March 2010.

# VAT

For companies, and sole traders for that matter, with annual turnovers exceeding a certain amount (currently £73,000), quarterly VAT returns must be completed and sent to HMRC along with any payment due.

**WANT TO KNOW MORE …**

For the most up-to-date VAT registration information: HMRC www.hmrc.gov.uk/ vat/start/register/ index.htm

The VAT form is very simple – just a single page – and often works in the company's favour. This is because, although you must pay VAT on any income generated, you can claim back VAT paid on some goods and services, such as office supplies, vehicle servicing, fuel and so on. So the extra accounting is definitely worth it and even companies with turnovers less than the VAT limit can still register voluntarily. Remember that the government increased VAT to 20% on 4 January 2011, in order to help tackle the UK's national deficit.

However, not all products and services attract the standard VAT rate, so ask your local HMRC office for its introductory video that explains the basics of VAT accounting. If that's not enough, you can also enrol on a brief course, again run by HMRC, which will go into greater detail.

*"Above all, tempting as it may seem, don't ever attempt to 'cook the books'"*

Try to keep track of changes to tax regulations. This means listening to the entire Budget speech! Your accountant should do this for you, but it doesn't hurt to know about VAT limits, along with changes in basic tax rates and company car regulations yourself. Above all, tempting as it may seem, don't ever attempt to 'cook the books'. Penalties for tax evasion are high. It's not worth the sleepless nights and feelings of guilt just to shave a few pounds off your tax bill, and there's always the chance that you will be found out, especially if you are audited.

Ultimately, you should remember that you are expected to account for every single business-related penny spent – this includes invoices for trade magazines and newspapers, for example. Although there may be some discretionary leeway, you are expected to show each month's transactions in sufficient detail that your profit and loss, income and expenditure – and therefore tax – can be clearly calculated.

*"Late payment erodes profits and stifles growth"*

## Credit control

Half of all new businesses fail during the first two years. All too often, the cause of failure is neither the quality of the product or service, the effort and talents of the people, nor the sales and marketing. It is quite simply down to financial failure – running out of money – which leads to closure, if not bankruptcy. In many cases, this failure could have been avoided by simple but effective planning from the outset. In too many new businesses, well-qualified people enthusiastically develop their goods or services, but pay insufficient attention to cashflow. Late payment erodes profits and stifles growth.

A sale is not really made until it has been paid for, so the discipline of ensuring prompt payment, called credit control or credit management, has to be a priority if a business is to succeed, rather than payment being an afterthought. Establishing it as a priority means you can then consider granting customers credit where appropriate. But this should be a calculated risk, never a gamble. You must know who you are dealing with, and this should be part of the preparation before a sale.

Granting credit to a customer involves the risk of non-payment and so should only be done after checking and assessing that risk. A bad debt means that a company could have to make sales five – or even 10 – times the value of that debt just to recoup the loss. Research shows that the longer a trade debt remains unpaid, the greater the risk that it will never be paid.

For many companies, their receivables – the money owed to them by their customers – are their largest assets. Figures from BACS – the banks' automated clearing system – show that growth businesses have a combined overdraft of £4bn. Reducing the amount owed by debtors cuts the overdraft and frees up capital to be used to finance the business, and reduces the stress of running the business.

You can get some basic training in credit control even before you have made your first sale. Local chambers of commerce usually have courses available, covering topics such as how to collect a debt over the phone. These are open to non-members. The government-sponsored Better Payment Practice Group (BPPG), which was formed to reduce late payment of commercial debt, also publishes advice on the subject.

**WANT TO KNOW MORE …**
Better Payment Practice Group
www.payontime.co.uk

From the outset, establish procedures for credit applications by customers:

- ⇢ Produce a credit application form: you can download an example at www.payontime.co.uk/collect/collect_cash.html.
- ⇢ Make credit terms very clear.
- ⇢ Ensure that all staff are aware of your credit policy.
- ⇢ Make payment terms a condition of sale.
- ⇢ Make sure that every buyer signs, agreeing to your credit terms.

Then, to help ensure you receive prompt payment:

- ⇢ Design a clear invoice, which will always state agreed payment terms.

-⇢ Send out invoices promptly and keep paperwork up to date.

-⇢ Establish a timetable for chasing debts, starting with the first request for payment: the invoice.

## Establishing customer credentials

*"Credit control is a continuous process. Always monitor your debtors as their circumstances may change"*

It is important to establish a potential customer's credentials. Obviously, if your sales are low value/high volume, this will not be practical, but many companies have a small number of major customers, the effective management of whom is crucial to success. In these cases, a visit to a potential customer's premises will usually tell you a lot. The annual report of companies is also useful (although the information could be out of date). For particularly high-value or high-risk orders, obtain a credit report from a credit reference agency. Such reports cost between £3 and £25, depending on the level of information.

For very small orders, buying a credit report may be uneconomical and you may wish to take the risk yourself, but for significant orders, it's well worth the expense. Bank and trade references should always answer specific questions, such as: can I grant £500 credit, or what proportion of this firm's payments to you are overdue? However, they should not be solely relied on.

If you have a new customer, confirm their address to avoid fraud, and find out how long they've been trading. If they are on a short lease, they could disappear with the goods. Also confirm that they have the cash to pay. There's no need to check their profit and loss account yourself, because a credit reference company will do it for you – and they will suggest a credit limit and a credit rating. For potentially high-value orders, take a credit report prior to negotiation, to avoid wasted effort. Credit costs and knowing the risks in advance also helps in pricing.

Remember that credit control is a continuous process. Always monitor your debtors as their circumstances may change.

## Deciding a credit limit

A credit reference agency may recommend a credit limit or you can do it yourself, deciding whether a firm is high risk – a late payer, for example with adverse information such as county court judgments against them or dubious individuals involved – or low risk, with a good payment record and strong credit references. If you decide to grant credit, set up an account and write to the customer confirming this. Always have delivery of goods confirmed through a delivery note and follow up with a phone call, confirming that goods were delivered satisfactorily. Then invoice immediately, re-stating credit terms, and quoting an order number if appropriate.

## Dealing with debtors

A new customer can equal more profits to your firm, but it could also spell disaster if they turn out not to be what they originally seemed. It may sound obvious, but it's vital to be sure of a customer's identity to help avoid the heartache of receiving a 'gone-away' notice in response to your invoice. Start by getting complete and correct contact details for every customer via a proper account opening form. This must include the correct address and telephone details, which should be checked against alternative sources, such as the *Yellow Pages*.

*"The longer a debt is outstanding, the less likely it is to be paid"*

In the case of a limited company, request the full limited name and registration number, and for a proprietorship and partnerships, ensure that you take private address details and telephone numbers. The Better Payment Practice Group has a sample account opening form on its website (www.payontime.co.uk/collect/credit_app_pre.html). Using a credit reference agency to check the credit viability of new and existing customers will often reveal any address anomalies, which can then be confirmed directly with your customer.

Once you have established the new relationship, maintaining regular contact means you quickly become aware if a debtor relocates. Do not just issue invoices and wait for payment. Contact customers by phone to enquire politely as to whether your invoices have been received, and in doing so, you can verify that the address and telephone details you have remain accurate. Ask delivery staff to alert you to anything suspicious about the way goods or services are delivered, such as if the customer insists on collecting the goods, without adequate verification of their trading addresses.

## Tackling late payment

Whether you have a manual accounts system or a computerised one, it is important to prioritise debts, chasing the largest first. It is crucial to establish strong relationships with major customers to ensure prompt payment. Remember, the longer a debt is outstanding, the less likely it is to be paid.

## Tracing a debtor

If a letter is returned via Royal Mail marked 'Addressee not known' or 'No longer at this address', never assume this is actually the case. Many practised debtors simply return a letter as 'gone away' to give themselves more time. Start by taking the following steps:

1. Check your own information to see if you have made any errors on the original details. If you identify an error, re-issue your invoice immediately using the correct details.
2. Dial telephone numbers and re-check via a directory enquiry facility to ensure that you have the correct number.
3. Try a recorded delivery letter, as this may be accepted and thus confirm occupancy.
4. If the debtor appears to be no longer trading from the premises you have details for, then consider the following:
   - Contact the debtor's local Royal Mail sorting office as it may have forwarding addresses, or may confirm that the subject is still at the original address.
   - If you operate in the vicinity, use your delivery drivers or staff to seek information from the address or from its neighbours. However, you must have due regard to the Data Protection Act 1998. In particular, do not divulge any information about a debt to non-interested parties. You should say that you are seeking general information on a 'private matter', asking if there is a forwarding address that they know of.
   - If you know any other suppliers that your customer uses, contact them to enquire if they have been notified of their change of address.
   - For businesses rather than individuals, use the *Yellow Pages* for the area of enquiry to identify and telephone businesses/newsagents in the locality which may well know the business or have useful information on the business' status. Again, you must have due regard to the Data Protection Act when making such enquiries.
   - Look at the status or credit reference report you obtained when opening the account as this may give you alternative addresses. In the case of a limited company, you are entitled to contact the directors, particularly the company secretary, who has an obligation to inform any interested party of the status of the limited company.
   - You can contact these individuals at their home address or an address lodged with Companies House, but you cannot make them individually liable for any debt. A polite question should help you establish whether, for example, the company has entered

liquidation, or a Company Voluntary Arrangement. If this is the case, you may need to seek professional advice about your rights as an unsecured creditor to a limited company. If these efforts fail then you could seek the help of a professional collection/tracing company who may quote costs, usually from £50 to £60.

Handling debt collection and your debtors professionally and effectively can help protect your company against a bad payment that could send the business under.

So when payment is due, don't be afraid to ask. After all, it's your money, and if you have done the job right, you are entitled to be paid. Any disputes or complaints that delay payment must be addressed immediately. Some customers will pay promptly whereas others are habitual late payers. Establish a timetable for chasing debtors (see the box below for an example) and to keep receivables under control. The suggested procedures should be supplemented with phone calls – one of the most effective methods of chasing debts – and faxes, emails and visits. Some businesses choose not to undertake their own credit control, but have someone else do all or part of it for them by outsourcing.

*"Some customers will pay promptly whereas others are habitual late payers"*

Techniques worth considering are using debt collecting agencies, credit insurance, factoring, retention of title or payment in advance. 'There are a range of ways in which third-party outsourcers are being used,' says **Colin Thomas**, managing director of debt recovery specialists STA Graydon. 'If you have limited resources, you can bring in an outsourcing company that can provide some immediate level of expertise. Future growth always depends on cashflow. Outsourcers can cover the entire order-to-cash cycle. You can choose whether your outsource partner operates in your name or in their own name. In the cash collections field, you may prefer them to operate in your name at the receivables stage and then in their own name for accounts that become overdue.'

**WANT TO KNOW MORE ...**
Credit Services Association
www.csa-uk.com

## Debt collecting agencies

'We're very much involved in advising small-to-medium-sized firms in ways to tighten procedures and collect debts,' says **Trevor Phillips**, CEO of credit and debt management specialists Credit Professionals. 'Debt collection requires pleasant persistence. It's a selling job. Companies have to persuade customers that they have to be paid. Once a debt is more than 60 days overdue, a company has probably exhausted all its own internal resources for collecting the debts, therefore, it is necessary to intervene with a third party.'

## Timetable for debt chasing

Here's a sample schedule for chasing money you are owed:

- The sale: send out invoice.
- 21 days: send statement reminding payment due after 30 days.
- 30 days: if not paid, send reminder statement, re-stating terms and pointing out payment is overdue.
- 45 days: send reminder, re-stating payment is overdue.
- 50 days: stop supplies until paid.
- 60 days: send final reminder.
- 90 days: assign debt to collection agency.

Many debt collection agencies have relationships with credit reference agencies giving them leverage to collect. Of course, there is a cost, typically between 1% and 5% of the sum, depending on circumstances. Under the Late Payment of Commercial Debts (Interest) Act 1998, a company can charge interest to its debtors on late payments. Many collectors have solicitors associated with them and can handle litigation if it is necessary to sue for a debt. It shouldn't be seen as a sign of weakness to pass on a debt to a collection agency. Simply view it as an extension of your business. A new business should be equally as professional as a large one in pursuing outstanding debts.

**WANT TO KNOW MORE …**
Association of British Insurers
www.abi.org.uk

## Credit insurance

Credit insurers will insure against the risk of bad debt. Insurance companies can be contacted through the Association of British Insurers.

## Factoring and invoice discounting

Factoring is a popular choice for new businesses because it helps avoid cashflow problems. In both factoring and invoice discounting, small businesses borrow against sales as a means of sustaining cashflow. Invoice discounting involves a company loaning you a large percentage of the money for each invoice as soon as it is raised, which is then repaid plus a commission fee when payment is received from your customer within a specified time period.

Under factoring, the company will also chase the debt for you, for a larger commission payment. The key difference between the two is that in invoice discounting you continue to chase the payments yourself and the service is usually undisclosed to customers. (For more information on factoring and invoice discounting, see Chapter 6).

There are two types of factoring: recourse factoring, which excludes bad debt protection, and non-recourse factoring, which includes it. In the latter case, if a credit-approved customer fails to pay an undisputed debt, the factor will credit you with the amount of the debt.

## Retention of title

Retention of title – keeping ownership of goods until they are paid for – has only limited application. It can't be used where you are supplying a service, such as cleaning or architecture, or where the goods supplied are then made into something else, such as flour in a bakery.

## Payment in advance

Credit is a privilege, not a right, and in some circumstances it may be appropriate to ask for full or part payment in advance – for example, when making a large order, which would extend the supplier's financial resources, or if a customer is not deemed creditworthy. In other instances, credit terms could be reduced to, say, one week, instead of the normal 30 days.

Public limited companies and their subsidiaries are obliged to publish the time taken to pay suppliers in their annual report and the Federation of Small Businesses produces annual league tables of companies' payment records, while credit reference agencies focus on recent payment trends. Adverse information, such as county court judgments or previous insolvencies involving directors, clearly indicate high risk. This information is available from official sources such as the Registry Trust or the Insolvency Service for a fee, and is also included in credit reports. Basic information can be obtained from Companies House, but, again, a credit report will include all of this. Good credit management should aid, not inhibit, the sales effort. The key is obtaining good information and setting up effective procedures. Making the effort at the beginning can save much wailing and gnashing of teeth later on.

**WANT TO KNOW MORE …**

Better Payment Practice Group
www.payontime.co.uk

Institute of Credit Management
www.icm.org.uk

Asset Based Finance Association
www.abfa.org.uk

Federation of Small Businesses
www.fsb.org.uk

Companies House
www.companieshouse. gov.uk

Trust Online (part of the Registry Trust)
www.trustonline.org.uk

"Credit is a privilege, not a right"

---

**Startups Tips**

**Assessing customer risk**

If your sales are high value and low volume make sure that potential customers can pay, by:

-> Confirming their address.
-> Establishing how long they've been trading.
-> Visiting their premises.
-> Consulting their annual report.
-> Running a credit check through a credit reference agency.

---

# Hiring an accountant

You might think that a start-up or small business isn't big enough to warrant an accountant, but unless you are an expert in tax and finance – in short an accountant yourself – this simply isn't the case. An accountant can provide your business with a great deal of essential support. If you are just starting a business, your accountant will take the form of another business adviser.

As mentioned in previous chapters, they can give advice on your business plan and the tax issues of registering your company. Some accountants offer bookkeeping services, but if they don't or if you wish to handle this yourself, you can get help with setting up manual or computerised bookkeeping systems. And most importantly, an accountant can advise on areas such as whether it is necessary to register for VAT or PAYE and the procedures involved. You can also ask them for help with budgeting and forecasting cashflow, as well as credit control and general financial advice, and they can offer you up-to-date information on any general or legal enquiries.

An accountant can also advise you on the best way to arrange additional finance without putting your business at risk. Once you have the finance in place, there needs to be some control to ensure the growth of your business is handled in the right way. Many of your concerns will be financial – adequate working capital, good stock control, invoicing and so on – and an experienced accountant's advice can prove invaluable in such matters. Furthermore, can you honestly say that you are on top of all the essential taxation issues? Well, that's also an accountant's job – taxation is a large business expense and an accountant can effectively minimise these costs.

## Finding an accountant

A simple internet search will throw up lots of accountants in your area. There are many ways to track down the right accountant for your new business, one of the best of which is through recommendation. Simply ask friends and contacts if they would recommend their various accountants. Also ask businesses around you if they use someone locally. Your solicitor and bank manager will be working with accountants all the time, and they will probably have a good idea of the firms most suited to your type of business, making them another good source of recommendations.

Make sure you ask people what they use their accountant for, as you might not need the same kind of services. You should also quiz them on what they would recommend about them, their weak points, and if they are always on-hand when needed. Most importantly, it is advisable to choose someone who is a member of one of the main professional accounting bodies. There is no legislation to stop anyone setting up as an accountant, so asking for member accountants in your area will ensure you are getting someone fully qualified.

## What to look for in an accountant

*"Your accountant should be a good investment"*

You need to make sure the accountant you choose for your company is at least familiar with your business sector so that they are aware of any specific legislation. Also, look at the size of the firm. As you are a start-up, look for a small to medium-sized business accountant as they will probably specialise more in small business work, charge less than a larger firm and give more direct access to more experienced partners.

Make arrangements to visit several firms in person to meet the people you will be working with and to make comparisons. 'A lot comes down to personal chemistry,' maintains **Paul Watts**, a partner at accountancy and advisory firm Baker Tilly. 'The accountant needs to be able to get into your business and show an interest in it, as well as just doing your accounts, if they are to advise you properly.'

You are likely to be working closely with your accountant, so if you don't get on at a basic level, your professional relationship may be more difficult than it needs to be. It's good to ask if you can speak to other clients, in the same way that you would ask for references, and this will be a real test of the calibre of the firm. If they are confident that their service has impressed, they shouldn't have a problem referring you to a few people.

Equally, a good accountant should want to make an appointment to come and see your business. 'It's important to go out and see clients,' says Paul. 'You can't fully understand a business until you have been taken round it.' And allow each accountant to pitch to you, as it isn't just about what you want, but also what they are prepared to offer.

## Agreeing terms

When you are considering taking on an accountant, it's important to establish who your contact will be at the firm and who you can speak to in their absence. This, along with the services they are offering you and the fees they will charge, should form part of the engagement letter. Like the contract, this should be signed by both of you, and will form the basis of your working relationship. As such, it is important to get as much information on it as possible. If the accountant is to handle your tax, your accounts and your payroll, it should say so.

This is also the point where you talk about money. Traditionally, accountants charge by the hour, with more for a partner than for a junior member of staff. However, many firms are prepared to be flexible with regards to payment, and you might negotiate a fixed one-off fee for a full audit, for example, or pay monthly rather than all at once at the end of the year. The latter should be popular with both parties as it ensures regular payment when the money is available.

However, going for the firm that charges the least can sometimes be a false economy, according to Paul. 'Don't always go for the cheapest firm, look for one that adds value,' he advises. 'For example, how much does the hourly fee vary for a partner and other staff and will photocopying and phone time be included in the cost or be extra?'

Most importantly, don't be afraid to question anything on the engagement letter or to ask for something to be added. As with most contracts, it is in both your interests. In exchange for an hourly fee, you should get someone who saves you money, prevents you sitting up late with accounts that won't balance and who can provide general business sense. All the more reason to choose carefully.

## Are you getting a good deal?

So you have followed all the rules and carefully chosen your accountant, but this is the first time you have had one, so how do you know if they are doing a good job, and what do you do if you think they are not? To gauge their performance, look at what you are getting from them. At a basic level, are your accounts and tax returns prepared on time? Are you being billed as agreed and are your phone calls and letters answered? On top of this, take note of the advice they've given you. Have they come up with ideas you wouldn't otherwise have thought of? And if not, is that because you haven't liked the ideas, or because there haven't been any?

It is possible just to say to an accountant that you no longer want to work with them – you can effectively 'sack' the firm. But don't rush into doing this at the slightest hitch, as it's important to build a relationship with your accountant, which is difficult if you are changing every six months. Problems can often be ironed out, so keep careful track of the service and speak to your accountant if you need to. But ultimately, remember that you are not paying for poor service.

## *Paying yourself*

Few people start their own business solely for the purpose of becoming wealthy, and even fewer actually succeed in achieving this. So right from the start, it's essential to consider how much you should be paying yourself.

*"You need to consider, right from the very start, how much you need to live on and what you can afford to pay yourself"*

When starting up you are likely to want to plough everything you can into making sure you give your business every chance of succeeding, but aside from the issues of needing to keep enough back for running costs and marketing, etc, you need to live. The first 12 months, or however long it is until you think you will be in profit, will be a difficult period – in fact, there are more people who scrimp by than make a bucket-load of cash straightaway.

Essentially, you need to be realistic. If you have given up the comfort and security of a regular salary, you can't suddenly survive without any income at all. You are also likely to have financial commitments that you will still need to meet, in addition to the new ones you will be taking on by starting a business, so it's important to make sure you take enough to support sensible living costs. If you don't, you may be tempted to borrow more or build up another debt on a credit card – something that will inadvertently place more pressure on your business. Starting a business is also one of the most stressful things you can ever do. Failing to ensure you have enough money to relax when you are away from it will only increase the strain, and again, will prove detrimental to your business.

So how much should you pay yourself? This will be dependent on the sector you are going into and this is probably the best place to start looking for answers. Talk to others in the trade or to people with similar sized businesses and ask how much they were able to pay themselves at first, and what they can afford now. If they are not willing to tell you, try contacting trade associations, who should be able to help.

Once you have some idea of what others in the sector are earning, try to fit a similar figure into your financial estimates and see if it's viable. If it isn't, it could be that there's a problem with your business plan as a whole, and it is something you will need to address before you take the plunge. The key is to plan ahead.

Don't be afraid to treat yourself every now and then, but don't go overboard. You will need every penny of your start-up funds and profits to put back into the business to help it grow. But don't under-calculate what you can live on either. Be honest about what you need to 'get by' and incorporate that into your costs and your business plan.

## Travel and expenses

Few people actually know how much they spend each year on travel and expenses and most would have to take valuable time researching to get the answer, and they should. Travel and entertainment – or T&E as commerce likes to call it – amounts to the third largest controllable corporate cost, just behind salaries and data processing, and as a small business, it could be a leakage in your profits and something you need to keep under control. You are also likely to spend more on T&E than advertising. So it's even more concerning that so few companies can actually put an annual total on such a vital part of their operation. As a start-up, this is your opportunity to redress the balance and keep a close track of T&E from the start.

With any travel policy, the balance is between the benefit of the travellers and the cost saving for the company. And this isn't simply a cost issue. Time out of the office has to be managed efficiently. No one can afford to miss too many important calls and it may be difficult to hand over to anyone else to 'hold the fort' while you are away. Then, of course, these days there is concern over a company's environmental impact, of which travel can play a major part, particularly with respect to air travel.

## Minimising travel costs

Whether you work by yourself or run a company employing several people, travel expenses will need to be minimised wherever possible. Here are a number of easy steps that you can take to help control your costs.

**Don't just take the most obvious route:** A business can save almost a third by sending an executive via Paris to Los Angeles instead of flying direct from London. If you operate away from London and would be paying for a connecting flight, say from Aberdeen or Manchester, it may well benefit you to skip London and go direct to Paris.

**Think about downgrading:** When arranging business flights, ask yourself if business class is really necessary. Of course, for many start-ups 'slumming it in the back' may well be the only affordable way to go – but it can make better business sense anyway. Equally, using secondary airports or 'no-frills' airlines can cut costs significantly. For example, a return flight to Geneva from London Gatwick is six times cheaper with a low-cost carrier.

**Loyalty schemes:** If you will be travelling to see the same client several times a year, there may well be an opportunity to negotiate a better rate. It is also important to remember that a travel policy is more than just about the flights. Using the same hotel chain on a regular basis can also cut costs with a negotiated rate. And for individual travellers, who happen to be with the company too, loyalty schemes are worth using. Free points towards flights and hotel bills all help the bottom line.

**Get in the professionals:** You could use a company, such as American Express, which will help you to implement and follow a travel policy, organising travel for you and negotiating better rates on your behalf.

## What to do next

- Make sure you're aware what records you need to keep from day one. It's far easier to sort and file these away as you're going along then tackle them all in one go at the end of the tax year.

- Put together a timetable for dealing with late payments. Unpaid invoices can be the death of even the most successful businesses so it's important to have a plan in place to deal with them

- Keep on top of any changes to tax regulations, especially if you don't have an accountant to inform you of them. At the very least, make sure you're aware of any changes announced in the annual Budget and pre-Budget reports

- Consider hiring an accountant early on. Yes it's an added expense, but a good accountant will save you far more money than they cost in the long-run

- Don't forget to account for your own salary. If you've given up a steady income you can't suddenly live on thin air. You need to make sure you've budgeted to pay yourself enough to live on

# ⌾ CHAPTER 9
*Marketing and PR*

##  What's in this chapter?

- → What is marketing?
- → Building a marketing plan
- → Marketing methods
- → Low-cost marketing techniques
- → Social media
- → Setting up a website
- → Search engine optimisation (SEO)

No matter how awesome your product or service is, it won't appeal to everyone. A crucial part of your research – both before you launch and as your business grows – is to find out who your most valuable prospects or customers are and what marketing methods will reach them. Armed with this information, you can put together a plan of action for promoting your business.

This chapter will look at how to create your marketing plan, as well as outlining some of the main marketing methods available, from media advertising to public relations. We will pay close attention to low-cost marketing techniques – one of which is social media. Read on for advice on creating your social media strategy, as well as how to get the most from your business' website.

# What is marketing?

Marketing is the means by which your business identifies, anticipates and then satisfies customer demand. If carried out effectively it will not only ensure that your business is seen and heard, but will also give it the flexibility to adapt to fluctuating customer demands and a changing business environment. Companies that really succeed are those where the owner has a vision for the firm and is dedicated to seeing it through. A marketing plan will help achieve focus and establish the vision. Marketing will also help you to understand who your potential customers are, place and price your product or service against the competition, and position the company in the marketplace. It will also help identify future opportunities for self-promotion.

Although there are established guidelines to follow, marketing can be a difficult skill to develop. But in terms of successful impact on the future commercial effectiveness of the business, it is worth cultivating. It can offer improved returns and profitability and a greater understanding of realistic business development opportunities. There are no hard and fast rules for timetables for your marketing. As a general rule of thumb, it's recommended that you think about what your business would like to achieve three years from now compared with where it would be if you didn't employ a marketing strategy.

With respect to how to set your marketing budget, there are several possible approaches, none of which can claim to be the right way. They include using a percentage of sales, the same spend as last year (which is unlikely to be relevant to a start-up), a similar spend to key competitors, and the dubious 'what we can afford' approach. Of course, in the end it will come down to what you can afford, but initially you need to plan your strategy to find out how much marketing you think is necessary, identify the essentials and go from there. Also, as you will see later in this chapter, there are some effective marketing methods that don't cost much at all.

**Sonja Garsvo**, former director of corporate relations at Apple and now an experienced business and communications consultant, recommends factoring the marketing budget into your business plan from the bottom up. 'If you can't afford a marketing budget, you have to ask yourself how viable your product is,' she says.

One of the major problems for start-ups when considering marketing is quantifying in advance the expected result for a given spend. But consider

---

## Sales versus marketing

Don't confuse sales with marketing. It's a common enough mistake for any small business to lump sales together with marketing under the perception that the two disciplines are different heads of the same beast. This is because tactics can overlap. However, they are not the same. The mission of sales is to increase turnover through a number of tricks, such as discounts, two for the price of one, special offers and so on. The mission of marketing is to identify the market, build the company and promote the product.

---

Microsoft. While your ambitions may be more modest than those of Bill Gates, his company's domination of the software industry is a testament to the power of successful marketing. Gates targeted potential competitors, undercutting rival Apple, while launching a sustained marketing blitz to become one of the richest men in the world, with PCs dominating the home computer market. Industry observers attribute Microsoft's success as much to its marketing prowess as Apple's lack of it.

Of course, in recent years, Apple has carved itself a lucrative niche in the technology sector thanks not only to wonderfully innovative and stylish designs, but also because of – yes, you guessed it – excellent marketing and branding.

# *Building a marketing plan*

Any marketing plan should include the four Ps:

- Product
- Pricing
- Position
- Promotion

Building a marketing plan means drawing up a blueprint for effective marketing. It can also be a useful way of ironing out differences between colleagues about where the business is heading and creating a common goal.

## Product and pricing

The key to product and pricing is research. The more thorough your marketing plan, the better. If your business is going to operate within a specific locality, will the market support it? For example, if you plan to open a restaurant, how many already exist, what type of service do they offer and what are their prices like? How do they position themselves – greasy spoon, haute cuisine or takeaway? Will the locality support another restaurant, or is the area already saturated? Check out your rivals' prices too, and position your product accordingly.

You need to establish whether once you have started your business and want to introduce new products or expand into other markets, the prospects for growth are viable. Perhaps there is a niche for the product/ service or the competitors have the market sewn up. Think about how you will sell the service (eg directly, via mail order or through an agency) and the distribution method you will use, where your office will be located and whether you will need to supply after-sales service.

## Position

Positioning means creating an identity for your business. You want to stand out from the crowd and be distinctive, so you need to develop a brand identity that is instantly recognisable. This will build a platform from which to launch your product. A business name is important and should reflect the value of the product or the service. See Chapter 4 for more on this subject. To create the brand identity, find a good local designer who can come up with letterheads, signage design, business cards and packaging.

Although design is one of those trades that many people think they can do themselves, a professional designer should be able to create a unique identity and appearance for your business. A good local designer need not be expensive and is likely to be a small business itself, sympathetic to your needs and ambitions.

*"You will need to give the designer a clear brief about your company and what you want it to achieve"*

To make sure that your logo and brand identity reflect the visions and values of your company, you will need to give the designer a clear brief about your company and what you want it to achieve, including the market you are targeting – as this should all influence the design they come up with. In fact, if a designer doesn't ask for details about the values of your company, your market and your competition – and perhaps examples of logos and branding you admire – then think twice about commissioning them. Ultimately, they should be producing a look and feel for your company that is significantly different from your rivals, appealing to your target audience and also right for your business.

All of these considerations have to be factored into a marketing plan and will form the foundation on which the fourth P – considered to be the classic marketing tool – promotion, is built.

## *Promotion*

Customer targeting is the first and most important step in planning any kind of promotional activity. **Jeff Holden** of the Chartered Institute of Marketing recommends asking the following questions to provide a clearly defined target audience:

*"Start by focusing on marketing your business to a core group of prospects well, rather than overstretching yourself"*

- → What kind of people buy or will buy your product?

- → What do your best customers tend to have in common?

- → Can you reach all of your customers through the same communication channels?

- → Do customers fall into different groups?

- → Are there different buying circumstances, for example, planned, impulse or special occasion?

On answering these questions, you will recognise who your customers are. The next step is finding effective channels to communicate your message. These fall into three categories: media advertising (above-the-line), non-media communications (below-the-line) and public relations. Media advertising includes television, radio, the press, cinema, outdoor and transport. Non-media communications include sales literature, direct marketing, sponsorship, sales promotion and point of sale. Public relations involves a range of activities that attempt to generate a positive attitude towards your company or products.

Initially, you are unlikely to be able to sell to all the people or businesses you have identified as potential customers, simply due to resources. This means that it's important to look at your audience and hone your niche by identifying the best prospects – those you are most likely to get business from. They will not only be those prospects who are most likely to need your product or service, but also those you can reach most effectively and efficiently in terms of both time and expense.

In my experience

**Company:** Any Junk?
**Owner-manager:** Jason Mohr

*Making it fun*
It doesn't really matter what angle you look at it from, rubbish just isn't sexy. Trying to build a memorable, and more importantly, appealing brand in waste disposal has obvious challenges.

**Jason Mohr**, who founded rubbish collection business Any Junk? in 2004, has overcome some of these issues by putting fun at the heart of his company. Two-man teams in bright red vehicles turn up at the customer's home or workplace and clear away anything they don't want hanging around. The vehicles alone, sporting funky elephant logos, have proved an effective marketing tool, helping the company stand out from the competition and increasing recognition of the distinctive brand.

More recently, the company launched a viral campaign featuring an Any Junk? team disposing of *X Factor* duo 'Jedward' on video sharing site YouTube. The video has proved extremely popular, receiving more than 41,000 hits to date. With the motto 'If it's rubbish, we'll clear it', Jason's plan is to make the company synonymous with rubbish clearance of any kind.

Since starting with one vehicle in the south-west London area, Jason has gradually built the fleet up to 30, and the past year has seen seven new national depots open, increasing revenues to just under £4m. Much of the recent growth has been fuelled by commercial clients including B&Q and Magnet, as well as work with local authorities. At present, the company diverts more than 70% of the waste it collects away from landfill, either through recycling or resale.

The strong brand, coupled with the national coverage the company boasts, should go a long way towards protecting the business from competitors. Jason says the firm is 'unique by a country mile' in the B2B sector as similar offerings with a national presence simply don't exist.

Think carefully about how much time and effort you can afford to put into promoting your business and evaluate the most effective way of getting your message across to the most appropriate people. The internet means that you can reach more people than ever and you have greater potential to take your business to the global level. But the reality is that you need the resources to be able to service such a demand, so initially it's worth scaling down ambitions. In some cases, if you are offering a service that requires your physical interaction with customers, geography will play a key role in delineating your audience, as you will be restricted to how far you can physically travel. So it's best to start by focusing on marketing your business to a core group of prospects well, rather than overstretching yourself, as this is likely to affect the quality of the message you are delivering, with the consequence of reducing its effectiveness.

**WANT TO KNOW MORE …**

Chartered Institute of Marketing
www.cim.co.uk
☎01628 427120

# *Marketing methods*

There are three key points to remember when promoting your business:

→ **Reach**

→ **Frequency**

→ **Impact**

Reach means getting through to the right audience, in the right circumstances, at the right time. 'Who wants to know about investment products when they are cleaning the kitchen floor and don't have the money to invest?' asks **Jeff Holden**. So, successful reach is about selecting the right media and scheduling advertisements for appropriate times. Frequency is about giving the audience a reasonable chance for the message to sink in amid the hubbub of everyday life, while impact pretty much speaks for itself. Your message must have impact to cut a swathe through the myriad of distractions that confront consumers every day, and it must be presented at the most appropriate time.

*"Your message must have impact to cut a swathe through the myriad of distractions that confront consumers every day"*

## *Media advertising*

The three major aims of above-the-line promotion are to inform, remind and persuade your customers about your products, services and the company itself.

The measure of advertising cost is the amount of business that you can generate per pound spent on advertising. A recruitment agency could benefit by advertising on panels on local transport and could reach thousands of people in the right categories every day. Online or local radio advertising could also be cost-effective mediums for small businesses. However, **Sonja Garsvo** warns against the scattergun approach. 'Shout as loud as everybody else and get attention but be focused about it, don't advertise for the sake of it; think about who you want to reach and the best way of reaching them,' she says.

## Non-media communications

Non-media communication takes a number of forms and its methods are within the reach of every start-up business. Sales literature is a familiar tool, ranging from the glossy company brochure to the single-sheet product flyer dropped through the letterbox, stuck behind the windscreen wipers of cars or direct mailed. It should be designed with a specific target audience in mind and should convey what the key features and benefits of the product or service are. Direct marketing can be the most effective means of communication, and it embraces all forms of promotion where the buyer is required to respond directly to the advertiser rather than through a retailer or dealer. It includes selling off-the-page as well as direct mail and telephone sales. Don't forget *Yellow Pages*, and you may want to consider online information services such as Scoot or Yell.com.

**WANT TO KNOW MORE ...**

Yellow Pages
www.yell.com

Scoot
www.scoot.co.uk

One of the advantages of below-the-line marketing over media advertising is that responses can be measured more easily (except perhaps where online media is concerned). However, it is worth noting that a 2%–3% return rate is considered the average, 5% is very good and 0% means something is seriously amiss. Sales promotion and point of sales can be used to offer something extra and build in loyalty, such as buy three curries and get one free during the following week. This also has the added advantage of blocking out the competition. Offers such as these can be made at the point of sale or via mail drops, and are often a useful means of giving a start-up business a leg up.

Sponsorship can also be an effective tool. Is there a local nursery or community project that needs some equipment in your area? You can provide it and in return work out a deal in which your company gets some promotion. If the cause is worthy it can generate positive word-of-mouth approval, too. However, do not make too much noise about the sponsorship and your generous donation, as this is often viewed cynically and considered opportunism.

## *Public relations*

PR takes a number of forms, with its purest form viewed as the means by which a company can communicate honestly and accurately with its audience. It includes media releases, product launches and premises openings. To do it effectively, there are simple guidelines to follow. Email a press release to the local paper or relevant publication, or hold a launch event and target the appropriate local reporters or trade journalists. To find the relevant trade titles, consult the business section in your local library, or search online and check out media directories such as *PR Newswire*, then call the title and find out which journalist covers your area.

*"Keep press releases simple. Journalists are bombarded with hundreds of press releases every week and have tight deadlines to meet"*

Keep press releases simple. Journalists are bombarded with hundreds of press releases every week and have tight deadlines to meet. If your press release is too long, there is a very good chance it will be deleted before the third paragraph is reached. Do not make any grandiose claims, as these are usually seen through very quickly. Simply explain concisely and clearly who, what, where and when. Invite the reporter along to an opening, but make sure it doesn't clash with press days because they will not turn up.

Try to build a relationship – you may have other information that a reporter could turn into a story and in return you may get a free plug. Remember that the editorial content in newspapers and magazines carries a lot more weight with readers than the advertising. So make the time and effort to send out regular press releases, try to identify individual journalists to cultivate relationships with, offer your services to publications as an expert commentator, propose that you will write a free series of useful (and short) articles or sponsor newsworthy local events.

Letters to the editor can also be a surprisingly powerful marketing tool, although its effectiveness may take time to develop. If you have a local market, you probably read the same local newspaper as your target audience does – and both of you are likely to read the letters page, as it is often one of the most popular parts of a newspaper. Don't write in unless you have something constructive to say, but you can make sure that you have by reacting to news items, commenting on new government policies and legislation, and any local issues (traffic and the environment are good candidates for a business' viewpoint). Your letter can apply a spin that reflects your business' concerns, and always ensure your business' name is part of your signature.

## Startups Tips

**Successful marketing strategy**

For successful marketing, bear these simple rules in mind:

→ Start by setting clear objectives for where you want your business to be, in say, three years.
→ Define your target market and identify your audience.
→ Decide on the brand and the values you want to transmit, which will be the platform for your business.
→ Plan your promotion strategy.
→ Set a budget.
→ Devise a schedule.
→ Decide how the strategy will be measured, such as through increased sales, direct responses, coverage received in local press, etc.
→ Implement the programme according to the schedule.
→ Monitor and evaluate the results, so you can assess effectiveness and make more informed future marketing decisions.

# Low-cost marketing techniques

*"Good business marketing is less about getting big bangs and more about producing smaller amounts very regularly"*

A good business marketing strategy doesn't have to cost that much. At its simplest, a marketing strategy is all about improving your chances of making sales – usually by making more potential purchasers aware of your products or services, or by making them aware of its desirable qualities (perhaps including its price). In any case, it makes sense to optimise your budget. Given the choice between big-bang and little-but-often, good business marketing is less about getting big bangs and more about producing smaller amounts very regularly.

You don't, however, need to spend big, as most of the ideas in your marketing strategy are likely to involve moderate costs. But it will require quite a lot of time and effort from you on a regular basis. The key is to choose the ones that best support your marketing plan, and mix them in with more expensive options to help keep your costs down. Most (but not all) take advantage of the fact that you have a computer and an internet connection.

## *Build a mailing list*

Collecting the names is the hard part, so give your prospects a reason for them to provide you with their name and address – competitions, an emailed newsletter, the promise of advance information and discounts, maybe even a loyalty card. Work at keeping your list accurate and up to date. Try to get hold of email addresses as well as (or even in preference to) postal contact details. Email is cheaper and more versatile than postage, and it can be integrated more efficiently with other aspects of your marketing, notably your website. If your database of names has been gathered in the normal course of business, you might not have to register under the Data Protection Act. This is a complex area, however, and you should check the situation with the Information Commissioner.

Once you have your list, use it. Concentrate on customers more than prospects as they will be more valuable to you, both for repeat business and because they will act as a reference. Looking after your customers so that you retain their custom is actually cheaper than attracting new ones. So be personal. Remember birthdays and anniversaries. Say 'thank you' when they buy (if only by email). Offer them the chance to comment and criticise. Give them special offers not available to anyone else. Make sure they know that your Christmas 'thank you' gift is going to a select few, and that they're in this group.

Ask them to check out new products or services, because they will appreciate being treated as special, and the risk is lower because they're more likely to buy. Look at their past purchase history if possible, and tailor special promotions to them. Find out whether they prefer you to use their first names or a more formal mode of address, and make sure all your mailings and other communications use the appropriate salutation.

## *Use discount vouchers*

A good way to bump up sales volume is to offer discount vouchers, but they can also send a message about your business. It could be customer care (distribute them to favoured clients only), but coupons work better as a value-for-money flag. Distribute them in print advertising ('cut here'), by direct mail, by hand (on the street corner, if appropriate, or at trade shows), by email or via the web ('quote this reference or enter this code to get your discount'). You can also include 'next purchase' coupons with customer orders. The coupon can be a fairly cheap production in terms of design and print, as its main selling point is usually the low price it offers.

**WANT TO KNOW MORE …**

Information Commissioner
www.ico.gov.uk

## Action points

### Keeping hold of your customers

☑ Looking after customers is far more important than attracting new ones, according to **Alastair Campbell**, managing director of The Ideal Marketing Company. 'It is far more cost–effective to target your resources towards holding onto a customer you already have than to spend a fortune trawling the country to attract a new one,' he says.

☑ 'After all, it costs seven times more to attract a new customer than to maintain an existing one. A whopping 75% leave because of "perceived indifference". That means that they stop doing business with you because they feel that you aren't interested in them; that you don't make them feel special anymore. So while you may think you are treating your customers well, most of them probably think otherwise and could be quickly tempted away by a competitor.' Here are Campbell's five easy–to–implement ways on how to keep hold of your customers.

☑ **Capture their details and keep in touch with them**: At least once a month write to them about a special offer, special product preview, clearance sale, new product line, open evening or whatever. This lets them know that you are thinking about them and looking for new ways to serve them.

☑ **Ask them how you are doing**: Conduct a customer satisfaction survey on an annual or regular basis depending on your customer base. You can even offer an incentive if they complete the form.

☑ **Conduct regular customer forums**: This allows you to tell your best customers more about what you are up to and to find out from your customers what they like about your service and products. It can also be a useful opportunity for customers to meet your staff (especially background staff), and of course, other customers. If you are feeling brave, let them talk about you while you are out of the room for an hour and then listen to their feedback on what they like and don't like about your company.

☑ **Develop more than one contact point**: If a buyer leaves or your contact leaves, the relationship between your two organisations disappears overnight, but if you have more than one point of contact, the relationship is far stronger and can withstand the odd member of staff moving on. When a company pairing system is carefully planned your two organisations become so closely intertwined that no other company will get a look in (as it does with Northern Foods and Marks & Spencer).

☑ **Be honest**: Own up to mistakes, and don't pretend to be something that you are not. You can't build a long-term relationship based on mistrust. A customer would prefer you to hold your hands up to making a mistake rather than trying to shift the blame where it doesn't belong.

☑ **Remember**: Most companies spend their marketing and sales efforts attempting to attract elusive new customers when they probably have most of the business they will ever need sitting on their database.

## *Distribute postcards*

Postcards are also cheap and easy to produce, especially if you use colour on one side only. They can be mailed to prospects, stacked in help-yourself dispensers, and you can use them for a variety of marketing messages, such as 'see our new product', 'gasp at our new prices' or 'look at our short-term cut-price promotion', and 'enter the competition or the free prize draw (and get two entries if you give us a friend's name and address)'. A reply-paid licence makes it easy for someone to return the card, and these are simple and economical to set up with the Post Office.

**WANT TO KNOW MORE …**
**The Post Office**
www.postoffice.co.uk

## *Run competitions and giveaways*

People love competitions, even if someone else wins. They are an excellent way to garner mailing list names, while sending branding messages, as the kind of contest you run implies the kind of company you are. Contests can also make for good PR, especially if there's a fun element that will attract media coverage. Of course, you can also simply give them something free, as people like to get gifts, even if they have to pay a premium price for a more expensive item to qualify for the freebie. This could be a free make-up purse with purchases, wine and fruit in your room if you book the weekend break, a CD of business tips with every seminar booking, or a pizza with every DVD film rented.

*"The aim is to boost sales and to tell the world that you are a generous, value-conscious supplier"*

The aim here is both to boost sales and to tell the world that you are a generous, value-conscious supplier. It also improves your competitive sell, since it becomes more difficult to compare like with like.

## Start a loyalty programme or club

The customer gets a good deal from a loyalty scheme, while you get a keen customer (and their contact details). A simple approach is to give customers a card that is marked after each purchase and results in a free or reduced-price offering after a specified number of regular-priced purchases. Easier to operate is a loyalty card scheme where regular customers get a discount on purchases on presentation of the card.

You can extend the programme into a full-blown club, sending out newsletters, launching exclusive special offers (great for shifting slow-moving stock), offering discounts on related products or services (it's generally easy to find other suppliers willing to give your club members a 10%–20% discount in return for capturing the buyer's details for their own database – with the customer's permission) and seminars and other get-togethers.

## Work on your elevator pitch

Every entrepreneur should prepare a short presentation that sums up the great things about their venture. As mentioned earlier in this guide, this 20–30-second piece is called an elevator pitch, as you could potentially deliver it while ascending a building in an elevator before the lift stops at your floor. Work on this so that you can recite it in your sleep – but not as though you are delivering a canned presentation.

When people say: 'So, what do you do?' the question they're really asking is: 'How do you make money?', but actually saying that is regarded as impolite. So your elevator pitch should answer the unspoken question, but in such a way that identifies the problems you solve or the benefits you can offer, and implies that your business is very successful because it's so good at solving those problems – and providing those benefits.

## Work on your references

Marketing should focus on benefits rather than features, meaning what you can do for your customer rather than how you do it, so use case studies and testimonials to prove your point. Ideally you need real clients. You can use a photograph and direct quotes to prove they exist. However, a start-up could get by with some hypothetical situations, but make it clear that these are not real. Customer stories are good business-to-business website content, and you can use clickable links for specifications and other non-chatty material to prevent the reader being inundated with statistics or technicalities. You can also produce them as single-sheet case studies and include them in brochures, but they should be both relevant and up to date.

## Keep up with your email

People who use email expect a speedy response, and providing one is a simple marketing technique that sends out lots of good messages: we're alert, responsive, aware of customer concerns, professional, up to date and so on. If you can't reply to incoming emails within an hour or so, use an automated system to provide an instant response of some kind. This could be a simple: 'Thanks, we'll get back to you as soon as possible'. But if you've organised your email addresses correctly, a more targeted response should be possible, meaning that incoming mail addressed to products@ yourcompany.co.uk could elicit an automated response that includes a PDF document containing product details or an appropriate website link. You can do quite a lot with Microsoft Outlook rules, or check out some of the auto-responder packages on offer.

## Always use email signatures

A couple of lines at the bottom of a message identifying you and your company is a simple way of sending out your contact details. Make sure every email carries your 'signature' (including replies to incoming messages) and that everyone in your organisation uses the same signature format. It shouldn't be too long, but should give two or three alternative ways to contact you and your company, your website address and include a marketing message of some kind, such as 'Sale now on' or 'Winner of the Best Company Prize 2007'.

## Email marketing

This is among the simplest and least expensive marketing options. You know almost immediately whether the email address is 'live' – still active, or spelled correctly – and most email marketing programmes enable you to track responses to see how many of your targets opened the email, and what they clicked on.

This doesn't mean that all email marketing is inherently good, however. For a start, it is indelibly associated with spam – unwanted and unrequested

*"The subject line is what will persuade people to read on, so put real effort into finding the right words"*

junk mail. Make sure that the people on your list actually want (and preferably are expecting) the material you are sending them and that your e-marketing activity complies with the Data Protection Act.

The 'From' and 'Subject' lines are crucial in email marketing. The recipient must recognise the sender — company name or brand are good options if your own name will mean nothing. And the subject is what will persuade them to read on, so put real effort into finding the right words. People don't read emails, they skim them. You still need good copywriting in an e-newsletter or a sales letter, but if possible you should also include clickable links or buttons for instant access to key online areas.

You can send a test mailing to a subset of your mailing list using two different subject lines. When you track the response, you can see which subject worked best and use that for your main mailing. The same holds true for other marketing methods, such as banner advertisements and paid search campaigns. You can start with a low investment, track your returns, and make changes before deciding whether to invest more or try a different tactic. Internet marketing is useful to marketers on a budget because it is flexible, measurable, and offers vast reach for little investment.

Finally, always include an 'Unsubscribe' option in your message, but you may as well make sure that people know what they're missing when they do unsubscribe. Clicking the unsubscribe button should take them to a webpage which asks them to confirm their decision and to identify what they specifically want to remove. They might not want to unsubscribe from everything and may want your occasional product updates, but not the regular newsletter.

## Social media

*"Users can chat to the real people behind the businesses, as well as sharing their own opinions and experiences"*

Social media has rocketed into business marketing over the last few years. With the proliferation of the internet have come many new methods of communication, which has led to increased user interactivity. Sites such as Facebook and Twitter provide platforms for businesses to connect with their customers on a more personal level, enabling them to post comments or tweets about the products and services they receive. Here, users can chat to the real people behind the businesses, as well as with each other, sharing their own opinions and experiences. Social media is a cheap and easy way for companies on a tight budget to market their business, and it is rapidly becoming a huge player in the promotional industry.

According to Regus, provider of workplace solutions, small businesses are more successfully utilising social media as a revenue generation tool than larger companies. Some 44% of small businesses have acquired new customers through their use of social networking sites, compared with 28% of large businesses. There are currently around 1.5 million small businesses with fan pages on Facebook, and around a quarter are now even dedicating their marketing budget to social media.

**Christian Nellemann**, founder of XLN Telecom, explains that when it was first launched in 2006, Twitter was dismissed by critics as a cult trend; however, the site now boasts 200 million users worldwide and has become a valuable platform for businesses to develop a dialogue with existing and prospective clients.

**Wendy Tan White**, founder of self-build web company Moonfruit, has found Twitter to be a highly effective marketing tool. In 2009, Moonfruit launched a Twitter campaign giving away a free MacBook Pro every day for 10 days – the only catch was that followers had to send a creative tweet to enter the draw. This brought a deluge of poems, jokes and cartoons; the campaign was one of the top discussions on the social networking site for three whole days.

However, despite the hype about social media in recent years, many businesses remain at the foot of a very steep learning curve, and are hesitant to take the plunge. See the box below for advice on how to create an effective social media strategy.

 **Action points**

## Creating your social media strategy

**Melanie Seasons**, social media strategist at PR agency Onlinefire, says that when shaping your social media plan you must bear the following in mind:

### 1. Audience

To get people talking about you, you have to know all the background. Research your typical customer – what are his/her online habits? What does he/she talk about online? What's the tone of voice? Are people already talking about you? Once you have a clear idea where your audience is and what they're saying, you'll know where you should have a presence.

## 2. Conversation platforms

Don't join Facebook or set up a Twitter profile just because you think you should. Think about who your audience is. You should be engaging on the sites that your customers are on.

## 3. Your presence

Your website is the face of your brand and often the hub of your business, and so it should be the hub of social media as well. Make sure all your social media channels are integrated and on the front page. Try to drive people back to your website, but equally keep your content 'out there' and circulating. You should be integrating with your customers' online lives.

## 4. Building followers

Unfortunately there's no quick and easy way to do this! It's all about having something interesting to say and giving your audience what they want. Chances are, unless you're Apple or the BBC, people aren't going to be interested in internal appointments and financial figures – they want to know about the people behind the company. Be personable, approachable, funny and smart. Promotions and giveaways for your social media fans can help boost your numbers, but it's your personality that will keep them there.

## 5. Integration

Social media is not an isolated channel. If you're not prepared to integrate social media with your overall marketing, digital, search, and/or customer service strategies, you're not ready for social media. Identify how the social media conversations you're having can be fed back into the business.

## 6. Measurement

Social media is highly measurable, but only if you're using the right tools. Make sure you've incorporated Google Analytics to track conversions from your social media sites. If you're using any social media monitoring tools, such as Radian 6, set out from the beginning some benchmarks. It's not just about sales – you also have to think about brand perception, buzz and sentiment.

# *Setting up a website*

As mentioned in previous chapters, it's also well worth setting up a website for your company. Getting someone to design and programme a basic site shouldn't be too costly, while keeping it simple can even be the best strategy, as overly complex websites can actually deter visitors.

You could also create one yourself, and these days there are lots of software packages around – such as Moonfruit, BaseKit and Microsoft Office 365 – that can guide you through the process even if you don't know how to code websites.

There was a time when creating a company website involved extensive consultation between designers, hosting companies and ISPs. If you want a bespoke graphic and flash animation heavy site this is still the case. However, if all you need are some company details, a few pages of product information and a location map, there are plenty of DIY and budget options where you can have an online presence in a matter of hours, or even minutes.

There are several cheap and often free services out there for small businesses that take minimal effort to set up and maintain. Bearing this in mind, there's really no excuse for not having an online presence. Whether it's a fully fledged site with your own domain name or a single page on a directory, if your business isn't online don't let your competitors steal your clients – do something about it today.

## *Getting the most from your website*

Like any other aspect of business, websites don't start with perfect success. They all start rough and improve with time. The key to this is web metrics – getting the numbers that tell you how people are using your site. Success on the web means getting people to do what you want when they visit your website. So the first thing you need to do is decide what it is you want them to do. This is called the target action. In most cases it's buying something or filling in a form.

*"By continually testing and learning, you will improve your conversion rates"*

Ask yourself if your site's design makes it easy for people to engage in your target action. Ease of navigation is consistently one of the top 10 complaints people have about web design. Once you have determined your target action, you need to determine how successful the site is. The key performance indicator of success is your conversion rate. This is the percentage of visitors to your site who engage in your target action. The average conversion rate across the web is 2%. Amazon is said to have the highest rate at 9%, though this is not a figure they will confirm.

## What makes a good website?

Nick Bramwell, founder of TwoLittleFishes web design, claims that the most important function of any small business site is to give customers (and potential customers) information about the business and what it does. A good place to start when creating a useful and successful website is to include information on:

- What the business does.
- The product/s or service/s the business provides.
- How the business can be contacted.

Taking these ideas one step further, you can allow customers to interact via the website. This could be as simple as having a contact form, or as advanced as allowing customers to buy products or services online via the website. You could also use your website to add value for your customers by providing them with additional support. For example, if you included an FAQ section, it gives your customers 24-7 access to answer common questions but can also free you up from answering the same question time and again.

To make your website successful you need to provide something of value to your customers. However, just creating a site with valuable content that remains static will not keep people coming back time and again. No matter how good the information, if it never changes people will get bored and stop visiting.

One of the things you could do is put up news items about your business. Another thing you could do is have a deal of the week or month with a voucher that visitors to the site can print out. The best content is often detailed information about your products and/or services – after all that is what your website is there to promote.

If you want to improve your site, you need to establish where it's failing. Google's free Analytics software will show you what users are doing on your website, where they came from, which pages they visited, and crucially, where they abandoned you.

**Nigel Muir**, MD of search and PPC specialists DBD Media, explains: 'You may find that 50% of visitors land on your homepage and then leave immediately, which would lead you to question the relevancy of the search terms you are using (in your search marketing), or the quality of your homepage. Or, you may find that 80% of people who place an item in your shopping basket then abandon the process before completing a sale – perhaps you are asking for too much personal information, or have a surprise credit card or delivery charge on this page.'

By continually testing and learning, you will improve your conversion rates. If you're an online retailer, try purchasing a product from your site. It's also worth asking friends, colleagues and customers to give you honest feedback on your site, as well as looking at your competitors' offerings to see what you can improve on.

## Search engine optimisation

Search engine optimisation (SEO) increases your website's visibility in the search engines, and can therefore increase your sales and growth potential. SEO is the process of altering a website so it ranks higher in search engines' listings.

Search engines use algorithms to decide which sites are most 'relevant' to the keywords entered by the user. The 10 most relevant sites are shown on the first results page – your goal is to persuade the search engines your site is relevant to the words potential customers will use to search.

The main search engines are 'crawler-based'. Like a spider, search engines create their listings automatically by 'crawling' through the web and reading every site. Everything the crawler finds goes into a huge index. When you search for a phrase, the search engine software sifts through the millions of pages recorded in the index to find the most relevant. How they decide this is based on highly complex, mathematical algorithms.

These rules are very closely guarded secrets. There's no way of knowing exactly how to get to the top of the listings, but here are a few tricks you can use to optimise your site that have been proven to boost rankings.

### 1. Be your customer

The best place to start is from your potential customers' point of view, by working out what they will be searching for. These are your keywords, which will form the basis of your optimisation.

**Nick Holmes**, from PR recruitment company, Parker, Wayne & Kent, says: 'We had a brainstorm to identify all the words that could describe our company. Because we work with clients as well as candidates, we had to ensure we picked up the words that people from both areas might search for.'

If you decided to hire the services of a specialist search marketing agency (and there are many), you would start with the same focus. **Jeremy Spiller**, MD of online marketing agency White Hat Media, explains: 'We discuss with the client what keywords they want to do well with. We take into consideration things like location, USPs and competitiveness of the words. For example, it's not worth bothering trying to be top with the word "houses" – it's too generic and competitive.'

Sites such as http://searchmarketing.yahoo.com/rc/srch and www.wordtracker.com will tell you for free how frequently your keywords are entered as search terms and suggest related, more popular phrases. Also try www.seochat.com, which contains an extensive list of free SEO tools.

## 2. Add keywords

Your site's text will need frequent instances of your keywords to attract the attention of search engines. Look especially at the first paragraph, headings and subheadings. But be warned: don't be tempted simply to insert a paragraph flooded with keywords. This is called 'keyword spamming'. The SEO world has developed its own code of conduct and spamming is viewed unfavourably. Google is especially good at spotting things like this and says that if a site does not meet its quality guidelines (www.google.com/support/webmasters), it may temporarily or permanently remove it from its listings.

A good rule of thumb is never to forget that the site is for its users, not for search engines. Spiller warns: 'There's a danger of getting obsessed with search engines, but the most important thing of all is making a good site – easy to use, with good content – and Google does recognise that.'

There is a wealth of frowned-upon behaviour used by sneaky SEO-obsessed site owners, such as putting white text on white background, so only search engines can see it. Resist such tricks – they will backfire in the long run.

## 3. Don't forget the awkward bits

Almost as important as the body text is your site's title. This is one of the first things search engines – and users – notice, so it's vital to have your keywords in the short, descriptive title tag.

Another element is the Meta Description tag. This allows you to describe your site to search engines, so a short description can be beneficial. But be aware that Google now ignores it and generates its own description of the page. Many people believe the Meta Keywords Tag can help. But the major search engines ignore it, meaning that you can too.

Now your site is woven through with search-engine attracting keywords, have a look at how navigable it is. If it's easy for users to get around, it is likely to be appealing to search engines too. If your homepage includes hyperlinks to the major sections of your site, search engines will follow them, finding more of your website as a result.

## 4.  Look at your links

Your site is already more likely to catch the wandering eyes of search engines. But you're not finished yet. Spiller says: 'We get lots of calls from people who have done all that and still haven't moved up the listings much. This is often because of links from other websites. It's important to get as many good ones as possible.'

Popularity is always attractive, especially to search engines. They will love your site if other reputable sites link to it. **Andrew Girdwood**, head of search at Bigmouthmedia, says: 'Google treats links like votes. So if you're lucky enough that a respected online magazine writing about your industry has a link to your site, then Google sees that you have a good site in respect of the keywords the article is about.'

For this reason, agencies often create link-building campaigns for your site, using techniques such as blogs and submitting papers and press releases to other sites. If your SEO is in-house, there are methods of getting your link on other sites, such as link exchanges, but be careful – often the people willing to exchange don't have great websites themselves. If you can find high-ranking websites related to the topics on which your site is based, and which are willing to link to you, your site is harder for search engines to resist.

However, avoid 'link spamming', the process of trying to get as many links on external sites as possible – another example of bad industry practice. Search engines will spot it and will be mighty unimpressed.

## SEO glossary

**Algorithm:** the criteria used by search engines to rank pages. Frequently updated to avoid black hat SEO techniques (see below)

**White hat SEO:** Ethical SEO techniques, ie good industry practice

**Black hat SEO:** SEO techniques that are seen as unethical, such as keyword spamming or hidden text

**In-bound links:** Links from other websites to your own. Another big factor in the ranking criteria

**Keyword:** The word(s) used by a search engine user to search for sites

**Keyword density:** The frequency of the keywords on the page – a key criteria in search engines' ranking

**Pay-per-click or paid search:** The paid-for links on the search engines. Your ranking will depend on the amount you bid – you will pay this amount whenever anyone clicks on the site. An effective, though often expensive option

 ## What to do next

- Put together a marketing plan you can refer back to including specific goals and accomplishments. If you don't have this written down, you won't be able to track how successful you've been and what methods proved most effective.

- Focus on targeting your marketing efforts at specific groups of consumers. The scattergun approach won't cut it. You need to identify exactly who you're trying to reach and tailor your marketing plan accordingly.

- Embrace the value of PR. It's far more cost-effective than paying for advertising and can get you even more exposure if done well.

- Make sure you have, at the very least, a basic website. Too many small companies neglect their online presence.

- Don't underestimate the importance of social media. Although a fairly new marketing channel, it can prove incredibly powerful for small businesses if used effectively.

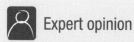 Expert opinion

# Do you really need marketing?

**Helen Murdoch from HM Marketing has some tips on your marketing strategy**

One of the biggest myths in business is that if you have a great product or service, business will come to you in floods.

But it's just not true. As many new businesses discover, if you don't market your business and promote it effectively, you won't achieve success – no matter how good your product or service is.

Marketing is making sure the right people hear about what you have to offer, understand what it is about, decide they want it, and know how they can find you to get it. It is more than just placing an advert, producing a brochure or designing a website – every contact you make with potential customers is a form of marketing. Your aim is to make these contacts as numerous and positive as possible.

*Three simple steps*

However, not everyone is a prospective customer, so to make sure you are not wasting your time and money on marketing that doesn't produce results, it is essential to plan what you are going to do. Here are three simple steps to follow:

1. Identify those people who show the highest potential for buying from you.

2. Make contact with them, so that they are aware of you and what you have to offer.

3. Make sure you are the first person they think of when they are ready to buy and make sure that they know exactly how to make contact with you.

*Not just anyone – focus on someone*

Forget trying to sell to everyone. I know it's very tempting to try and sell to anyone and everyone, particularly when you are starting your business. However, no matter how appealing your product or service may seem, it is never going to be bought by everyone.

Instead of wasting your time and money trying to sell 'to the world', research your market so that you know specifically who your product or service will appeal to.

Use these questions to guide you – Why do they need your product? What are their problems and how can your product or service solve them? What is it about your product or service that will appeal to them? What drives them – price, quality, prestige? Does your product or service meet their criteria? Where can you reach them? How can you reach them on a consistent basis?

Focus your attention and efforts on appealing to the people who are most likely to buy from you. To do that you must know what their needs are, what they really want and what their problems and concerns are. Address those needs, wants, problems and concerns directly in your marketing. Demonstrate that you know what they want and that you have a solution to their problem, and they'll come running to you.

### Grab their attention

How do you grab and hold the attention of prospective customers? And how do you get them to respond?

Well, it's not all about the biggest and flashiest advert, and it doesn't have to cost thousands. The key is not where you market but what you say, how you say it and who you say it to. Getting the message right is critical to your success.

Look in *Yellow Pages* or in a local newspaper and you'll see that typically an advert starts with the company name or logo, then simply lists the products or special offers and ends with the company address, telephone number and website address.

Wow, isn't that exciting! Is there anything in that sort of advert to make you want to contact the company, want to find out more or want to buy? Probably not. What prospective customers want to know is how they will benefit from your product or service – what will it do for them?

For example, if you are a company selling replacement windows and doors, most people are not interested in 'Buy One Get One Free' or 'Styles and Sizes to Suit Every House'. They are more likely to be interested in saving money on their heating bills or in being more secure. A headline such as 'Save 15% on Your Heating Bills' or 'So Secure, We've Never Had A Single Forced Entry' is certainly more appealing. Both of these statements directly address the problems or concerns that are in your prospective customers' mind. By focusing on the benefits or the solutions to a problem, you create a powerful message that engages your customer.

*Knock seven times if you want me*

Too many times I've talked to small business owners who have sent out one email campaign, run one advert or sent out one sales letter and when they get little or no response, claim marketing doesn't work. Let me tell you a secret – relying on just one type of marketing won't work; marketing takes patience and persistence.

The rule of thumb is that on average it takes seven contacts with a potential customer before they take action. That doesn't mean that someone will automatically buy if they see your advert seven times. No, it means you have to give your prospect lots of opportunities to see your message. That means using a range of different methods from emails, sales letters, phone calls, speaking at an event, networking, leaflets, your website and so on. Create a drip, drip campaign to stay in front of your best prospects and you'll soon see the results.

Remember it takes time – don't expect overnight success with one small advert, one email or one leaflet drop. After all, do you buy a McDonald's every time you see a McDonald's advert or pass one of their restaurants? No, the advertising and marketing is there so that when you want a burger, you think of McDonald's first. Make sure your business is the first people think of when they want what you provide.

*Does a car need an engine?*

Without an engine, a car may look good, but it doesn't get very far. The same is true of a business that doesn't do any marketing. You may have the best products and services in the world, but if no-one knows about them and no-one buys them, the business isn't going anywhere.

**Helen Murdoch has spent 25 years uncovering the marketing mistakes that are costing small businesses £1,000s. Find out if you are making these same mistakes in her FREE report 'The 5 Big Marketing Mistakes and How to Avoid Them'. Simply go to www. HelenMurdochMarketing.com and download your personal copy.**

# CHAPTER 10

*Making a sale*

 **What's in this chapter?**

→ Making a sale
→ Your sales story
→ The sales pitch
→ Negotiation
→ Repeat sales

Not everyone is a natural born salesperson, but as an entrepreneur you need to learn how to sell your products and services if you want to win business in the early days. You also need a clear sales strategy. This chapter will take you through the key stages of the sales process, from drawing up a list of potential customers and making contact with them, to establishing your sales story and delivering a winning sales pitch.

In addition, with the pressure to realise value from deals higher than ever in the current financial climate, understanding the art of negotiation has never been more important. Read on for advice on how to close the deal – and how to keep your existing customers coming back for more.

## Making a sale

Some people seem like they were born to sell, while for many the mere thought brings them out in a cold sweat. But if you want to make your business a success, then you need to sell what you do – at least until you have the resources to build up a sales team. And even if you may not consider yourself a salesperson, if you can launch a new business you can probably also sell your product or service. In fact, when you speak to your bank, and potential recruits and suppliers, you are essentially selling your business to them to get them to work with you.

A lot of businesses – from clothes shops and online retailers to cafés, bars and restaurants – don't need salespeople in the classic sense, with sales driven more by marketing, such as advertisements in the local press, calls to action on websites, direct mail flyer drops, etc. But for many more businesses, salespeople are a key aspect of generating income and driving profit.

In many cases, simply having the best product or service is not enough. You still need a marketing strategy to raise awareness, and once you've launched, you will need a sales plan alongside it to build up a list of key prospects and sell directly to them.

## Knowing your customer

Before you can think about selling a product or service, you need to clearly define and understand your customer. It may sound obvious, but it is crucial to every aspect of starting up, from writing a business plan, to designing a website, and of course trading – and by that we mean selling!

Although it sounds counter-intuitive, you don't want to sell to everyone. This will mean you spread yourself too thinly, when you could be focusing on the people that will be the most valuable customers. A more efficient use of your time will be to focus on the people who will spend the most money with you over the long term, so you can forget about customers who are only likely to spend a negligible amount and buy from you only once or twice.

So how do you identify this perfect customer? The answer is to do some research. You could use market data, demographic information, industry and trade knowledge to identify who is buying what you're selling. Look for common characteristics in your key customers or even customers of your competitors. If they're individuals, how old are they? What's their geographical or income demographic? What are their buying patterns? Why do they buy your product or service? Be sure that the target market is big enough for you to achieve enough sales, however.

Even if you're selling business-to-business (B2B), there's still an individual that buys from you, not a company. Once you've identified as much information as possible about this target customer, B2B or business-to-consumer (B2C), ask yourself questions such as: what problems does this individual have that I can help with? What are their priorities? What information should I be getting from them? Is there a gap in the market of interest to them?

This should help you structure your offering, your sales approach and your marketing to be much more focused and appealing to your most valuable customers.

## Buying data lists

Acquiring new customers is never an easy task. One approach is to buy 'customer data' from specialist data providers. This data provides details on individuals who might be interested in purchasing your product or service. It usually includes contact information as well as lifestyle data, for example, what car a person has, so you can determine how likely it is that this particular individual will buy your product or service.

To be sure that you have prospect data that adheres to the guidelines, check how the data was collected and if prior consent for contact was provided by the individual. There's no point, for example, spending £500 on customer email addresses when none of the people on the list have opted-in to receive information via email or SMS as it's a waste of your time and money.

You can also get lists that have been verified post sign-up. These will cost more but are undoubtedly more valuable.

*"There's no point spending £500 on customer email addresses when none of the people on the list have opted-in"*

## Keeping customer records

The simple administrative task of keeping records of your customers will pay dividends in terms of your business' success. Knowing who is buying from you, how often, and having contact details allowing you to keep in touch with them will be invaluable in sales, marketing, customer service, even financial forecasting, and will keep your business customer-focused.

This is especially true in a small business, where customer relationships are everything. If you can keep on top of names and preferences and offer a friendly service as a result, you'll see a significant amount of repeat business. People like a personal touch, so you can also keep personal details: names of family, preferred football team and so on.

These records might be as simple as a spreadsheet comprised of names, companies, and contact details, or you could install something much more sophisticated. For example, customer relationship management software (CRM) can help you track and analyse customer data as your business grows. CRM isn't just for big businesses however — software has been specifically designed for small firms too.

The software will keep records of sales history, preferences, contact details and more, and will let you access this information in an easily manageable way, allowing you to target the most valuable customers. The software can also link to accounts software, giving you a more holistic view, and can record people's spending patterns, budgets and more.

## *Your sales story*

*"Knowing what you want to say and having an engaging story will give you confidence"*

A good sales story is vital. Whether you're on the phone, making contact with potential customers or closing a deal, you need to make your customer buy into the idea. They have to want to use your service or buy your product. You need a watertight bona fide story of why they need you. Too many businesses offer complex services and products without ever exploiting the most basic human message. Why?

Furthermore, knowing what you want to say and having an engaging story will give you confidence. If you can tell your story well, the customer is more likely to want to know more, and additionally, not worrying about what to say next will mean you're able to listen more and make a deeper connection with the customer. This story can obviously be adjusted depending on who you're talking to, but the key points will probably remain the same.

So how do you create this story? The goal is to let the person on the other end of the phone know what you can do for them. What benefits will they receive by buying from you? Use what you know about your existing customers to help you. If you base the sales conversation on their priorities, concerns and needs, you will have a better chance of communicating the benefits of your offering to the new potential customer. It's vital that they know that you actually care about what they want or need, and that they can be sure you will make a real effort for them.

As soon as you know what the individual could gain by being your customer, you have to communicate that effectively. You have to address some of the potential customer's questions and fears. Why should they believe you? Will they enjoy doing business with you? What's different about what you're offering?

And when your sales story is engaging, convincing and concise, make sure everyone in your business is familiar with it.

## *Knowing your product and the competition*

It's absolutely vital to know your competition in order to sell your products to their best advantage. It's advisable to keep one eye on them at all times, since knowing who they are and what they're offering can mean you are much better placed to stand out and maximise your sales.

*"It's vital to know your competition in order to sell your products to their best advantage"*

It's arguably unprofessional to criticise your competition when selling, but you can certainly play it to your advantage if you have a clear idea of their weaknesses. For this reason, if it is possible to get information from the customers about previous experiences with the competition, it could be very valuable.

It is also important to know if there are any new entrants to the market to ensure you retain your USP. If you have a good grasp of your industry, you're likely to hear about it if someone comes along with something new to offer, but use internet research and your contacts as well.

Don't just learn about the competition's product and pricing, however. Whatever you use to sell your offering is important – the level of customer service, how it is sold, any customer loyalty devices, for example. And it also useful to know about the company itself – age, size, number of staff, even their accounts which are accessible at Companies House. Ask them for brochures, price lists, or any other marketing products.

From an entrepreneur's point of view, if it turns out that your competition is making more sales than you with good reason, you know things need to be changed. From the salesperson's point of view, there's no better way of finding out how to make your offering irresistibly different and convincing than knowing you're better than the competitors. Of course, this is what makes competition a healthy thing – driving you to be the best you can be.

## Cold calling

*"Cold calling gets around a 5% success rate if done very well, so you need to develop a thick skin"*

It is likely that at some point you will have to pick up the phone and attempt to convince strangers of the strength of your product or service. It's a business fact of life, but inevitably, so is getting rejected – cold calling gets around a 5% success rate if done very well – so the most important thing to do is develop a thick skin.

Cold calling is not all about making an instant sale. It can often be used for gathering information, or trying to arrange a meeting, so launching straight in with the breathless description of your product may not be the right approach. Calling to confirm names, titles and contact details can be a good way to start. You get information confirmed, and you might be able to take it further.

If cold calling isn't something that comes naturally, then consider a script. But be very careful – sounding like you're reading from a piece of paper is off-putting to the person on the other end of the line, as you probably know from being cold called yourself. Perhaps a better way of using a script is to remind you of the points you need to make, rather than being a word for word recital tool. You have to be able to be flexible, and listen to the needs of the person you're calling.

### In my experience

**Company: CURB Media**
**Owner-manager: Anthony Ganjou**

*CURB Media and the cold call*
**Anthony Ganjou** founded CURB Media in 2008, after spotting a gap in the market for delivering a marketing message using 'natural media', such as snow, sand or grass.

While the company has achieved impressive growth, many people needed convincing of the viability of Anthony's new venture in the early days – not least the advertising agencies he visited. Anthony made a conscious decision not to target 'green' customers – while he acknowledges this would have been a far easier sell, he felt this would create the wrong impression of his offering and limit his growth prospects: 'I made an active decision not to go after the typically green clients – this did make the pitch harder but we never wanted CURB or natural media to be pigeonholed as just a "green thing" or fad,' he says.

To make the venture work, Anthony made up to 150 cold calls a day in the initial stages, relying heavily on word-of-mouth to build a profile. Then, in February 2009, the big freeze brought his vision to boiling point: 'At that time, London experienced its worst snow in almost 100 years – everything ground to a halt. But I saw it as the chance to try out snow-tagging – we had received a sample logo from Al Gosling, founder of the Extreme Group, and, with his blessing, we went out into the snow and started imprinting it on cars outside our office. Within an hour I was on Oxford Street, placing hundreds of snow tags across the West End.

'The next day the media went bananas. The images went literally everywhere, featuring in nationals, trade mags and even US titles like *Ad Age*. Conservative estimates put the value to Extreme of the snow-tagging campaign at £750,000, and it even received the Cannes Lion Gold award (like the Oscars of the ad industry) in 2010.'

Since taking a giant leap in the snow two years ago, CURB has grown rapidly. Interest has flooded in from media planners and ad agencies, and a number of projects have grabbed the headlines. Anthony's strategy of targeting mainstream rather than 'green' clients – and not being afraid to cold call – laid the foundations for the company's future success. CURB has now created striking campaigns for some of the world's leading brands, including Microsoft, Nike and Lynx. The company has also installed natural media in the White House, helped Sony launch Michael Jackson, and even done work for the Queen.

One problem is getting through to the right person. If the list you've bought is what it claims to be, this should be easy, but as people frequently change job or roles within an organisation it's important to ensure the contacts are up to date. However, there is often someone – the 'gatekeeper' – standing between you and your contact. This could be a receptionist or PA who has

*"If you befriend the gatekeeper, you are more likely to get through after a few calls"*

been instructed not to put salespeople through. This means the less you sound like a classic salesperson the better, so clearly introduce yourself and where you are from, and be polite and friendly, perhaps saying you have only a few questions and won't take up much of your target's time.

Don't open the conversation by asking them how they are and not telling them who you are – this will be highly unproductive, even though it is standard cold-calling fare. Ultimately, if you befriend the gatekeeper, you are more likely to get through after a few calls.

You will get people who put the phone down straight away (don't you do that occasionally?) but don't be scared of this outcome or let it get to you when it does happen. It's not personal. Keep calm and smile, and this will come through in your voice and make people more receptive. Monitor your success rate and attempt to strategically perfect your approach.

If you ask for information by using open questions, and keep your voice friendly and inquisitive, you're more likely to get people's interest. The aggressive sale usually won't work in this context because people are so wary of cold calls. Offer meeting times if it looks like you won't be able to make a sale, and confirm in writing.

## The sales pitch

*"Always begin by taking a deep breath and smiling, as this will help to relax both you and your audience"*

Once you have a meeting arranged, you need to work on a short, engaging presentation that adds key points to your initial phone conversations. Try to keep your presentation to no longer than 20 minutes – even shorter if possible – and then be prepared to field questions.

First impressions do count, so it's important to come across well at that first meeting. Good preparation will help build your confidence and calm your nerves, and always begin by taking a deep breath and smiling, as this will help to relax both you and your audience.

### Do your homework

To mis-quote Tony Blair: Preparation, preparation, preparation. Sales pitches should have been worked on extensively before they're wheeled out to prospective customers. Make sure you know your figures. Write down all the major points that explain what you do and what sets you apart from the competition. Then pick out the best three or four, which could vary depending on who you are going to be pitching to.

Construct your sales story around these points, then practise telling it – if possible to people who know a bit about the sector. Honest feedback will help you improve this story. And trust your own instincts. Pitch to yourself. What questions would you ask?

Also do your homework on who you're pitching to. If you understand their business and their needs, and how what you're offering is suitable for them, it will make your job easier and impress the client.

## How to pitch

As an entrepreneur, you're likely to be filled with huge enthusiasm for the product or service you're offering. This is a great advantage and will come across well in your pitch. But be careful – there will be a temptation to keep talking, but this would be a big mistake. Try and base your pitch on listening instead. Ask questions and tailor your pitch to the answers you receive. The intelligence you will glean could also be vital on a more long-term basis.

*"Don't be scared to say you don't know the answer to a particular query; this is better than bluffing your way through"*

Also, throughout your pitch remember to speak clearly and slowly, maintain eye contact (though not too much – don't stare unnervingly), and smile. Your mood will affect the mood of the buyer, so be happy and relaxed. Be receptive to changes on their part too – make sure you know if they're losing interest, becoming irritated or showing signs of interest, and adjust your pitch or style accordingly. Keep it short and sweet too. There's no ideal length but don't push your customer's patience.

Once you've finished and invited questions, try to answer confidently and knowledgeably, but also don't be scared to say you don't know the answer to a particular query, as this is better than bluffing your way through, and won't come back to haunt you later. You can always research the answer and get back to them.

Finally, close the meeting effectively. Find out what the next steps are, what additional information they need and what factors they will be basing their final decision on. This will help you at the next meeting, if necessary.

Of course, rejection is just as (if not more) possible as clinching a sale, so be prepared for it and take it on the chin. Try to ask your audience the reasons for them not wanting to buy from you, as this can be key information in the development of your offer, and will mean you will get something productive from the meeting. Also ask your audience if they would mind if you contact them in six months or a year's time to review the situation.

### Using presentation software for sales

There's no consensus on whether you should use presentation software, such as PowerPoint, in your sales pitches. Some people find it extremely helpful, others hate it. If you find it helps you structure your pitch then by all means use it. But be warned against the potential pitfalls – the time taking setting it up, the fact that it can make the conversation slightly less personal and more formal, and the danger of becoming dependent on it. You should be able to do your pitch without it. That way if the worst happens and it doesn't work, you'll be able to put on an impressive performance in adverse circumstances.

Keep the presentation short and sweet and don't include too many slides. More than 10 is usually too many. Also make sure you're not putting too much information on each slide. Everything should be concise, clear, and immediately understandable. If your customer is reading the slides, then they're not listening to you. For the same reason, don't hand out printouts of the slides until the end of the meeting.

Also be warned against the presentation looking amateur and ruining your professional image; it could be worth getting a professional to design your slide templates for you if you will be using this method a lot.

*"Believe in what you're selling and the benefits it will give to the buyer"*

## Negotiation

Negotiation is one of the most vital skills any entrepreneur can have. It's not just in sales meetings, but in everyday situations where you'll be using negotiation skills – for example, negotiating with staff over time off or department budgets, or with suppliers who want to hike prices and so on. But most of all, you'll need those negotiation skills in securing a deal.

The skills used in a sales meeting will be the same as those used in all the other situations. First of all, whenever you're entering a negotiation, make sure you're prepared. Know what you want to get out of the meeting, and what you're prepared to offer to prevent you from going too low on price or promising things you can't deliver.

Through previous contact with the buyer, you should also have a good idea of what they want out of the negotiations too. In the negotiations, remain confident. Believe in what you're selling and the benefits it will give to the buyer, and communicate this clearly. Don't undersell under pressure. Try and keep the negotiations under your control – within your price range, delivery time or profit margin.

Listen. If you're listening carefully, you'll work out what it will take for you to close the deal, and be able to answer their concerns, as well as reinforce the personal relationship with the buyer. You might even learn other things of interest about them or your competition.

Be careful about how much you discount, as discounting can backfire if you're undervaluing your product by doing so. If it's a deal breaker then tread carefully to ensure you still get a sensible margin. And no matter how tempting, don't over-promise. If the buyer has agreed to purchase at full price, don't get carried away and promise to deliver in terms of stock and timings things that aren't possible.

Throughout your negotiations, think of the long-term relationship. Negotiating fairly and getting a positive outcome for both parties will strengthen your relationship with the buyer.

## How to close a deal

Closing a deal is where everything rests. The pressure's on for any salesperson at this point, so it's important to know how to maximise your chances of finalising the sale. Too many business owners do all the legwork of meetings, preparation, pitches and so on, then don't get that all-important signature.

*"There are no hard and fast rules about when you should lean to a close"*

The first thing to know is that there are no hard and fast rules about when you should lean to a close. Only you will be able to judge when the moment's right, and if you do recognise the time, don't leave it too late. For example, if there have been positive signals from the buyer all the way through the meeting, it's natural to start closing.

Closing will obviously be much easier if you've done your preparation. If the customer doesn't want the product at all, or is already sourcing it from someone else and is happy with the provider, or has no budget, you should have already found out about this. If there's no way round these problems, which often there won't be, then there's no point in continuing trying to sell.

However, if none of these problems exist, you know you could in theory be making a sale here. So how do you start? It's up to you how direct you want to be. A question such as 'Are you able to sign the contract today?' is obviously very direct, but can often be effective. Alternatively you can sum up the benefits in a way which concludes the meeting, leading naturally to a sale, or you can ask a question about what the buyer wants, for example, 'Do you want this in red or blue?' Find whichever way is most natural for you.

Then comes asking for money, something that even the best salespeople can still find difficult. But as an entrepreneur it's something you're going to have to be good at. If you find it difficult to talk money, practise telling the customer what the total price will be until you can say it in real life without finding it awkward. Be honest and not afraid to talk money. It's an issue for both sides so address it openly.

Don't talk too much – don't be afraid of silence. Produce an order form, don't rush anything, remain confident and make eye contact. When the customer signs, and the sale is made, keep friendly and resist any urge to sell them anything else. Leave on a friendly note so you can keep a long-term relationship.

## What next?

It is easy to think that once you have closed a sale, you can relax. But the reality is far from it. Often, shaking hands is simply the first in a series of steps to ensure the deal goes through smoothly. Remember to enter the sales negotiation armed with information. If the value or risk of the business transaction is high, it's wise to get as much financial information about the client as possible, to minimise the level of risk to the business and protect against bad debt.

Closing the sale is not simply a matter of asking for an order, and establishing terms of delivery and payment. You should also re-state your credit terms to the buyer and present them with your credit application form (free samples are available at the Better Payment Practice Group website: www.payontime.co.uk/collect/collect_cash.html), while establishing a named contact responsible for payment.

Once you've got your first few sales under your belt you will start to build up a network of customers, and further sales should be a little easier – you could well have some good testimonials to back up your pitch.

## Saving a seemingly lost sale

The art of getting a sale back is a difficult one to master. It could happen at any point, but the customer could start to backtrack during the close. Occasionally you won't be able to save it, but by staying calm and confident you'll heighten your chances. Remember the points that you established with the customer thus far, and briefly run through them again. Be clear and friendly and remind the customer of the benefits they will get out of the sale. Be confident in the product and the reasons that someone would want to buy it. Think on your feet to meet any objections, and take your time.

*"Be clear and friendly and remind the customer of the benefits they will get out of the sale"*

Look out for 'buying signals'. If the buyer appears reluctant but is also indicating through what they're saying that the product is needed, you're still in with a chance, and you have to listen and work out what you need to offer to make your business the one to provide what they need. However, don't be desperate! They need to want you, not the other way round.

Even when objections are raised, this isn't necessarily a problem. This is your chance to shine by being well-prepared and being able to meet these objections. The buyer is actually showing interest through raising objections so you can steer them around to seeing benefits instead.

If things don't go how you hoped, it's easy to feel a blow to your confidence or be too disappointed. But the fact is that this will happen. Try and learn from it, and ask as much as you can about why you didn't get the business. Who did you lose it to and why? Ask if you can have a chat in a few months and leave it amicably – there may be future business to go for. So record the customer's information!

# Repeat sales

You'll probably find that a large amount of your business is repeat business, particularly if you're doing things right! So how do you maximise the chances of a customer returning to your business?

*"Remember the value of communication with your customer"*

Obviously, the whole sales process should be geared towards long-term relationships as well as the individual sale. If you've been honest with the customer and built up a good relationship with them all the way through, there's a high chance they will be a repeat customer.

If you've had a successful transaction with a new customer, you're in a perfect position to make this customer keep coming back to you. Trust is difficult to get but once you have it, you need to use it as much as possible. It may sound obvious, but the simple act of asking for more business can be extremely helpful. Your aim is to make your business the first thing the customer thinks of when they need what you're offering.

As well as a healthy focus on after-sales, remember the value of communication with your customer. Is there anything you could improve or that would make them more likely to buy from you again? Take advantage of your customers – they're an excellent source of information. If there are any complaints, then show that you're taking them seriously, and actually taking action to make sure buying from you is as easy as possible.

And use your customer records to keep in touch with customers, especially the ones you've identified as potentially most valuable, so your business' name always easily comes to mind. Build relationships with them – set six-monthly catch-ups – and build discourse using tools such as mail lists, competitions, newsletters and so on. Look after your most valuable clients, maybe the top five, by taking them out every now and again. Let them know they're valued.

## The value of after-sales

*"It costs a lot less to keep an existing customer than to find a new one"*

After-sales is also about customer service and how you want your business to be remembered. This is all about carrying on even once you have the money. It's very easy to close the sale then walk away, but letting clients know you value their custom is an invaluable marketing tool. Additionally, if you impress customers with your after-sales service, you may reap the benefits of word of mouth referrals, which cannot be underestimated.

Providing a strong after-sales service is relatively straightforward. Do you offer a comprehensive guarantee and returns policy? Can customers contact you easily if they have a complaint about the product or service? Will this complaint be treated promptly and seriously? Can your staff handle after-sales calls professionally and in a friendly manner? You could even make follow up calls or letters making sure everything is OK a few weeks after the sale.

Remember that it costs a lot less to keep an existing customer than to find a new one so don't neglect repeat customers. After-sales really is one of your most cost-effective marketing tools.

## Cross-selling

Cross-selling is a very simple sales technique. If you've made a sale to a customer and you have other products they may be interested in, it's simply selling them the additional products too.

In terms of the benefits, it is a very time and labour efficient way of selling – as the customer already has the trust in you as a salesperson and a business. Most businesses know how much it costs to acquire a new customer, so cross-selling has significant cost savings. And for the customer, it can often be better to limit their dealings to as few providers as possible, so if you offer another product or service they need, it can be beneficial for them too.

Cross-selling generally refers to selling items that are related or can be integrated with the item being sold. Rather than simply trying to get as much out of the customer as possible, cross-selling can be a demonstration that you understand and care about their needs, and can suggest other items that will help them.

For that reason, for the good salesperson, many cross-selling opportunities will arise naturally. Don't, therefore, offer a lot of unrelated products since the customer will realise their needs are not being taken into consideration. If you keep the customer's needs in mind, you will benefit them, making them a more likely repeat customer, and maximising the potential of each sell.

Examples of cross-selling are all around us. Do the words 'Do you want fries with that?' sound familiar? Or what about online bookshops such as Amazon who tell you that the other people who bought that book also bought *War and Peace* and the autobiography of Victoria Beckham? Or perhaps you once bought some new shoes and came away with the shoe polish too. As you can see, cross-selling can serve a practical purpose for the customer too.

 **What to do next**

- Identify whether you have the appropriate sales skills yourself or whether you need to bring in outside help. The ability to sell effectively is not a talent possessed by everyone.

- Do your research before you approach your customers. Make sure you know your products inside out, and arm yourself with information about the competition too.

- Look after your customer details and go back to them later. It's far cheaper to sell to existing customers than acquire new ones.

- Don't underestimate the value of after-sales care. Your efforts shouldn't stop once you've secured payment. Customers need to be well looked after or they'll go elsewhere next time.

# CHAPTER 11

*What's next?*

## 📖 What's in this chapter?

→ *Time management*
→ *Delegation*
→ *Self-motivation*
→ *Personal development*
→ *Finding a business mentor*
→ *Over to you ...*

Once your business is up and running, it's vital to maintain your energy and drive. A key part of this involves making the most of your time and skills. You may well find yourself doing everything at first – and working all hours – but if you're exhausted and bogged down with administrative duties, then growth, strategy and even customer relationships could suffer.

The key is to learn to work smarter, thus freeing up your time to focus on the things you're best at – such as winning new business. This chapter will explore some key techniques and skills to help boost your efficiency and motivation – from time management and delegation to personal development. We'll also look at why a mentor can be a major asset to a new business – and where to find one.

# Time management

It's not just owners of small businesses who claim that 24 hours are just not enough in a day – but do they seem to complain about it more than most! It almost seems obligatory that, when starting out, you will be at your desk late into the night, early in the mornings and throughout the weekend. Can you operate in this way for long at an effective level? The European Union (EU) obviously thinks not, as its many rules on working hours suggest that the evidence shows that people do not work effectively at such a pace, and it is unfair to expect your staff to do this. So why do owner-managers do it themselves?

## How many working hours?

A recent Bank of Scotland survey found that entrepreneurs work on average a 50-hour week, compared with the EU norm of just 35 hours a week. For those businesses growing at over 10% a year the average working week is 52.3 hours. The survey reported that overall, Britain's 1.4 million small businesses are collectively putting in a staggering 31.2 million extra 'working weeks' each year. Seven in 10 (71%) small business owners claimed to feel stressed by running and managing their business, compared with only half (54%) in the previous year.

Without doubt, new business owners want to be efficient, and one way of keeping costs down is to take on as much of the workload as possible. And if, during the regular nine-to-five working day, you are handling customers or clients, then it is more than likely that the administration will follow in the evenings or at weekends. The increasingly global nature of business, particularly for anyone running a website as part of their business, for example, also means that working hours are extending – a work phone call at 9pm or even 4am is not unusual for website owners. But the key to making it all work is time management.

**Imogen Daniels**, an adviser at the Chartered Institute of Personnel and Development (CIPD), believes 'time management can make an enormous amount of difference to small businesses'. However, she also believes that you have to find the right solution to suit your business and your personality. Managing your time more effectively can be as simple as being more organised, such as keeping your desk tidier and having a more efficient filing system, or a good software package. However, if you are the kind of person who hates tidying, there's no point forcing yourself to keep everything on your desk neat, as you will simply resent it and soon stop making the effort. There will be another solution that suits you better, such as placing key documents in a certain place on your desk. As long as the important stuff is in one place, it doesn't matter if your desk is cluttered.

You are likely to have gone into business because you have a particular skill or want to do something you enjoy under your own supervision. Getting bogged down in all the administration and other chores that come with running your own company can be frustrating, preventing you from enjoying what you do, and could result in you ultimately losing interest in the business. What's more, you won't be dedicating enough time to what you do best, which is running your company. And if you are stacking up the hours so you can fit it all in, you will be far from your best most of the time. So for the sake of your health, sanity and business, it is worth applying a few time management techniques to reduce time spent on administration and free up time to dedicate on the work you are better at and enjoy more. In the end, it's your business that will benefit.

**WANT TO KNOW MORE ...**
Chartered Institute of Personnel and Development
www.cipd.co.uk
☎020 8612 6200

## *Work rate*

Any self-employed person, and certainly any new business, will agree that it is practically impossible to turn down work. Even if you are manically busy, it is very difficult saying 'No' because of the fear that all existing work will dry up and that you will be left with nothing. Unfortunately, although understandable, this approach has been responsible for bringing down many a good company. That's because, although business may be booming, individuals and companies that overstretch themselves are in serious danger of missing deadlines along with the faith of their clients – which means business won't be booming for long. However good the work, it is of little use when the deadline has passed. Clients are also quick to point out this failing to others and may recommend you, but with the words of warning: 'Good, but a hopeless timekeeper'.

The key is to be honest with yourself and your customers, as well as making sure that the people who are employed to carry out the key work that delivers your products and services – one of whom will be you – are doing just that, rather than taking on less productive roles that don't make the most of their skills. This will have the impact of maximising your work rate, allowing you to get through as much of it as possible, and so turn down less.

Ultimately, if you aren't confident that you can deliver good-quality work within the required timescale don't take it on, for the reasons outlined earlier, or be clear about your existing workload when talking to your customer. Being honest and saying you need a little more time doesn't necessarily mean the work will go elsewhere. A customer may decide to be more flexible and give you the time you need to do the work properly – and will appreciate your honesty and commitment to only delivering the best possible product or service.

Photographer **Jonathan Pollock** has built up a team of freelance assistants, who he calls on at busy times. This frees him up to concentrate directly on his primary function, photography, and allows him to take on as much work as possible, without cutting corners. His assistants help with building sets and also answering the telephones when he is at work. 'You don't want to miss a call from your next potential client because you are too busy to answer the phone,' he advises. In terms of balancing work and personal life, which is essential to prevent you from becoming jaded, and maintaining your work rate and hunger for the business, he advises that everyone books a holiday well in advance and sticks to the dates. This will give you plenty of time to book in any necessary cover for when you are away or plan work around your break.

Jonathan also suggests the following: 'Of course, as well as busy times, you also need to prepare for quieter periods. Although you should never lie to customers, avoid revealing that you have no other work. Simply say that you can fit them in.'

## Be prepared

Another common mistake made by inexperienced owner-managers is underestimating the time a job will take and consequently undercharging. It is easy to think that a job will be cracked in a day or two, but it is much better to add on extra time to cover any changes that a client might request. Some people are afraid of charging for that seemingly unnecessary day in case they lose the work to someone else, but experience does prove that clients will be prepared to pay a little more for the confidence of knowing that a job will be done properly.

Often clients will ask: 'How much will you charge?' at a very early stage of negotiation. One tip is to throw the question back and ask what size budget they have and, if appropriate, how long they expect the job to take. Imply that you are flexible. You do not want to lose the work in a haggle over fees, but also stress that you want a decent rate for the decent job that they will get. Try to gain as much information as possible about what is required before naming your fee and timescale. Questions that may have seemed unnecessary at the outset can save a lot of embarrassment and heartache down the line.

Another recent survey, conducted by MORI and British Gas, showed that owner-managers of small businesses are setting aside more time to plan. Commenting on the findings, a British Gas spokesman said he believes this is because owner-managers are 'working smarter'. Owner-managers are seeking more external advice and keeping a careful eye on spending as two ways of managing their time more efficiently. This is because they feel that forward planning is allowing them to allocate the right time to jobs and employ the relevant number of staff to achieve deadlines, as well as giving them time to chase up new contracts.

## *Keeping on track*

Staying on top of your working schedule is hugely important, particularly with a newly launched company, as you won't have slotted into any kind of routine or work pattern, and taking your eye off the ball can harm your reputation before it's even built. It is all too easy to forget to send an invoice as one job is completed and the next deadline is on top of the list in your mind. Losing control of the cashflow in that way is bad enough, but worse still, a disorganised owner-manager could easily lose sight of a whole commission.

Time management consultant **Gerard Hargreaves** is a great believer in lists. When working with British Gas on its biannual Time survey of small and medium-sized companies, he suggested making lists as a top tip because it helps organise the tasks in your head and helps prioritise the tasks ahead. Keep the diary up to date, make sure that conversations with clients are logged and that agreed actions are noted somewhere prominent, so that those actions do actually go forward.

**Jonathan Pollock** has a page-a-day diary for just this purpose. 'It was one of the first things that I did when launching on my own,' he says. 'It sounds a little silly, but it is so crucial.' Each day is split into hours so Jonathan can log meetings in the correct order and it has space for him to include priority tasks. He keeps this diary up to date all the time, filling it in as he speaks to clients. 'I keep lists of props that are needed and tasks to be done, and I tick them off as they are completed so that, at a glance, I know what still has to be worked on,' he explains.

**Imogen Daniels**, from the Chartered Institute of Personnel and Development, is also a great believer in lists, claiming they organise events in your own mind, regardless of whether you actually keep the list beside you through the working day. She also finds that 'people gain a great deal of satisfaction from achieving listed goals and being able to tick things off'. Again, the answer lies in finding the solution that suits your character – some people prefer to use Post-it notes, sticking them around their computer and office, while others prefer accessing a complex diary on their computer. 'There is an enormous amount of fire-fighting that goes on in small businesses,' says Imogen. 'Keeping lists and being aware of what is needed next does help to reduce the stress.'

## Delegation

One of the biggest challenges facing entrepreneurs is delegating tasks effectively. When it is your own business, it is very hard to let go, but delegation is a sign of sound management. Even early on in the life of your business, it is pretty difficult to do everything and there comes a point when the cost of employing someone else to help is less than the cost of work lost because you can't cope.

Chartered surveyor **Simon Smith** has first-hand experience of this. After setting out on his own he quickly found plenty of demand, but a merger with another business placed extreme pressure on his time. Instead of being out and about winning business and handling the tricky side of the operation, he found himself bogged down in administration and routine jobs that were taking up disproportionate amounts of his day. With a wife and three young children at home, he also found it hard to justify spending weekends at the office. 'I knew I needed someone to help out, but there has to be a balancing act between cost and help,' he says.

In his sector, Simon knew there was a history of recent graduates receiving low salaries and a consequent backlash of students unwilling to enter the profession. After months of seeking out the right person, he appointed a recent graduate who was going to spend the next two years working towards full qualification. Simon knew he would have to give time to the new recruit to ensure he was in the best possible condition to pass his exams – and also give him the right sort of work to meet industry criteria. But he still got the benefit of having time to return to his core business and concentrate on doing what he did best.

Of course, you may not need to actually take someone on but simply to delegate the work to someone already within the business. And this shouldn't just be done for the more menial tasks. Passing on responsibility to staff can be a great motivator and often people rise to the challenge if given the chance. As long as you monitor the situation carefully and build in review processes, little damage to your business is likely to be done. 'Often owner-managers have a strong emotional attachment to their business and it will have affected them in a lot of ways, from financial to family,' says Imogen, 'but they do have to learn to let go and trust others to take on some of the burden.'

*"Learn to let go and trust others to take on some of the burden"*

# *Self-motivation*

The key to the continued success of your new enterprise is maintaining the levels of motivation that drove you to launch the business in the first place. Motivation is more important than a business plan, or funding, or even business skills, according to entrepreneur **Len Tondel**, director of the Home Business Alliance. He believes that self-motivation is something you either have or haven't got. Successful owner-managers have it whereas frustrated employees don't.

However, as time goes on, entrepreneurs can suffer from a drop in self-motivation. This can be brought on by anything from too much success (if there is such a thing!), which can cut the drive to succeed, and delegation, which can result in a reduced sense of control, to failure and excessive stress, which can sap motivation. The key to avoiding this, and therefore maximising your potential, is to understand what motivates you. Ask any self-employed person what drives them, and the answer is likely to be simple: 'Money'. But owner-managers who think purely financial factors keep them motivated may be fooling themselves. 'Enthusiasm that's purely profit-based wears thin very quickly,' advises Len. 'So if you are going to start a business, make it something you will enjoy doing.'

Experts believe that the real source of motivation is likely to be rather more complex. Being your own boss comes top of the list for most small business owners, followed closely by flexibility and flexible hours, according to research by **Andrew Oswald**, professor of economics at Warwick University. Money comes a poor third for most self-employed people, including those who believe they are driven by the clatter of pound coins and the rustle of large cheques. A whopping 49% of the thousands of self-employed people he has studied call themselves very satisfied, compared with 29% of employees, and yet the popular view that self-employed people are happier to take risks is unfounded, Andrew argues. 'Their gambling behaviour is no different from the rest of the population,' he says.

*"Enthusiasm that's purely profit-based wears thin very quickly; so if you are going to start a business, make it something you will enjoy doing"*

311

Studies by **Cary Cooper CBE**, professor of organisational psychology and health at Lancaster University Management School, and director and co-founder of Robertson Cooper consultants, confirm Andrew's findings. 'People who start their own businesses have typically worked in a larger organisation and enjoy the amount of control and autonomy that self-employment gives them, when they see the direct rewards for their labour,' he says. But although that autonomy may make most self-employed people happier than the average employee, Cary's studies of top businesspeople have shown that the desire to prove themselves is often what drives them rather than money. 'Many top entrepreneurs have had unhappy experiences in childhood, and are motivated by something negative. They want to go on and prove they can succeed, and are driven by control and power,' he says.

Although those negative experiences may drive many to set up their own businesses in the first place, motivation grows with the enterprise, argues Cary. 'As the business expands and they employ people, it's like an extended family with everyone depending on your success,' he explains. 'The drive that keeps you going then comes from your feelings of responsibility to everyone who depends on you.'

Although small business owners' lives have become more stressful, with increasing red tape and too little time to finish too many tasks, most would never contemplate working for anyone else, studies show. Running a business now means longer working hours, less free time and a negative effect on family life, but the attraction of being your own boss still outweighs going back to working for someone else.

Once the business is up and running, stress can undermine self-motivation unless you find some way to control or channel it. Set yourself targets, recommends independent business adviser **David Street**, former director of the Institute of Business Advisers, and dig out that business plan, too. 'Small businesses tend to use business plans only when they're trying to raise money,' he says, 'but they can also help you set realistic performance targets.' **Jason Oakley**, former head of business banking at the Royal Bank of Scotland and now managing director of Acorn to Oaks Financial Services Ltd, agrees, saying: 'Your business plan should be the life and soul of your business and the key to targets you set.'

Formulating realistic goals for you and your team means you are more likely to achieve them, which will feed motivation all round. Gradual delegation of the jobs you don't enjoy or excel at will also boost your self-motivation, enable you to play to your strengths and boost the performance of your business.

**Startups Tips**

**Staying motivated**

⇨ Find a mentor to help you steer your self-motivation in the direction of success.

⇨ Set yourself realistic targets, and draw up a checklist.

⇨ Think positively by congratulating yourself on all the things you have achieved.

⇨ Visualise success by thinking in terms of what you will achieve rather than the obstacles in your way.

⇨ Make time for family and friends as strong relationships can help support your success.

⇨ Recognise that breaks are beneficial.

⇨ Look after your health – if it breaks down, so does your business success.

⇨ If you work from home, separate your working time from your leisure time.

⇨ Identify what really motivates you – money, independence or a fresh challenge – then pursue that goal.

⇨ Take a step back to gain a broader perspective.

## *Enhancing performance*

In the early days of a business you are likely to be highly motivated, which will drive you to work very hard. If you are not motivated you should seriously consider why you've launched your own business. Having said that, racking up the hours alone doesn't mean you are performing to your optimum level.

*"You need to analyse the quantity and quality of what you do in the day"*

If you are working long hours, make sure the effort you are putting in is as effective as possible, and that you are not wasting your time. So, look at how you are spending your time during the day, and work out just how much of it is actually being spent productively. Then think of ways that you may be able to carry out certain tasks more effectively. For example, if you are spending a long time doing an essential, but rather repetitive or highly intense activity, there will be a maximum period when you will be at your most productive before you become jaded and distracted and your performance level starts to fall off. Try to recognise when this occurs and recharge your batteries by taking a short break and then switching to another task, returning to the original work with more vim and vigour later on.

A great way to monitor the time you are spending on each task is by completing a time sheet for yourself. This is simply a sheet of paper (or you can do it on a spreadsheet on your computer) divided into the days of the week, under which you record the time spent working on a particular job and the nature of that work, building up a list throughout the day. Many companies use time sheets not only to ensure their people are spending their time productively and to keep on top of which projects they have been working on, but also to assess the time – and therefore cost – spent in terms of person-hours on certain jobs (and therefore the job's profitability) to inform decision making and assist customer charging.

'In the early days of a business you need to put the hours in to make it work, but you also need to analyse the quantity and quality of what you do in the day,' says management consultant **David Broad**. David also recommends networking as a great way to gain the necessary insight to improve your performance levels. 'Managers in larger companies have to motivate their staff, while in very small businesses often the owner just has to motivate themselves,' he points out. 'Going on a course or networking helps you to find a group of people who are all speaking your language, and can help enormously.' Networking can help to direct your motivation towards properly defined goals, and generate more business too.

'Keep in touch with other businesses and find out how they've managed to keep things fresh and meet their targets,' advises **Jason Oakley**. 'Exchanging views can inspire new ideas that apply to your business and may be proven winners.'

*"It might be hard to envisage needing a career pattern when you are your own boss, but personal development is still important"*

## *Personal development*

Sometimes, it can be hard to get up in the morning when you are your own boss – late night drinking, a young child and extreme tiredness can all contribute. Motivation is one of the essentials for anyone working for themselves, but there is far more to it than simply gearing yourself up to start the day, and it isn't enough to keep your career on the straight and narrow. It is equally important to establish a career path that you work towards maintaining. It might be hard to envisage needing a career pattern when you are your own boss, but in reality, personal development is still important, and the same also goes for your staff – an employee who receives training will see that they are moving forward by gaining key skills, feeling valued and satisfied in their position, making them far less likely to leave than an untrained member of staff.

## *Move on up*

It's important to bear in mind that once you are your own boss it won't be enough to simply keep working – as anyone who has survived a recession can tell you. As mentioned above, standing still in career terms should never be an option, no matter how small your business. Take the example of a copy typist. There was plenty of work in the past on old style typewriters, but those who weren't able to become computer literate would have quickly found themselves, quite literally, redundant.

If you worked for a large company, you may have been offered training as required, with follow-up opportunities where necessary. Your employers might have even been prepared to give you time off for outside course work or even contributed towards the cost of independent training. Although your business may be no more than a one-man band, you can still adopt the same strategies for yourself. The only difference is that you will have to be more organised than if you were part of a large organisation. As a small business, attending a block release course will mean that no one is back at your desk, keeping the business going. The financial and practical implications need to be carefully thought out, too, but there is still no reason why you shouldn't better yourself and the same goes for your staff.

Personal development can help your business in several unexpected ways:

→ Not only will you be able to carry out the related task better, but it may also help motivate you through a rough business period or provide fresh ideas if the business becomes stale.

→ You never know when you might think of taking up a job again, for example because you have sold your business or you have been asked to join at board level – so by keeping up to date with developments in the sector and by being seen as an industry leader, you have a better chance of winning a lucrative position.

→ Your own business may be so successful that others will want you on their board as a non-executive director.

→ If you sell your business on after the first flush of success, you may well want to start afresh and need to have developed your skills along the way.

315

## Legal requirements

Besides personal development aimed at becoming better at the job and gaining confidence in your own ability to handle various situations, there is also an increasing need for gaining knowledge about the latest statutory requirements. The government has placed a lot of emphasis on the need for improved quality at all levels of business. New laws on corporate bribery (the Bribery Act 2011 introduces a new form of corporate liability for failing to prevent bribery, while individuals found guilty of bribery offences could now face up to 10 years in prison) are just one example of where individuals are being forced to take responsibility. **Mark Redfern**, director of training at Searchlight Solutions, has seen increased demand for senior management training to keep abreast with new legislation. 'People are having to become very well versed on the legal side and keep up to date with current and forthcoming legislation, such as the Companies Act, the Data Protection Act and the Human Rights Act,' Mark reports. He adds that Searchlight tries to address problems before they arise, so that trainees are in the best position to manage their businesses correctly.

Professional director **Martin Pedler** has strong views on the need for better quality directors and believes that recent legislation on corporate manslaughter, in particular (where a company can now be prosecuted if there is a gross breach of duty of care by senior management which leads to a person's death) will give a wake-up call to the nation's bosses. 'I think people have a fear factor about what they are taking on,' he says, adding that ignorance will be no defence for directors who haven't kept a close eye on what is happening within their businesses. Although business owners and senior managers can't be prosecuted personally under the Corporate Manslaughter Act, individuals can still be prosecuted for gross negligence manslaughter and health and safety offences.

The laws put pressure on all bosses to adhere strictly to health and safety regulations. If companies and directors can show they have tried to maintain proper standards, the courts will have no grounds for conviction, but cutting corners or non-compliance in any way will open the door.

## Personal and staff training

Developing the skills of your workforce through training boosts morale and helps provide a better service to customers. They, in turn, are happier and more likely to return swelling profits, which then benefits the business and encourages higher salaries. This is very much a win–win situation, and should encourage new owner-managers to view training less as a drain on resources or an annoyance that takes up employees' valuable time, and more as a useful investment.

In addition, it can help attract and retain the right people for your business. While unemployment is currently high, making it easier to find applicants, recruiting is often expensive, disruptive and time consuming. So when you do hire the perfect candidate, it makes sense to try and hold on to them. Having a training programme or 'people development' strategy in place can help to both attract and retain key members of staff, giving your company a positive profile in the recruitment marketplace.

As mentioned earlier, bosses can also benefit from career development. Completing a course will provide a boost in self-confidence and renewed interest in developing the business. A better-trained boss will be more motivated, and this is reflected throughout the business, whatever its size. The former director of development at the Institute of Directors (IoD) and founder of strategic management consultancy StellaNova Consulting, **John Weston**, calls it a virtuous circle: 'Better directors run better businesses and as a consequence you create wealth and employment,' he says. John believes that by starting at the top, the professionalism will filter right through the business.

One of the IoD's prime missions is to improve professional standards across the UK, and the organisation offers a series of courses designed to cover most aspects of running a business, which are available to members. They are designed for like-minded people and many who have been through an IoD course say that the most valuable part was not the formal course work, but learning about other directors' experiences.

## Choosing training courses

There are two ways to go when choosing courses: you can follow the structure of your chosen career or develop across a spectrum of skills. The options led to the development of an IoD chartered director qualification, because, as John points out: 'Most directors have followed vertical career ladders, but [IoD] membership comes from a horizontal level of achievement and [the organisation] needed a qualification that would appeal to that.' In other words, when you have become an accountant, lawyer, etc, you have a career structure that takes you up to the boardroom level, but once there you may well need the skills of a completely different career.

*"Developing the skills of your workforce through training boosts morale and helps provide a better service to customers"*

*"Having a training programme or 'people development' strategy in place can help to both attract and retain key members of staff"*

To follow your chosen career you need to make specific decisions about what to learn. Most fields have relevant industry qualifications and there will be a well-trodden route – one that you are likely to have done or have followed before you decided to go solo. Learning a new set of skills is likely to be more of a challenge. For example, it is easy enough to employ an accountant, but it might also pay dividends if you understand the basics of it as well. The UK has a raft of colleges offering full and part-time courses and you can find out more by searching the internet. Bear in mind that different rules of entry (and payment) apply for mature students, and take into account your current workload before committing to a course – one or two evenings at college a week may not be feasible.

Local councils are another good source of courses. Many run a variety, specifically designed for part-timers. These are often evening classes that require a little, but not too much, homework between sessions. These could vary from a basic accountancy course to learning a new language – or a completely unrelated skill, such as upholstery, which could provide another source of income should the tough times arrive.

However, if you are looking for a more academically inclined qualification, then check out your local university, although part-time courses are usually limited. The other alternative that is quite popular is the Open University, as it allows you to work at a distance and at your own speed.

## Should you consider an MBA?

If you want to learn more managerial skills, a Masters in Business Administration (MBA) might provide the solution. An MBA often takes several years to complete, but can be combined with a full-time job. Students complete course work in a series of block releases. An MBA is usually divided into 12 modules, comprising eight compulsory sections and four optional ones in which a student might choose to specialise in a work-related subject.

Nottingham University Business School has a variety of MBA courses, and according to its centre director **Chris O'Brien** most students are in full-time work. Some choose to concentrate on the course – and there are attractive bursaries to help them afford the tuition. Most students are in their 30s, although there are both younger and older exceptions. Chris stresses that the aim of the course is to give a framework from which students can help run businesses. 'They have an understanding of business, which allows them to move businesses forward in a changing environment,' he says.

## Online training

The time spent getting to and from a course and the inflexible times of lectures is often the reason why owner-managers don't take up training or executive education. This is where online training comes in, where you can work over the internet from any location, starting and stopping lectures when you choose. This mode of study is becoming increasingly attractive. Companies such as Elearnity work closely with an employer to provide the necessary training package for its staff. Others such as REDTRAY also offer courses on an individual basis. The downside is many of the courses are technology based, but this is beginning to change. Another criticism is the lack of one-to-one help, but a lot of online courses now offer telephone support, while tools such as Windows Meeting Space help course members share questions. The Open University is just one academic institution to make use of the internet as a way of reaching students.

**WANT TO KNOW MORE …**

**Institute of Directors**
www.iod.com

**Association of MBAs**
www.mbaworld.com

**Elearnity**
www.elearnity.com

**REDTRAY**
www.redtray.co.uk

 Action points

### Key ways to improve your business

You may think that once you have started up your business a lot of the hard work is over, but successful owner-managers are the ones who continually try to improve their enterprise. This is particularly important in a downturn, when you need to be able to respond to changing market conditions. Sitting on the sidelines while competitors make progress could prove to be disastrous for your venture. To help, here are 10 ways from startups.co.uk to help you get ahead:

☑ **Take on experienced staff:** Since October 2006 it has been illegal to discriminate against workers on the grounds of age, so incorporate this change into your thinking when recruiting. Older staff offer maturity and experience, which could provide the keys to success for your business. Don't believe that old dogs can't learn new tricks and remember that they might have a thing or two to show you.

☑ **Train up:** The skill levels of your staff will have a direct impact on the performance of your company, so it pays to continually develop your employees through training to make sure they are up to speed on the latest workplace innovations, such as IT, and on those in your particular sector. This is also

319

vital during the current economic climate, as you need all possible resources at your disposal to attract business and fight off competition.

☑ **Expansion through recruitment:** Not every company is doing badly as a result of the recession, and if yours is one of those that is performing well, perhaps you could update your business plan and take on a few extra staff. If demand is great enough and you can budget carefully, new workers could drive your business onwards and upwards. It will also mean you are ready to push on further when the recovery kicks in.

☑ **Expand your offer:** How about branching into other areas? If there is a niche market being ignored in your local area and your business is doing well, why not exploit it? Do some market research on demand and how any potential expansion would fare, but be careful not to over-stretch yourself. However, a targeted, well-thought-out expansion into a closely related field could prove to be very profitable — particularly if your existing market is slow due to the recession.

☑ **Don't just bank on banks:** Although research has shown that the majority of small firms go to their high-street bank whenever they need new finance, many are now having to look at other options as the credit crunch has resulted in bank finance being difficult to come by. Equity investors, such as venture capitalists and business angels, are a possible alternative, but they too have been hit by the downturn and have less to invest. This makes asset-based lending the best current option, where assets such as invoices, equipment, or even intellectual property can be used as security. See Chapter 6 for more details about finding finance.

☑ **Go public:** The government has announced that red tape on securing public sector contracts will be cut and that work will be awarded on a regional, not national, basis. Both measures are good news for small firms, who can now compete against a reduced field at a fraction of the cost for government contracts. From pavement maintenance to IT work, there is around £13bn worth of contracts out there.

☑ **Get your message across:** If you have spent the last year relying on local newspaper advertisements or the Yellow Pages, it may be worth widening your options slightly to help boost your business. Cinema advertising often proves effective, as do panels on the sides of buses. Or you may want to put together a radio advertisement to reach out to local customers. If you come up with a targeted, attention-grabbing campaign at a reasonable cost, you should be able to boost takings significantly. See Chapter 9 for more on marketing.

☑ **Get supplied**: Getting quality, affordable stock is essential in making your business profitable. If you feel that you aren't getting the best deal from your wholesaler, do something about it. Most are happy to negotiate over prices, particularly at the moment when business can be hard to come by, and good wholesalers reward loyalty by offering money off or extra products to repeat customers. If yours doesn't, try to find another one. Do some research on suppliers in your local area, and if none of them offer good value, then look further afield, as the savings you make could be critical. See Chapter 7 for more details on handling suppliers.

☑ **Get paid on time:** Now more than ever it's vital that you do all you can to maintain a healthy cashflow through your business. A big obstacle to this is that late payment has been seen by many businesses as acceptable practice for many years, putting small firms in debt that they can ill afford. So, it's important that you act to get what's owed to you. See Chapter 8 for more details on tackling late-paying customers.

☑ **Keep the cash flowing**: Debt is not necessarily a bad thing for small firms attempting to grow. However, it's essential that you keep up with repayments or your whole business could be at risk. Make sure you operate a well-organised cashflow system. Try to negotiate repayments so that you can pay in instalments when it suits you best, try to use a business debit or credit card to cut down on paperwork, make sure your records are well looked after, and ensure that you are aware of all outstanding debts.

## *Finding a business mentor*

A mentor is essentially a 'wise or trusted adviser or guide'. The word has its origins in Homer's *The Odyssey*. Before leaving to fight the Trojan War, Odysseus leaves his son and estate in the care of his friend Mentor, who then guides the young Telemachus.

*"Successful entrepreneurs will often attribute much of their achievement to the support and guidance they received from a mentor"*

To give it a more modern context, a mentor is someone with more experience or wisdom, sharing and imparting his or her knowledge to someone younger or less experienced. The concept works incredibly well in a business environment, where an entrepreneur may have a great idea for a business but needs a bit of guidance turning it into a successful and profitable venture.

Successful entrepreneurs will often attribute much of their achievement to the support and guidance they received from a mentor. Most notably,

321

billionaire airline and entertainment industry mogul Richard Branson was mentored by the British airline entrepreneur Freddie Laker. Mentoring does not involve employing a consultant or employee to help run your business. It's a relationship between you, the entrepreneur, and someone with business experience that can guide you through tough decisions, point out ways of improving your business and offer general support within a trusted relationship. It's a two-way communication process which gives more experienced entrepreneurs who have possibly taken a step back, or even retired from their business, the opportunity to share their wealth of skills, experience and expertise with those hungry for knowledge and guidance.

There are plenty of mentoring organisations where you can request a mentor for your business. However, you don't have to go through formal channels to bring a mentor on board to help your business. Friends, contacts and fellow entrepreneurs can all end up as informal mentors, sometimes without you even realising.

## Maintaining a good relationship

Like any relationship, the bond between mentor and mentee has to be worked at to prevent it from turning sour. Here are five ways to keep your mentor/mentee relationship as sweet and fresh as the day you met . . .

### 1.  Build up a relationship

While you're there to get as much business advice out of your relationship as you can, a mentor will always be more forthcoming if you take an interest in them as a person, rather than just as a machine to dispense advice. Make sure you ask them a little about their life, their partner, or their children. Similarly, one good turn deserves another, and a little reciprocation will never go amiss. If you think you have the skills to help them out, let them know – even if it's just a magazine article you think they'd like to read, the smallest gestures will be appreciated.

### 2.  Don't ask to be spoon-fed

Your mentor is there to help you out with his or her knowledge and experience. They are not there to run your business for you. If you have a problem, try to work it out on your own before turning to your mentor – and once you have, explain to them exactly what you've done and how you did it before asking for their advice. Your mentor will appreciate your dedication, and is likely to take you far more seriously.

### 3. Communicate

Business is a time-consuming thing, and as a result, the mentor/mentee relationship is no longer as hands-on a thing as it may once have been. While the wonders of modern technology mean you can gain access to your mentor's experience from anywhere in the world, it also means you can get your wires crossed from anywhere in the world – a sure-fire way for things to turn sour.

When you write your mentor an email, read it back to yourself, or get someone else to read it. Does everything make sense? Is there anything that could be misconstrued? Similarly, if your mentor's reply seems curt, go back over your previous email – was there anything which could be confused?

### 4. Take their advice

Your mentor will inevitably dispense some advice that you don't like – whether it's because their suggestion will require sacrifices you would rather not make, or because it seems too hard. Of course, that is not to suggest that they are completely infallible, but there is potentially a considerable amount of experience and knowledge behind their suggestion. At the end of the day, you are there because you have asked for their help, so make sure you listen when they give it to you.

### 5. Value their time

Like you, your mentor is likely to be a businessperson with very little time on their hands. In order to get the most out of your relationship, make sure you don't make excessive demands of what little time they do have: make your emails short and to the point, keep your phone calls brief, and don't waste their time with questions which you know you could resolve after five minutes on Google. Finally, always thank your mentor for their time. As the old adage goes, good manners cost nothing, and it could mean your mentor will give you more time when you next speak.

## Finding a business mentor

Here are three organisations that can help you in your search for a business mentor:

*Horsesmouth*
Launched in January 2008, Horsesmouth is a not-for-profit social networking site which offers free one-to-one online mentoring for members. The site is a network made up of entrepreneurs looking for advice and entrepreneurs willing to give it.

Each member's profile is picture-free and users are encouraged to come up with an alias instead of their own name to maintain anonymity. Each profile lists the areas of expertise of each member. The site's search functionality allows business owners to locate mentors who have first-hand experience of the issues they need help with, ranging from raising finance to improving their marketing techniques.

**www.horsesmouth.co.uk**

*Rockstar Group*

The Rockstar Group offers a very structured mentoring programme to entrepreneurs that sign up, allowing them to pair up with a mentor that suits the level and type of guidance they're after.

Entrepreneurs browse the Rockstar site and are able to see profiles and photos of all the mentors signed up with the programme. There's a membership fee to join but once signed up, each entrepreneur is contacted to find out exactly what they're looking for from a mentor and given an explanation on how the process will work.

Entrepreneurs are then assigned to an appropriate mentor who contacts them to arrange a face-to-face meeting where they establish a realistic 12-month goal. Objectives are laid down for the first month after which they'll meet again. From then on mentoring can either continue face-to-face or via the phone. Email conversations between the mentor and entrepreneur are also encouraged.

**www.rockstargroup.co.uk**

*The Prince's Trust*

Founded in 1976 by the Prince of Wales, the Prince's Trust is a charity that provides training, personal development, business start-up support, mentoring and advice to around 40,000 young people a year.

Its business programme is aimed at helping people aged 18-30, who are unemployed or working under 16 hours a week, to start up in business. The Trust's mentoring scheme works in three parts:

**Part one:** The Trust works with the young person to help them develop their ideas and put together a business plan.

**Part two:** This is the funding stage where the applicant goes through a 'friendly' ***Dragons'***

*Den*-type process.

**Part three:** If the applicant successfully gets funding for their business they are then assigned to a suitable mentor.

The Trust encourages them to meet at least once a month but generally takes a back seat to the actual proceedings unless the mentor asks for them to have further involvement. They report back to the Trust each month and let them know if the mentee needs any specialist advice they are not able to provide.

**www.princes-trust.org.uk**

# *Over to you ...*

If you've read this far you must be serious about setting up your own business, but now it's up to you. You've taken the journey through this guide from idea to launch, and now it's time for you to put all the theory into practice – and perhaps flick back through these pages along the way to make sure you are on the right track.

You should now be under no illusions about the task ahead, and have a much better idea of what starting up involves. You will also have read plenty of examples of those who've gone before, and how they've overcome obstacles and faced challenges along the way, finally achieving what they set out to do – running their own company on their own terms.

Remember, no one has launched their own business without making mistakes along the way. This is all part of the process, and it's how you deal with these situations and learn from them so you avoid them in the future that matters. As for the challenges, you are bound to face plenty, but approach them in the right way and they'll make you even more determined to succeed.

This should be an enjoyable, liberating and ultimately exhilarating experience. And hopefully you will be making the webpages of startups. co.uk in the not-too-distant future as one of our entrepreneurial success stories.

Good luck!

# *Index*